CAMBRIDGE LATIN AMERICAN STUDIES

EDI

DAVID JOSLIN

8

ECONOMIC DEVELOPMENT OF LATIN AMERICA

A SURVEY FROM COLONIAL TIMES TO THE CUBAN REVOLUTION

THE SERIES

ECONOMIC DEVELOPMENT OF LATIN AMERICA

A SURVEY FROM COLONIAL TIMES TO THE CUBAN REVOLUTION

BY

CELSO FURTADO

TRANSLATED BY
SUZETTE MACEDO

CAMBRIDGE
AT THE UNIVERSITY PRESS
1970

Published by the Syndics of the Cambridge University Press
Bentley House, 200 Euston Road, London N.W.1
American Branch: 32 East 57th Street, New York, N.Y.10022

Library of Congress Catalogue Card Number: 74–121365

ISBN 0 521 07828 8 clothbound
0 521 09628 6 paperback

Printed in Great Britain
at the University Printing House, Cambridge
(Brooke Crutchley, University Printer)

To my students at the University of Paris

A meus alunos da Universidade de Paris

CONTENTS

Contents

viii

Contents

Contents

TABLES

Tables

xii

PREFACE

The study of the economic development of the Latin American countries has been attracting increasing interest, both in Europe and in the United States and in the countries of the Third World generally. An independent political life, which began practically at the same time as the Industrial Revolution, and an even longer experience of the international division of labour system as exporters of raw materials, single out this group of countries from among the now numerous family of nations with so-called underdeveloped economies. To these reasons must be added the growing awareness that, to a greater extent in Latin America than in any other important areas, obstacles to development are mainly of an institutional nature, a circumstance that makes it doubly difficult to try to identify evolutional trends in the region. Moreover, the problems posed by economic development at its present stage are leading Latin American peoples to see their situation in more truthful terms and to value those aspects that constitute the features of a common cultural personality.

This book was written with the dual purpose of helping students outside the area to form some idea of the socio-economic profile of the region and of contributing to the provision of a wider perspective for studies of the development of individual Latin American countries. In seeking to avoid dealing with each country in isolation—which would be to ignore the existence of a cultural reality in process of becoming homogeneous— I have also tried to avoid giving the false impression that there is a Latin American *economic system*, which would be the result of manipulating aggregate data for the region as a whole. So far as possible, each country is dealt with as an autonomous economic reality, whose experience, at a given historical moment, can be regarded as typical of regional evolutional trends.

C. F.

Paris, April 1969

xiii

ABBREVIATIONS

BNDE   Banco Nacional de Desenvolvimento Economico

CIDA   Interamerican Committee for Agricultural Development

ECLA   United Nations, Economic Commission for Latin America

FAO   United Nations, Food and Agriculture Organisation

IDB   Interamerican Development Bank

IMF   International Monetary Fund

LAFTA   Latin American Free Trade Area

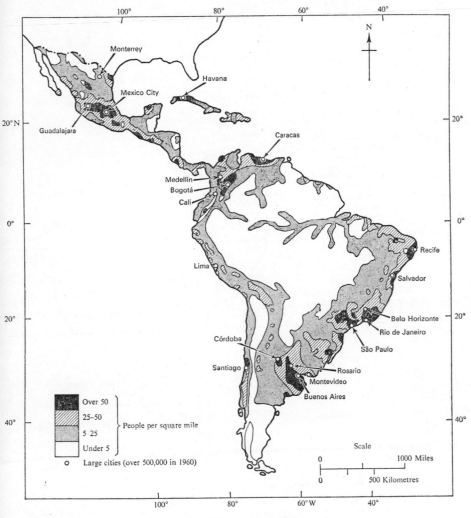

Map A   *Latin America: Population Distribution*

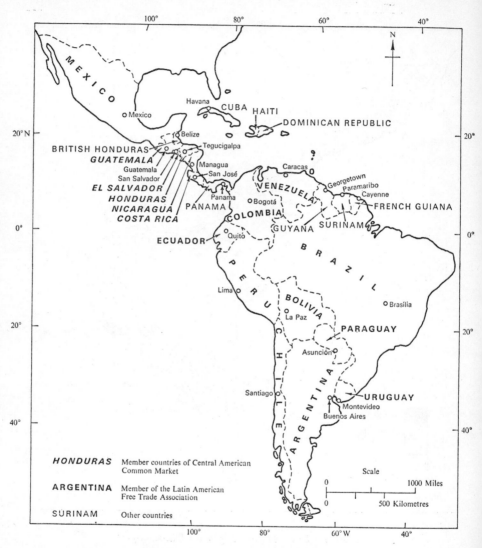

Map B *Latin America: Political Divisions*

I. FROM THE CONQUEST TO
THE FORMATION OF NATION-STATES

CHAPTER I

INTRODUCTION: THE LAND
AND THE PEOPLE

LATIN AMERICA: FROM GEOGRAPHICAL EXPRESSION
TO HISTORICAL REALITY

For a long time the term 'Latin America', coined in the United States, was used only in a geographical sense to designate the countries situated south of the Rio Grande. Far from showing any interest in what they had in common, the nations that emerged from the Iberian colonisation of the Americas sought to emphasise their distinctive characteristics in an effort to define their own national personalities. With the exception of Brazil, colonised by Portugal, and Haiti, colonised by France, the remaining Latin American republics share much of their colonial history and, in Spanish, a common language. Nevertheless, the fact that the pre-Columbian cultures, in themselves so strikingly different, contributed in such widely diverse ways to the formation of the present national personalities makes the differences between countries such as Argentina and Mexico as great as the similarities. The same can be said of the African ethnico-cultural contribution, which is no less unevenly distributed. Even leaving aside the case of Haiti, whose African–French origins place it in a category of its own, the differences between the countries of the Caribbean region, where there is a marked African ethnico-cultural influence, and the Andean countries, where indigenous ethnico-cultural elements predominate, are as marked as is possible for countries sharing part of their history. None the less, the emphasis on diversity was less a reflexion of the real extent of the differences between the Latin American countries than of their awareness of a common origin. It was as though the new nations felt themselves threatened, in their formative process, by superior forces that would lead them, sooner or later, to be reintegrated in the web of a common history interrupted by the circumstances in which the Spanish colonial empire finally collapsed.

I

Economic Development of Latin America

The growth of a Latin American consciousness is a recent phenomenon, deriving from the new problems posed by the region's economic and social development over the last three decades. Generally speaking, traditional development, based on the expansion of exports, had transformed the countries of the region into competing economies. Exporting the same primary products and importing manufactured products from outside the region, they failed to forge any economic links with each other. Thus, in the context of the international division of labour created in the Colonial Pact period and consolidated during the first stage of the Industrial Revolution, the traditional form of development helped to foster regional fragmentation. The disruption of international trade in 1929 had profound repercussions in the region. It is the attempt to find the solution for the problems that have arisen since then that has paved the way for the emergence of the present Latin American consciousness. The shortage of manufactured goods, which became more acute during the Second World War, gave rise to a regional trade in manufactures, opening the way to a better understanding and the emergence of common interests. Regional trade became particularly significant between countries exporting temperate-zone products, such as Argentina, and those exporting tropical products, such as Brazil. The traditional exchange between these two countries had been characterised by a marked imbalance in favour of Argentina. However, the new conditions, favouring the creation of a flow of exports of Brazilian manufactures, stimulated Argentina to begin diversifying her own exports. With the end of the war and the reopening of normal channels of trade, intra-regional trade declined significantly, but the experience had served to create contacts and crystallise possibilities that were to be explored at a later stage.

Since the second half of the 1950s, when industrialisation based on import-substitution began to reveal its limitations, for the first time in Latin America the obstacles to regional development created by the small size of the national markets began to be widely discussed; this discussion has greatly contributed to the growing awareness of similarities and the creation of a regional consciousness.

Lastly, mention must be made of the role played by Latin America's changing relations with the United States in shaping this regional consciousness. Control of a large part of the region's sources of raw materials by United States companies created close dependent links with the United States for most Latin American countries, particularly those in the Caribbean area. After the First World War, United States capital ousted European capital from control of the public services in almost all

2

The Land and the People

the countries of the region. Finally, after World War II, American penetration gained considerable momentum in manufacturing, which was the region's fastest-growing sector. Thus Latin America as a whole was clearly in a position of economic domination by the United States, a situation which tended to become institutionalised in the proliferation of 'Pan-American' organisations. This institutionalisation obviously helped to consolidate the system of tutelage already established, but it also served to precipitate the realisation that only by seeking closer ties could the Latin American countries hope to bring about any significant change in the conditions of their dialogue with the United States.

In summary, 'Latin America' ceased to be a geographical term and became an historical reality as a result of the belated process of industrialisation now under way in the region, and of the particular form of dependence established between the Latin American countries and the United States.

PHYSICAL BACKGROUND

The Latin American republics cover an area of almost 8 million square miles, an area equivalent in size to that of the Soviet Union or of the United States and Canada combined. Crossed by the Equator, much the larger part of Latin America lies in the Southern Hemisphere: its southern tip is in latitude 55° S, whereas its northernmost extremity extends only as far as the 33rd parallel. From the geographical viewpoint the region is made up of three sub-regions:

(a) northern Mexico, in which the basic relief features of the United States are prolonged;

(b) the American isthmus, which extends for more than 2,000 km, narrowing southward to a width of only 70 km in Panama; and

(c) the South American continent, whose relief is dominated by the Andean Cordillera, the great interior plains, the Guiana and Brazilian massifs, and the Patagonian plateau. The Andean barrier extends from the extreme north to the extreme south of the South American continent, sheltering extensive plateaux such as the Bolivian Altiplano—over 800 km wide—and reaching altitudes of more than 6,000 m. The great South American plains are formed by the basins of the Orinoco, Amazon and Paraná rivers.

The existence of extremely complex general conditions and of certain highly significant peculiarities determines the extraordinarily wide variety of climates found in the Latin American countries, taken as a whole. The two major conditioning elements in the regional pattern of climate are the position of the Equator, which crosses the region close to its widest part,

3

Economic Development of Latin America

and the importance of the Andean Cordilleras and the Sierra Madre in Mexico—an importance reflected in the fact that several of Latin America's largest cities are situated more than 2,000 m above sea level (Mexico City: 2,240 m, Bogota: 2,591 m). The pattern of climate can be roughly characterised as follows: a humid tropical climate prevails in extensive areas, which are also the least densely populated. A tropical climate with a dry season and a hot semi-arid climate prevails in areas no less extensive but with a more concentrated population. Finally, mountain climates, subtropical climates and temperate climates characterise the most densely populated areas.

POPULATION PATTERN

The Latin American population, which at present exceeds 250 million, represents about 7 per cent of the world total. Excluding China, it accounts for 28 per cent of the Third World's total population. Two features of the Latin American population distinguish it from any other population grouping of comparable importance. The first is its rapid rate of increase, which is at present around 3 per cent a year.[1] In the period 1950–60, the average annual growth rates for the world's major population groupings already placed Latin America in a leading position:

	%		%
Latin America	2·8	U.S.–Canada	1·8
Africa	2·0	Soviet Union	1·7
Asia	1·9	Europe	0·8

The second salient feature of the Latin American population, closely related to the first, is its age structure, which is characterised by a large proportion of children and young adults. Persons under 15 years of age

[1] This average obviously conceals wide differences between the various sub-regions. Thus, in Argentina and Uruguay, both the birth and death rates have already declined significantly and the natural rate of increase of the population is approximately 1·5 per cent. Chile and Cuba are in an intermediate position: with a substantial decline in the mortality rate and the birth rate also beginning to show a downward trend, the rate of population increase is nearly 2·5 per cent but has started to decline. In some special cases (Haiti and Bolivia) the crude death rate has not yet been significantly reduced and this, combined with a high but stable birth rate, produces a rate of population increase of the intermediate type (2·5 per cent), but with a tendency to rise, in contrast to the second group for which rates of increase show a downward trend. Finally, in the remaining fourteen countries, representing 79 per cent of the region's population, the combination of a high and stable birth rate with a mortality rate that has already been significantly reduced results in a rate of population increase which is generally higher than 3 per cent and in some cases even higher than 3·5 per cent. For details, see: Carmen A. Miró, 'The Population of Latin America', in Claudio Véliz (ed.), *Latin America and the Caribbean: A Handbook*, London, 1968.

4

The Land and the People

now make up more than 70 per cent of the Latin American total, whereas in the United States and Canada they account for about 30 per cent, and in Western Europe for an even smaller percentage. The rapid growth of Latin America's population is a relatively recent phenomenon. Although the basic data still await a more systematic analysis, it is now generally accepted that the population of Spanish America at the time of Independence was smaller than when America was discovered.[1] It is widely held that the total Indian population in the areas occupied by the Spaniards must have been not less than 50 million at the time of the Conquest. The particular circumstances of the Conquest and of the subsequent occupation of the more densely populated areas produced what amounted to a virtual holocaust of the indigenous population. To understand this extraordinary phenomenon, almost without parallel in the history of mankind, one must bear in mind that the native populations at the time of the Conquest were supported by handicraft industries and agriculture in economies characterised by complex systems of social organisation. The mining economy introduced by the Spaniards, which required a wide-scale dislocation of the population, seriously disrupted the pattern of food production and led to the break-up of the family units among a sizeable proportion of the population. The actual process of conquest resulted in the forcible dislocation of great numbers of people, particularly adult males, who were practically wiped out by the long marches and forced labour imposed upon them by the *Conquistadores*. On the other hand, the need to exact a food surplus from the population remaining on the land, in order to provide a steady food supply for the mining communities and cities, made heavy demands on the diminishing rural population and shortened its average life span. Finally, the ravages of epidemics caused by contact with peoples carrying new contagious diseases played a no less significant part in bringing about a holocaust of the Indian population. It has been estimated, for example, that the Mexican population, which probably numbered about 16 million at the time of the Conquest, was reduced to one-tenth of this total in the course of a century.[2]

[1] For a general survey of data relative to the growth of the population of Spanish America in the Colonial period, see: Rolando Mellafe, 'Problemas Demográficos e História Colonial Hispanoamericana', in *Temas de História Económica Hispanoamericana*, Paris, 1965. For data relative to Brazil, see: Celso Furtado, *Formação Económica do Brasil*, Rio, 1959; English edition: *The Economic Growth of Brazil: A Survey from Colonial to Modern Times*, tr. Richard W. de Aguiar and Eric Charles Drysdale, Berkeley, Univ. of California Press, 1963.

[2] The wholesale destruction of Brazil's aboriginal population was equally drastic. The Jesuit, José de Anchieta, observed that 'the number of people used up in this place (Bahia) from twenty years ago until now (1583) seems a thing not to be believed', and proceeds to give figures that reveal a destruction of population on a scale similar to that carried out in Mexico. See J. Capistrano de Abreu, *Capítulos de História Colonial*, 5th ed. Rio, 1934, p. 79.

Economic Development of Latin America

Towards the middle of the seventeenth century the decline of the mining economy, and its replacement by subsistence agricultural and pastoral activities, opened a new chapter in the demographic history of Latin America. Attached to large agricultural estates with abundant land resources, the population began slowly to increase. The establishment of an export trade in agricultural products in the eighteenth century made possible the continuation and even acceleration of population growth.

Brazil's demographic history contrasts sharply with that of Spanish America. The aboriginal population was relatively sparse when the Portuguese began to colonise Brazil, which led them to bring in large numbers of Africans who were to provide the basis of the labour force for the tropical agricultural economy established in the Brazilian Northeast in the first half of the sixteenth century. The discovery of alluvial gold and precious stones in the early years of the eighteenth century prompted a strong current of immigration from Portugal to Brazil. This influx of immigrants altered the demographic and the ethnic patterns in Brazil. Up to that time the population had been concentrated in the region of tropical agriculture between Bahia and Maranhão, with the African contingent in the majority. The mining economy, which in Spanish America had brought about the depopulation of certain regions, produced the opposite effect in Brazil. Since what was involved was not the full-scale operation required in the case of silver, but simply the working over of placer deposits, Brazilian gold provided opportunities for the small entrepreneur. Even the slaves, who generally worked under strict supervision, enjoyed far better living conditions than the slave workers on the plantations. By the end of the century dominated by the mining economy, Brazil's population structure had undergone striking changes: the population of European origin now outstripped the African contingent, and the largest and most rapidly expanding population cluster had shifted from the northeast to the centre-south. At the close of the eighteenth century Brazil's population numbered 3 million, whereas that of Spanish America was slightly over 16 million.

During the nineteenth century Latin America's population increased at twice the overall rate estimated for the growth in world population. In effect, the ten-year average for Latin America was as high as 12·8 per cent, as against a growth rate of 6·4 per cent for the world as a whole. Nevertheless, compared with the rate of population increase in North America, for which the ten-year average was as high as 30 per cent, the Latin American growth rate was relatively low. In 1800 the population of the United States and Canada combined totalled 6 million, whereas that of Latin America was over 19 million. By 1900, Anglo-Saxon America had a

The Land and the People

TABLE I.I. *Area and Population of Latin American Countries*

	area (km²)	population in 1967 (000)	population densities (inhabitants/ km²)
Argentina	2,766,656	23,031	8·3
Bolivia	1,098,581	3,801	3·5
Brazil	8,511,965	86,580	10·2
Chile	741,767	9,010	12·1
Colombia	1,138,338	19,215	16·8
Costa Rica	50,900	1,536	29·7
Cuba	114,524	8,033	70·2
Dominican Republic	48,442	3,889	81·0
Ecuador	270,670	5,508	20·3
El Salvador	20,935	3,151	147·3
Guatemala	108,889	4,717	43·0
Haiti	27,750	4,515	165·0
Honduras	112,088	2,445	21·8
Mexico	1,969,300	45,611	23·6
Nicaragua	130,000	1,778	14·0
Panama	75,650	1,329	17·5
Paraguay	406,752	2,121	5·1
Peru	1,280,219	12,385	9·6
Uruguay	186,926	2,783	14·6
Venezuela	898,805	9,352	10·4
Latin America	20,019,000	250,950	12·0

SOURCE: Instituto Interamericano de Estadística, *Boletín Estádistico*.

population of 81 million and Latin America only 63 million. It is only in the present century that Latin America has taken over the lead in world population growth. Between 1900 and 1930 the decennial average of Latin America's population increase was 20 per cent, whereas that of Anglo-Saxon America was 18·6 per cent, and the world rate was 7·8 per cent. Between 1930 and 1960 the Latin American rate rose to 24·8 per cent, easily overtaking that of Anglo-Saxon America (14 per cent) which for the first time fell below the world average of 14·3 per cent. As a result of these changes in the rate of increase, Latin America's population, which at the turn of the century was approximately one-fifth below that of Anglo-Saxon America, now exceeds it by about 15 per cent.[1]

[1] For data on the growth of world population since the nineteenth century see Simon Kuznets, *Modern Economic Growth*, Yale University Press, 1966.

CHAPTER 2

ECONOMIC AND SOCIAL BACKGROUND
OF THE TERRITORIAL OCCUPATION

INDIVIDUAL ACTION AND THE
'ENCOMIENDA' SYSTEM

The essential features of what was to become the social structure of the
Latin American countries originated in the Spanish conquest itself and in
the institutions established by the Spaniards and Portuguese to create an
economic base which would consolidate their conquest of the new lands.

The circumstances attending the lengthy process of Spain's reconquest
of her territory from the Moors permitted the creation of a highly centralised state, although the different regions of the Peninsula retained markedly
feudal characteristics. Compared with other regions of Europe, commercial capitalism had made a belated appearance in the Iberian Peninsula. In
Portugal the development of commercial capitalism was intimately bound
up with the monarchy from the very beginning. By basing its strength on
commercial activities and becoming the promoter of a grand commercial
design, the Portuguese monarchy achieved autonomous development
within the Peninsula. However, placing commercial activities under the
the aegis of the State led to a centralism not very different from that of
Spain.

Adventurous spirits from all over Europe had been attracted to Spain by
the war against the Moors and, at the time of the discovery of America,
which coincided with the end of the Reconquest, Spain had large numbers
of men able and ready to embark on military adventures likely to bring
them handsome rewards.[1] The conquest of the American lands was organised along the same lines and guided by the same principles as the long
struggle to reconquer the homeland from the Moors. The essential difference lay in the fact that at home, the enemy possessed considerable technical
resources for the time which rendered individual action completely in-
effectual. Thus, the religious–military Order became the key factor in
organising the struggle. Bringing together knights from very different
cultural areas, united by their religious ardour and spirit of adventure,

---

[1] The Conquest of Granada, the richest of the Moorish kingdoms, was the culmination of a
war lasting eleven years; it capitulated in 1492, the year Columbus discovered America.

8

Economic and Social Background

Orders such as that of Calatrava, Santiago and Alcantara appropriated extensive territories reconquered from the Moors and laid the patrimonial and centralist foundations of the future Spanish monarchy. With the union of Castile and Aragon in the persons of Isabella and Ferdinand, and with Ferdinand's successful bid to impose himself as Grand Master of the religious–military Orders, the conditions were created for the establishment of a highly centralised state, in a society where commercial capitalism was only just beginning to emerge. Thus, in different ways, Spain and Portugal had created conditions that enabled the state to assume control of economic activities at the very outset of the commercial revolution.

In America, the weakness of the peoples to be conquered and the distance of the Central Power—allowing the conquest to become on many occasions simply acts of pillage—made it possible to organise the campaigns on a far less elaborate basis than that of the religious–military Order. In fact, individual initiative was responsible for most of the action, promoted by men of relatively modest means who organised groups of hardy adventurers eager to share in the spoils of conquest. Thus, the real driving force behind the shaping of the structure of the new empire was the private interest of the Conquistador. 'L'expression *Ost des Indes*', writes a contemporary historian, 'est devenue la meilleure définition du caractère privé des expéditions de conquête. L'État espagnol vérifia en pratique que la meilleure façon de protéger ses intérêts était de céder aux particuliers la possibilité de découvrir et de soumettre les nouveaux territoires à incorporer à la couronne. Les expéditions d'État furent l'exception et quant elles ont eu lieu, elles ont été justifiées par des causes très particulières.'[1]

Individual action, the basis of the occupation of American territories, was carried out within a contractual framework strictly defined by the Spanish or Portuguese State.[2] In the case of Spain, since territorial

[1] Alvaro Jara, *Problemas y Métodos de la História Económica Hispanoamericana*, Universidad Central de Venezuela, Caracas, 1969, pp. 1 and 2. 'Se ha establecido,' writes Jara, 'que los intereses privados de los conquistadores—los componentes de la hueste indiana—fueron el verdadero motor expansivo del amplio movimiento de ocupación del continente americano.' For a more complete version see his *Guerre et Societé au Chili*, translated by Jacques Lafayette, Paris, 1961.

[2] The absence of treasures which could be easily plundered lessened Portugal's interest in Brazil in the early years, particularly as her trade with the East Indies was then at its height. To attract private capital for her American colony, the Portuguese Crown divided it into twelve hereditary captaincies, placed under the direction of proprietary landlords (*donatários*), who took over many of the royal privileges. The want of any economic base, except in the region where the cultivation of sugar cane had been introduced, led to the collapse of this experiment. The Crown had to assume direct responsibility for the cost of defending vast territories which long remained of little economic value. Although formally modelled on Portuguese feudal institutions, the system of hereditary captaincies should be seen as an

9

expansion was almost always the result of the conquest and subjugation of native populations, later exploited as a source of labour, the nexus between individual action and State patronage assumed greater significance. Through the system of *capitulaciones* or concessions, the State ceded certain prerogatives to the individual Conquistador against the fulfilment of certain obligations. The rewards granted by the Spanish State assumed their definitive form in the institution of the *encomienda*.[1] This term had been used in Spain to designate the lands and rents ceded as a reward to the commanders of religious–military Orders. In America a nucleus of the native population was 'commended' or entrusted to a Conquistador who was to be responsible for ensuring that his 'wards' were instructed in the Roman Catholic faith.

The grantee, or *encomendero*, as guardian and protector of the native population entrusted to him, came privately to exercise public law functions, which placed him socially in a position comparable only to that of the feudal lord in medieval Europe. And, like the feudal lord, he had military responsibilities and had to organise local security at his own expense. In regions where the Indians were quickly 'pacified', the *encomendero*'s military obligations became merely formal. But in regions where the war against the Indians dragged on for a very long time, as in the case of Chile, these responsibilities proved a heavy burden.

Social organisation based on the *encomienda* was most effective in regions where there was a relatively dense native population which had achieved a certain level of material development and had a measure of social stratification. The existence of a local ruling class, traditionally entitled to the surplus produce, and in a position to finance wars or public works, facilitated the establishment of the *encomienda* system. In fact, *encomenderos* who were allotted native communities managed to persuade the chieftains to increase the traditional surplus and hand over most of it to the new masters. In regions where the Indians had a very low level of material development, the possibility of expropriating their surplus produce through traditional leaders was ruled out. In such cases the *encomienda* proved ineffective as a form of social organisation and the *encomendero* resorted to more direct forms of slavery, forcing the men to perform

endeavour to attract private capital for the task of commercial expansion directed by the Crown, comparable to the trading corporations set up in England and Holland during the latter half of the sixteenth century.

[1] On the *capitulaciones* and *encomiendas*, see the classic work by Silvio Zavala, *Las Instituciones Jurídicas en la Conquista de América* (Madrid, 1935). For a short bibliography on the *encomienda* see Jacques Lambert, *Amérique Latine: Structures Sociales et Institutions Politiques*, Paris, 1963.

intensive labour in conditions very different from those to which they had been accustomed. This system resulted in a rapid depletion of the population.

Unlike the feudal lord, who extracted a surplus from the population under his control which was used in one way or another in the same region, the Spaniard who undertook the Conquest or received an *encomienda* was mainly concerned to appropriate a surplus which could be transferred to Europe. Either because he was accustomed to forms of consumption which could be satisfied only by imports from Europe, or because his ultimate aim in embarking on the American adventure was to achieve a coveted economic and social position in Spain, the *encomendero* was not interested in a surplus which could only be used locally. In fact, his aim was to mobilise the surplus so that he could discover, produce and transport precious metals. Apart from gold and silver, little that could be produced in the Americas during the first century of colonisation was marketable in Europe. Unlike the East Indies, which produced articles of great value per unit of weight, such as spices, silks and muslins, the Americas produced nothing that could become the basis of a lucrative trade. The Portuguese who, in the first two centuries of colonisation, had failed to find precious metals in the lands they occupied sought to overcome this handicap by starting commercial production of a tropical crop, using the experience gained in the Atlantic islands since the middle of the fifteenth century. Finding only a sparse and scattered population, ill-suited to the hard work of the sugar plantations, they decided to import African labour, a step calling for considerable investment and hence limiting private action to groups able to mobilise fairly substantial financial resources. It was this that gave the Portuguese action its character of 'colonisation' rather than 'conquest', and it was this that created the distinctive features of the social structures of the Portuguese territories in the initial stage.

In the case of Spanish America, the search for precious metals—and their production following discovery—was the determining factor in the action of the private individuals who played the leading role in shaping the structure of the new Empire. On the other hand, the *encomienda* system provided the framework for the emerging colonial society, composed of a small minority of Spaniards and the native masses who had managed to survive the population holocaust referred to earlier. In the Portuguese settlements, the establishment of tropical agriculture created distinctive conditions at the outset, requiring substantial investment and co-operation between the men who settled permanently on the land in which they had tied up their investment.

Economic Development of Latin America

The evolution of the production of precious metals in Spanish America was subject to marked fluctuation. In the early years the treasures accumulated in Mexico and Peru were systematically plundered, an activity serving chiefly to excite the imagination of Spain. The second phase, which lasted until the middle of the sixteenth century, is characterised by the Spaniards' efforts to discover the sources of the precious metals. Production was limited to the alluvial gold which was discovered in several regions, and tended to be rapidly exhausted. In most cases Indians were coerced or cajoled into leading expeditions organised on the initiative of an *encomendero* to rivers or streams with placer deposits from which the Indians had traditionally extracted gold. Indian gold-workings were nearly always found near by. Production was started and rapidly intensified, to be followed by an even more rapid decline once the gold-bearing gravels had been completely worked over. The tardy discovery of gold in Brazil was not due to its greater scarcity. In fact, the output of Brazilian gold in the eighteenth century was to outstrip the total gold production of the Spanish territories in the two preceding centuries. The slowness of the Portuguese was due mainly to the absence of a gold-working tradition among the Indians of Brazil. Since gold was unknown to the natives, the Portuguese had to roam the vast Brazilian territory in search of rivers and streams with gold-bearing gravels.

Silver production became paramount towards the middle of the sixteenth century. Unlike alluvial gold production, which declined very rapidly, silver production, involving the opening of mines, attained a much higher level of development and great stability over a long period. The 1570s witnessed a revolution in American silver mining with the introduction of the amalgamation technique. This technological advance made it economically possible to use poorer-grade ores and to reach levels of production undreamed of in earlier periods. On the other hand, the discovery of a quicksilver deposit at Huancavelica in Peru made it possible not only to meet local needs but also to supply part of Mexico's quicksilver requirements. Quicksilver production, restricted to a single mine situated in an isolated part of Peru, was carried out directly by the Spanish Crown, which was thus in a position to exercise indirect control over silver mining. Transportation was in private hands, and the quicksilver was sent 2,500 km over the mule trail to Potosí, in what was then Upper Peru. Silver mining was controlled by private groups, who were obliged to make heavy investments, particularly in hydraulic works. The Spanish Crown claimed one-fifth of all the precious metals produced. Thus, at least 80 per cent of the output remained in private hands.

The external trade of the Spanish colonies was subject to strict control by the metropolitan authorities. It was restricted to official convoys, under naval escort, which sailed only at certain times of the year between a Spanish port and two American ports. If we analyse the data on this trade, taking into account bullion exported by private individuals and the goods imported from Spain, it becomes apparent that the value of the imports covered only a fraction of the exports. The averages over long periods indicate that the value of the precious metals shipped by the private sector was about four times that of the total imports.[1] It seems, then, that there can be no doubt that the foremost objective of the work carried out in the Americas was to create a flow of resources for accumulation in Spain. Since production costs could be covered locally by mobilising the labour force of the *encomienda*—which produced the food supply for the men working in the mines and in transport—the imports from Spain essentially reflected the way in which the *encomenderos* used their own income, which included 80 per cent of the bullion output. Had this income been spent locally, whether in consumption or in productive or unproductive investment, the level of imports would have had to be much higher. The highly favourable balance of trade clearly indicates that the *encomendero* class was able to save a substantial proportion of its income, which was transferred to Spain.

GROWTH POLES AND THE ORIGINS OF LATIN AMERICAN 'FEUDALISM'

Although destined chiefly to produce a surplus which was transferred to Spain, the production of precious metals had an important multiplier effect on economic activities. The regions producing these metals—particularly silver—acted as genuine growth poles. The demand for food, rough textiles and draught animals required the organisation of satellite economies. Thus, settlement in Chile, which was at first supported by the production of gold, found a permanent basis in export agriculture for which the market was the Peruvian growth pole. Similarly, the regions of northern Argentina, with their relatively dense Indian population, tended to become a centre for supplying Upper Peru with textiles and draught animals.

A chain of economic interrelations was formed between the silver-

[1] For the statistical data see Alvaro Jara, *Tres Ensaios sobre Economía Minera Hispanoamericana*, Santiago, 1966.

producing region, situated in what is now Bolivia, the quicksilver-producing region, in present-day Peru, the Arica region, from which silver was shipped to Lima, Lima itself, which was the chief administrative centre, and the Cordoba–Tucuman region in Argentina, which supplied craft manufactures and draught animals. The dynamic pole of this system was, of course, the production of silver, based on Indian labour drafted by means of the *encomienda* system, which was used for this purpose throughout Spanish America.

The organisation of the Indians to create an agricultural surplus is closely related to the introduction of another institution which was to play a fundamental role in shaping the structure of Latin American society: the large agricultural estate. Grants of land were made in the same spirit as grants of Indians: as an incentive to private action so as to pave the way for the Conquest and produce a surplus for the benefit of the Crown. Land, in itself, was not an attraction. However, given the demand for agricultural products, it could become the source of a surplus to be exacted from the population ceded to the *encomendero*.

The period of great prosperity for Spanish America's silver production came to an end towards the middle of the seventeenth century. Mexico was still to experience a brilliant phase, as a major exporter of silver in the last century of the colonial era, but for Upper Peru the great days were definitely over. The decline of the mining economy marked the weakening of the dynamic pole of the economic system which had emerged in this vast region. This loss of vigour in the dynamic pole was profoundly to affect the region's subsequent social evolution. With the decline in demand for an agricultural surplus and for Indians to work in the mines and in transport, the institution of the *encomienda* tended to lose its importance. In fact, underlying the institution of the *encomienda* was the idea that part of the surplus exacted from the Indians belonged to the Crown, the *encomendero* acting simply as an agent for collecting this tribute. With the atrophy of the markets which had formerly made it possible to monetise the surplus, the transference of part of this surplus to the State proved an onerous burden. As a result, the institution gradually declined and was formally abolished at the beginning of the eighteenth century.

The decadence of the economic system that had grown up around the poles producing precious metals took the form of a progressive decentral-isation of economic and social activities, which tended to transform the ownership of land into the basic institution of social organisation. In effect, once the *encomienda* system had been abolished, it was the control of land that made it possible to continue extracting a surplus from the native population. Since this surplus, by its very nature, had to be used almost entirely locally, the social structure tended to assume the form of isolated or semi-isolated communities. These vast rural domains, essentially based on a subsistence economy and almost entirely cut off from the authority of the State, were to become one of the most characteristic features of Latin American society. The ownership of land became the basis of a system of social domination of the mass of the people by a small ethnically and culturally differentiated minority. External economic contacts were limited, and social contacts with the outside world were confined to the ruling class.

The social evolution of Brazil had its own distinctive features, but its results differed little from those described above. The decadence of the large plantation dependent upon slave labour and export markets began in the second half of the seventeenth century when the Brazilian sugar monopoly was broken and prices started to tumble.[1] Sugar production in the French and English Antilles expanded rapidly after this period, while mercantilist policies closed a great many European markets to sugar from the Portuguese colonies. The loss of foreign markets led to the partial break-up of Brazil's export agriculture and its transformation into a subsistence, or mainly subsistence, economy. The sector producing meat, draught animals and firewood for the coastal communities declined even more rapidly, disintegrating into a number of semi-closed estates. The working population for these estates, unlike that of the large coastal plantations which consisted chiefly of African slaves, was largely of Indian origin. However, given the rudimentary community organisation of the Brazilian Indian, this population was no longer organized in settled native communities. In both cases the tendency was to extract a surplus in kind, whether in the form of a share of the produce or in the form of unremunerated labour, for a specified number of days per week.

In areas of dense population the ruling class established relations with the native community's traditional leaders. In the sparsely populated areas relations were established with isolated individuals, giving rise to the dual pattern of *latifundio*–Indian community and *latifundio–minifundio*, which

[1] The marketing of Brazilian sugar in Europe was carried out from the very beginning under the control of Dutch interests responsible for refining the product and organising its distribution. The occupation of Portugal in 1580 and Spain's war with Holland made it difficult to carry out satisfactory marketing operations, and the Dutch West Indies Company finally occupied the Brazilian sugar region in 1630. In 1640 Portugal regained her independence, and twelve years later the Dutch were expelled from the Brazilian Northeast. Many of them went to the Antilles where they organised a new sugar-producing area. Thereafter sugar prices showed a persistent downward trend. For a detailed account and bibliography, see C. Furtado, *Formação Econômica do Brasil.*

were to leave a permanent mark on the Latin American agrarian structure. Since the Indian communities tended to break up into *minifundios* as their communal lands were gradually appropriated by the ruling class, the similarities between the two patterns became more pronounced. Thus, in different ways, a large proportion of the rural population came to be scattered in small structural units, self-sufficient from the viewpoint of the organisation of production, subject to the tutelage, whether direct or indirect (the latter when the authority of traditional native leaders was preserved) of a ruling class that extracted from it a surplus in a manner resembling the pattern generally known as *feudalism*.

The discovery of gold in Brazil at the beginning of the eighteenth century changed the overall trends of this country's evolution.[1] It opened up an important market for draught animals and provided new opportunities for the underemployed labour force of the sugar economy. The São Francisco River, linking the cattle-raising region of the Northeast to the mining area, became an important line of communication. The growth pole formed by the gold- and diamond-producing areas was to have considerable significance in the development of the Brazilian economy. In contrast to sugar production, only feasible for those in a position to mobilise substantial financial resources, alluvial gold could be exploited by lone prospectors and large-scale operators alike. The mining region thus attracted immigration on a far greater scale than that of the preceding two centuries. The rapid development of urban life created an expanding market for food, which was added to the even more important market for draught and pack animals used in the extensive transport network linking the vast gold region to the port of Rio de Janeiro. The market for cattle and mules was supplied mainly by the southern regions whose pastoral potential was soon recognised. Thus the growth pole created by the mining industry made it possible to establish economic links between Northeast, Central and Southern Brazil already in the eighteenth century, i.e. in the period immediately preceding independence. As we have seen, in this same period the links centring on the growth pole constituted by the silver-producing region of Upper Peru, established in the first century of colonisation, were beginning to slacken.

[1] For an analysis and bibliography of the gold period in Brazil see C. R. Boxer, *The Golden Age of Brazil 1695–1750: Growing Pains of a Colonial Society*, Berkeley, Univ. of California Press, 1962.

Economic and Social Background

The decline of silver production and the weakening of the Spanish State had far-reaching consequences for the colonial empire. The fleet system had to be abandoned at the beginning of the eighteenth century and at the same time important commercial concessions were made to England, whose penetration in Portobello and Buenos Aires was beginning to bulk large in the pattern of colonial trade. Buenos Aires was the natural gateway to Upper Peru, but this access was closed to facilitate the supervision of commerce by the Crown. From 1680 Portuguese traders had settled in the colony of Sacramento, opposite Buenos Aires, to exploit the commercial advantages offered by this strategic position. In 1713 the Treaty of Utrecht authorised the English to establish themselves in Buenos Aires with a monopoly over the slave trade.

Faced with the new situation created by the decline of mining and the advent of English commercial interests, the Spaniards reacted by attempting to diversify regional production and liberalise the conditions of trade. Trading companies were created with responsibility for developing certain areas, financing the importation of African slaves when necessary, opening up markets for new products, etc. These companies confined their activities to the Caribbean region, where conditions were favourable for the production of tropical commodities. However, given the difficulties encountered in European markets, defended by the Colonial Pact, the success of these companies was limited. In the course of the eighteenth century two new Viceroyalties were created—New Granada and Rio de la Plata—indicating Spain's interest in agricultural and commercial activities, just as the Viceroyalties of Mexico (New Spain) and Peru (New Castille), created at the time of the Conquest, had symbolised the pre-eminence of mining interests.

Taking an extremely schematic view, it can be said that the first 150 years of the Spanish presence in the Americas were marked by the spectacular economic successes of the Crown and the Spanish minority that had participated directly in the Conquest, by the destruction of a large part of the existing population, by the worsening of the living conditions of the population that survived the Conquest and, finally, by the impact on vast regions of the development of growth poles whose main function was to produce a surplus in the form of precious metals, which was transferred to Spain on an almost entirely unilateral basis. The 150 years that followed were characterised by the decline of mining, by the slackening of pressures on the population, which slowly began to increase and improve its living conditions, and by the weakening of links between the regions, which gradually became less interdependent. In the first phase the ruling class was composed of men directly connected with Spain, integrated in the apparatus of the State and in key positions of control of the production system that yielded the surplus transferred to the mother country. In the second phase the landowning class, having little connexion with the mother country and a strictly local horizon of interests, became increasingly important. In Portuguese America these two phases were to some extent reversed. In the first 150 years an export agriculture economy was set up, made up of isolated units directly linked to the exterior and cut off from all the other areas of the country, with the exception of the pastoral interior which developed as a dependency of the sugar economy. The first third of the second 150-year phase was marked by an economic depression which advanced more rapidly and had profounder repercussions than any experienced in the Spanish Empire in the course of its history. The last century of the colonial era was characterised by the emergence of a growth pole centred on the production of gold and diamonds, which performed the dual role of accelerating settlement of European origin and creating a market that linked up the country's various regions. The ruling class in the first phase consisted of the owners of large sugar plantations who had direct connexions with the metropolis. In the second phase, the ruling class included a sizeable group of individuals whose connexions were with domestic commercial activities and the flourishing mule trade, a sector of economic activity linking together the various regions involved. There is thus some evidence that whereas the structural evolution of the Spanish Empire fostered the tendency to fragmentation, that of Portuguese Brazil created conditions favouring the preservation of territorial unity.

CHAPTER 3

FIRST HALF OF
THE NINETEENTH CENTURY

END OF THE COLONIAL ERA

The break-up of the Spanish and Portuguese Empires at the time of the Napoleonic Wars was the last act in the complex historical process that unfolded throughout the eighteenth century, and was intimately related to the economic and social changes that had taken place in Europe. Spain's attempts to diversify the economies of her American colonies encountered two major obstacles: the protectionist barriers erected in the principal European markets as a result of prevailing mercantilist policies and her own inability to supply the colonies with manufactured goods. The colonies sought a way out of this situation by trying to find direct markets (through the contraband trade) or by producing domestically the articles they needed. Both attempts involved direct conflict with the metropolis. In regions with a developed export agriculture, such as Venezuela, or with a flourishing trade, such as Buenoes Aires, awareness of these problems had crystallised very early under the influx of liberal ideas from England and France. With the outbreak of the Napoleonic Wars, Spain's isolation and the rapid penetration of British commercial interests precipitated changes difficult to reverse after the establishment of autonomous local authorities in various regions. In most cases, these governments arose in circumstances which did not involve hostility to the metropolis, then occupied by the French. But the very dynamic of the process led to breakaway movements, which in some cases took the form of prolonged and cruel struggle against the obstinate attempts of the Spaniards to restore a situation which had long ceased to exist. The true nature of the problem is clearly revealed by the fact that in this same period Brazil broke away from Portugal, although the seat of government of this country, an ally of England's, had been transferred to the colony itself and remained there from 1808 to 1821. The new conditions created by the rapid advance of the Industrial Revolution in England, and by the progressive control England was able to exercise over world shipping, were bound to lead to a policy of opening the American ports to international trade, a policy incompatible with the type of relations prevailing between Spain and her colonies. The vast extent of the colonies, and the mother country's inability to supply them with manufactures, called for radical changes in the structure of an empire organised three centuries earlier around the exploitation of precious metals.

In the case of Portugal, the transition had begun much earlier. The Methuen Treaty, signed in 1703, had given England a privileged position in the Brazil trade. By this treaty, Portugal took the irreversible step of opening her own market and that of her colonies to English manufactures in return for the advantages her wines received on the English market. Brazilian gold production, which began in the second decade of the eighteenth century, had a dynamic impact on the Luso-Brazilian demand for manufactures, thus creating exceptional opportunities for English manufacturers. The result was that virtually all Brazil's gold found its way to England, enabling that country to build up the substantial international reserves without which she would have had difficulty in conducting the war against Napoleon.[1] English penetration into Brazil enabled Portugal to survive as a colonial power in the eighteenth century, but it also hastened the break in the link between the colony and the metropolis, whose position as a superfluous entrepot had become increasingly apparent. With the transference of the Portuguese Crown to Rio de Janeiro in 1808, English interests became directly involved in the Colony, which had become the seat of the Portuguese Court. In this case, too, the process proved irreversible, and set in motion a train of events affecting the Portuguese Crown itself, when one of its members assumed the leadership of the separatist movement.

The first half of the nineteenth century is marked in Latin America by the struggles for independence and by the process of formation of the nation-states. In the Spanish colonies the independence movement spread out from three centres: Caracas, Buenos Aires and Mexico. The first two were centres of regions that had developed most rapidly during the eighteenth century, a development that was largely a reflexion of Spain's weakening naval power and the penetration of English interests. In these regions, independence permitted the rise of a mercantile bourgeoisie, liberal in outlook, progressive in the sense that it was European-influenced, but hopelessly wedded to the concept of *laissez-faire*.[2] In Mexico the situa-

---

[1] Cf. W. Cunningham, *The Growth of Modern Industry and Commerce: Modern Times*, Part I, Cambridge, 1921, pp. 460–1.

[2] A conspicuous representative of this liberal current is the Liberator, Simón Bolívar, who issued decrees in 1824 and 1825 from Trujillo and Cuzco, dissolving the native communities, establishing private ownership of land by peasants, and ordering the 'so-called Indians' who were owners of the lands in their possession 'to sell them or dispose of them in any way they

tion was different, since silver mining, still in a relatively prosperous phase, continued to be the basis of the regional economy. Moreover, the indigenous Mexican Indian population, which had begun to increase again in the last century of colonial domination, was starting to exert pressure on the latifundian structure, whose power was based on the ownership of large estates and the exploitation of indigenous communities. The element of social unrest thus introduced into the independence struggle remained, and marked the country's evolution for more than a century. Thus two distinct movements, which were to remain present in Latin America's subsequent evolution, are discernible in the struggles for independence: on the one hand, the rise of a European-influenced bourgeoisie that sought to wipe out the pre-Columbian and colonial past with its decrees and to integrate the different regions into the expanding flow of international trade; on the other, the emergence of forces tending to challenge the domination of the colonial regime and seeking to integrate the native masses into the political and social framework, in an attempt to create a distinctive and independent cultural personality. The first of these movements dominated the greater part of the nineteenth century but, as we shall see further on, it was only in the latter half of that century that it finally bore fruit. The second movement entered the foreground in the present century which, for Latin America, began with the Mexican Revolution.

FORMATION OF NATION-STATES

In nearly all of Latin America the building of nation-states proved a formidable task. The liberal bourgeoisies who had led or supported the independence movements in Buenos Aires and Caracas were in no position to organise systems of political control capable of replacing those of the former metropolis. We have seen that the colonies had been evolving in the direction of regional autonomy, the result of the weakening of the former growth poles. In the absence of significant new economic links, political localism tended to prevail. In the North, where the growth pole of the mining industry remained comparatively vigorous and where a tradition of administrative centralism antedated the Spanish conquest, the political unity of what had been New Spain was preserved. In the South the captaincies of Venezuela and Chile became independent political units,

deemed fit'. These measures were not implemented at the time but clearly reflect the European-influenced outlook of the leaders of the wars of independence. For relevant comment see Arturo Urquidi Morales, 'Las Comunidades Indígenas y su Perspectiva Histórica' in *Les Problèmes Agraires des Amériques Latines*, Paris, 1967.

New Granada split up into Colombia and Ecuador, while the recently created Viceroyalty of the Rio de la Plata broke up, giving rise to the present-day republics of Argentina, Uruguay, Paraguay and Bolivia.

Once the ties with the metropolis had been severed, power tended to shift to the landowning class. The structuring of the new states was conditioned by two factors: the absence of genuine interdependence between the landowners, who joined forces or submitted to whoever succeeded in the power struggle and the action of the urban bourgeoisie, who maintained contact with the outside world and explored every possibility of expanding external trade. This second group was gradually joined by parts of the rural sector. Thus, as opportunities for different types of export lines arose, the urban group tended to consolidate itself and at the same time to become integrated into the appropriate rural subgroup, creating the conditions for building up an effective power system. In countries such as Mexico, Peru and Bolivia, where mining dominated the economy, the control of mining was enough to define the power of the State. There was hardly any connexion between this power and the population masses organised on the large estates. None the less, no regional landowner was powerful enough to challenge the authority of the State, control of which was the main objective of the political struggles. In regions with an agricultural economy, the consolidation of state power was dependent on the opening up of new export lines which, by favouring one region, enabled it to dominate the others. In Colombia, where none of the regions had managed to achieve a sufficiently solid economic base to become dominant, there were prolonged civil wars which decimated the population. In Argentina, the privileged position of the port of Buenos Aires enabled the coastal region to impose itself as the centre of a national power system, after prolonged civil wars.[1]

We have seen that events in Europe, which isolated Spain from her colonies, hastened the wars of independence, led by the local bourgeoisie which had emerged in the areas benefiting from the diversification of trade in the last century of the colonial era. Mexico is a case apart, in the sense that its isolation from the metropolis had more far-reaching consequences, setting in motion a process that challenged the social order itself, giving another dimension to the power struggle and creating a situation of instability that was prolonged throughout the nineteenth century. We have also noted the part played by the English in breaking the

[1] For an account of the role of the 'unifying autocracy' in the formation of the nation-state in Argentina see Gino Germani, *Política y Sociedad en una Época de Transición*, Buenos Aires, 1962.

22

trade monopoly and creating Europe-orientated urban interests. It must be pointed out, however, that English penetration, in the first decades of the nineteenth century, contributed to the disruption of the existing social and economic order rather than to the consolidation of the emerging nation-states. The English were essentially involved in organising an import trade. Numerous English import houses were founded, responsible for the wide distribution of English-manufactured goods, which changed consumption habits and led to the disruption of local craft activities. The influx of imported goods forced many countries to depreciate their foreign exchange rates, and governments had to apply for foreign loans to ease the balance of payments situation. On the other hand, the commercial houses importing British goods were able to accumulate liquid reserves and establish powerful financial concerns. The local bourgeoisies, who had connexions with English import interests, had to face the problem of an inadequate external payments capacity. The accumulation of the external debt and the recurrent balance of payments crises created fiscal and foreign exchange problems which were met by issuing inconvertible paper currency, entailing the constant deterioration of the domestic and foreign purchasing power of the national currencies. The urban populations, hardest-hit by the periodic price increases, were at times driven to open revolt. The export drive that this situation demanded led local bourgeoisies to turn to the interior for exportable products and to foreign countries for potential markets. However, during the first half of the nineteenth century external markets were limited and access to them proved difficult. This was largely because the Industrial Revolution, in this early phase, displayed two features that had a negative effect on the Latin American countries. The first was its concentration in England, a country with colonies of her own able to supply her with primary products, particularly tropical commodities. The second was the key role of the cotton textile industry, for which the raw material could be produced on a large scale in the United States, using slave labour. The shorter distance involved was also a direct advantage in an age when maritime transport was precarious.

By and large, the Latin American countries experienced great difficulty in opening up new lines of trade in the three or four decades following the wars of independence. Apart from precious metals, hides and skins, no other export managed to find favourable market conditions. Although cotton consumption in England had risen from two thousand to a quarter of a million tons, cotton prices had tumbled and it was difficult to compete with growers in the southern United States. Moreover, the prices of sugar and other tropical commodities had fallen steeply after the end of the Napoleonic Wars. It has been argued that expansion of exports was handicapped by the political instability that prevailed in almost all the Latin American countries. But it can be argued that the causal direction was opposite: the difficulties encountered in finding foreign outlets for their export lines left the urban groups, who had led the independence struggles, in no position to organise a stable power system. An interesting exception to this rule—and the exception proves the rule—is the case of Chile. This country, an autonomous captaincy in colonial days, was distinguished by the fact that it had been neither an exporting centre for precious metals (its gold production had declined very rapidly) nor a region exporting agricultural and livestock products to foreign markets. In fact, Chile was an agricultural and cattle-raising region focusing on the Peurvian growth pole. Unlike other commercial bourgeoisies, established through the contraband trade and under strong English influence, Chilean export interests were integrated with the region's agricultural and livestock interests, and had emerged within the legal framework of the monopoly organised by the metropolis. As a result, the Chilean ruling class was not subject to major internal conflict and managed to build up a stable power system in the decade following the wars of independence. In 1833 the *Portales* Constitution formalised a representative oligarchic power system, which remained stable until the late nineteenth century. On the other hand, Chile was able to take advantage of particularly favourable conditions for her foreign trade. First, she had the nucleus of a mining economy based on silver and copper, which expanded during this period. In the second place, she produced a surplus of temperate agricultural commodities, notably wheat, which gave her a distinct advantage in the Pacific zone at the time when gold was discovered in California and Australia.[1] Thus, for a brief but crucial period, Chile became a strategic food supplier to the West Coast of the United States. To what extent Chile's stable political structure enabled her to take advantage of the favourable foreign market conditions, or whether these conditions made it possible to consolidate the emergent political structure, is a matter of secondary importance. Obviously there was some interaction between these two factors. But one cannot ignore the fact that the foreign market conditions experienced by Chile constitute a special case. No other Latin American country in the Pacific zone could match Chile's agricultural potential and export 'knowhow' in this particular sector. On the other

[1] For an outline of the evolution of the Chilean economy in the nineteenth century see Aníbal Pinto Santa Cruz, *Chile, un Caso de Desarrollo Frustrado*, Santiago de Chile, 1962.

hand, given the transportation difficulties of the time, no Atlantic country, Latin American or otherwise, offered any serious competition.

The Brazilian situation during this period also displays distinctive features worth analysing for a better understanding of the political structures on which the Latin American States are based. In contrast with what occurred in the regions occupied by the Spaniards, agricultural activities in Brazil and the exportation of surplus produce were the Colony's very *raison d'être*. The Portuguese monopolised commercial activities, preventing the emergence of a local bourgeoisie with foreign trade connexions. In the gold- and diamond-producing region the metropolis exercised an even stricter control of external activities. Meanwhile, this same region, which offered a ready market for draught animals, saw the rise and consolidation of a class of cattlemen and mule traders with connexions in various parts of the country. These men brought large convoys of mules from Rio Grande do Sul to São Paulo, where the bustling livestock fairs attracted dealers who supplied the mining regions through the network they maintained with the coastal area. After independence, foreign trade interests remained in the hands of the Portuguese, protected by the continuity of the Crown, or were taken over by Englishmen. There was thus little change in the sugar region where the old structures were maintained under the more direct control of English interests. The most significant changes occurred in the south, where the mining economy had been on the decline since the end of the eighteenth century. The dwindling gold output, which shrank to a third or a quarter of the quantity formerly produced at the same time as administrative expenses were rising sharply as a result of the transference of the Court and the subsequent establishment of independent government, created an overall imbalance in the economy. This was countered by contracting foreign loans and issuing paper currency which rapidly depreciated.

Inflation bred dissatisfaction in the urban zones and centrifugal forces began to manifest themselves in several regions. None the less, the development of coffee production, whose possibilities became apparent as early as the 1840s, permitted the formation of the nucleus which was to become the basis of the new power structure. The men responsible for establishing the connexion between the mining areas and the coastal zone played a major role in setting up a coffee economy in the Paraíba Valley, from which it spread to the São Paulo highlands half a century later. Thus coffee developed outside the latifundian structures established earlier, through the initiative of individuals with a mercantile outlook. Consequently the economic activity that was to be the mainstay of the Brazilian State in its

Economic Development of Latin America

formative phase and throughout its period of consolidation was from the outset an agricultural-export activity. As in the case of Chile, planters and merchants came to have joint interests and presented a perfectly united front. The traditional *latifundio*, or large estate, with its mainly subsistence economy, was destined to have a marginal place in the power system that took shape in Brazil. None the less, since the new export agriculture was also modelled on the large unit, it achieved a basic solidarity with the established *latifundio*. The latter were thus able to retain control of local power in their respective regions while leaving hegemonic control of national power to the new interests.[1]

[1] For a synthesis of Latin American history in the independence period see Victor-L. Tapié, *Histoire de l'Amérique Latine au XIXe Siècle*, Paris, 1945. The book includes detailed bibliographies. For general bibliographies consult Jaime Vicens Vives, *Bibliógrafia Histórica de España y Hispanoamérica*, Barcelona, 1953. See also Robert A. Humphreys, *Latin American History: a Guide to the Literature in English*, London, 1960. The revised second edition of Jacques Lambert's *Amérique Latine: Structures Sociales et Institutions Politiques*, Paris, 1968, is also a valuable bibliographical source.

II. ENTRY INTO THE SYSTEM OF INTERNATIONAL DIVISION OF LABOUR

CHAPTER 4

THE TRANSFORMATION OF INTERNATIONAL TRADE IN THE SECOND HALF OF THE NINETEENTH CENTURY AND ITS IMPACT ON LATIN AMERICA

INTERNATIONAL DIVISION OF LABOUR

During the first half of the nineteenth century, the Industrial Revolution was essentially an English phenomenon. For this reason the structural evolution of the English economy provides the key to the radical changes which took place during this period in the world economy as a whole. The economists who witnessed the beginnings of these changes, and interpreted them from the English viewpoint, immediately realised that it was in England's interests to become a vast factory, opening its doors to primary products from all over the world. In fact, industrial activity, violating the law of diminishing returns, stimulated qualitative changes without precedent in economic processes.

In economics in which technology had made little or no progress—based essentially on agricultural activity—it was evident that there were limits to the degree to which the relative proportions of the productive factors employed could be altered. Beyond a certain point, the output obtained per unit of agricultural land necessarily tended to decrease, regardless of the amount of labour added, which meant that availability of land governed the use of the other factors. Industrial activity made it possible to break this barrier, since growth itself, by creating the possibility of further specialisation in labour and equipment (greater division of labour additional and more complex machinery), became the source of increased productivity, which meant increasing returns. In such circumstances,

27

even if prices of imported agricultural products remained stable and were the same as those of home-produced goods, it would still be to the advantage of a country like England, where land was scarce, to be able to pay for them with industrial products. On the other hand, once England had established an important industrial nucleus and consolidated its advantage over other countries, it would not be difficult to demonstrate that, in terms of the principle of comparative advantage, considered from the static point of view, it would be in the interests of other countries to buy industrial products from England and pay for them with raw materials. However, despite the enormous advantages it represented for England (since it implied nothing less than the concentration in this country of those activities in which rapid technological progress was being made), this pattern of development met with resistance on the part of agricultural interests, and its acceptance was much slower than is generally supposed. Throughout the first half of the nineteenth century, English agriculture continued to enjoy effective protection through an adjustable tariff mechanism which permitted customs barriers to be automatically raised whenever world prices fell below a certain critical point. However, faced with the growing power of the industrial bourgeoisie, resistance gradually broke down and, between 1846 and 1849, England eliminated barriers to external trade without expecting other countries to follow suit.

The complete victory of free trade ideas in some ways marked the end of the first phase of the Industrial Revolution. During this phase a dynamic nucleus was formed and consolidated in England, which was to lead, in the second half of the nineteenth century, to the establishment of a system of international division of labour, based on a world market. Of decisive importance in the transition from the first to the second phase of the Industrial Revolution was the application to the transport sector of technology originally developed in connexion with manufacturing industries. Railroads made possible the rapid integration of the domestic markets in European countries, while the mechanisation of maritime transport brought about radical changes in the conditions of international trade. The propeller was invented around 1840, and in the course of the following decade the introduction of iron hulls, reducing the resistance of water, permitted an increase in the size of vessels. From then on, the total world tonnage of the merchant marine was to increase with extraordinary speed: from 6·7 million tons in 1840 it rose to 12·8 million in 1860, and to 43 million in 1913. The impact on long-distance freight charges was dramatic, and in many cases ocean freight rates were cut by as much as 70–90 per cent. The consequent fall in the prices of raw materials, particularly of cotton, reinforced England's competitive position. By pursuing a policy of free trade and substantially reducing her own agricultural activities, England was able to extract the maximum advantage from the fall in raw material prices brought about by the cut in shipping costs. In this way, English manufacturers managed to 'internalize' the external economies resulting from the technological revolution in transport. It should be recalled that in the first few decades of the second half of the nineteenth century, two-thirds of the manufactures circulating in the world market were made in England.

The century between the 1820s and the outbreak of the First World War saw the establishment of an international division of labour and the shaping of a world economic system. The economic activities of a growing proportion of the world's population became interdependent elements of an integrated complex. The new pattern of the world economy displayed some notable features. The first was the rise in the economic growth rate of many of the countries that made up this pattern. This applied not only to countries which specialized in activities benefiting from rapid technological progress, but also to those making more rational use of their natural resources. This phenomenon had far-reaching historical consequences. Up to this time, growth rates had been irregular and, even when they showed a long term upward trend, were too weak to bring about really significant changes in standards of living within the lifetime of a single generation. It seemed natural, therefore, to assume, as did the mercantilists, that the enrichment of one community inevitably meant the impoverishment of another. With the Industrial Revolution, the accelerated output of goods and services made it possible to double a community's purchasing power in the course of a single generation.

The second significant change was the dramatic rise in the rates of population increase brought about by urbanisation, improvements in public services and the rise in real incomes. Immediately afterwards, the striking advances of medical science greatly improved life-expectancies. Expectation of a longer life and the possibility of seeing it dramatically altered produced a new outlook, based on the awareness that the horizon of possibilities open to mankind could be vastly extended on both individual and social planes. The great collective movements, which in the past had had a religious or military inspiration, became increasingly orientated towards understanding and mastering the physical world and reshaping social structures.

The third noteworthy characteristic is the creation and rapid expansion of a fund of transmittable technical knowledge related to the forms of production.[1] In the pre-industrial epoch, production techniques were the result of the gradual accumulation of empirical knowledge, handed down from generation to generation through apprenticeship in the skilled trades. Productive activity gave rise to further productive activity, just as one generation gives birth to the next. With the growing importance of an equipment industry based on advanced technology, the situation was radically altered. Transmission of techniques took the form of a straightforward commercial transaction, and it became possible to transform an entire productive sector at a hitherto-undreamed-of speed. By creating a transport equipment industry, England set in motion a process that was to transform the means of transport throughout the world. Further, by providing adequate financing for this industry, it created a mechanism for exporting capital which was to be a decisive factor in shaping the world economic system and in creating new forms of hegemony outside the traditional framework of colonial administration.

The result of the interplay of these factors was the growth and integration of the world economy in the nineteenth century and the intensification of international specialisation. World trade expanded rapidly: its growth rate was far higher than that of the domestic products of the nations that took the lead in bringing about the transformation of the world economy. The value of world trade, which was no more than 1·5 billion dollars in the 1820s, rose to 3·5 billion in the 1840s and to 40 billion just before the outbreak of the First World War. This growth was reflected in the growing 'internationalisation' of the industrialised economies and more particularly of the British economy. Thus, Great Britain's external trade coefficient,[2] which was 8·5 per cent in the period 1805–19, rose to 29·4 per cent in the period 1910–13. Generally speaking, the external trade coefficient rose in all the European countries that started industrialising in this period. The same phenomenon occurred in countries exporting primary products—the case of the Latin American countries—in which exports were developed at the expense of subsistence economic activities. This was not the case in countries whose development was essentially an expansion of the European economic frontier, i.e. countries such as the United States,[3] Canada, Australia and New Zealand, whose development

[1] Simon Kuznets, *Modern Economic Growth*, p. 286.
[2] The coefficient of external trade is defined as the ratio between the average value of imports and exports and the domestic product. For historical data see C. P. Kindleberger, *Foreign Trade and the National Economy*, Yale University Press, 1962, p. 180.
[3] The reference to the United States is restricted to the expansion of its agricultural frontier, particularly in the cereal-growing region. By the time the American provinces gained their

Transformation of International Trade

was dependent on an inflow of European labour and capital. In these countries development took the form of incorporating new territories and was an extension of the European economic space, whose basic natural resources, thus enriched, permitted a rise in agricultural productivity. The tendency to diminishing returns in agriculture was avoided by increasing the supply of good agricultural land. Thus, Britain could curtail agricultural production while prices of agricultural products could be reduced thanks to the incorporation of land in the temperate zones of North America and Oceania. The economy that developed in these new areas was specialised from the start, that is, it had a high coefficient of external trade and a high level of productivity and income. These conditions made it possible to attract the European immigrants on whose labour these developing areas depended. The result was that when they entered the world economy they already had effective domestic markets for industrial products and a labour force equipped for industrial activity, a circumstance which accounts for their early industrialisation. Since the newly established industries competed with imported manufactures, the external trade coefficient, which was high to begin with, showed a tendency to decline or level off, rather than follow the upward trend noted in the first two cases.

In summary, the following features of the formative process of the world economic system are worth emphasising, because of their significance in shaping international relations:

(a) the existence of a nucleus which achieved a considerable advance in the process of capital accumulation, concentrating a large proportion of industrial activity, practically all centred on the production of equipment; this nucleus was also the finance centre for world exports of capital goods,

Independence, they already had a nucleus of manufacturing activities, including iron and steel works and shipbuilding. During the Napoleonic Wars, the United States benefited considerably from her position as a neutral country and became the possessor of the world's second largest merchant fleet, consisting entirely of vessels built in her own shipyards. Modern textile industries were established at the beginning of the nineteenth century and by the 1820s a textile machinery industry had already been set up. On the other hand, the marked increase in cotton exports produced on the basis of slave labour made it possible to maintain a high level of imports, benefiting regions of the country which were in the process of industrialising. The great expansion of agriculture in the Mid-West was supported by the markets provided by the commercial-industrial Eastern region and the region of specialised agriculture in the South. It was the interconnexion of these three dynamic poles—the industrial-commercial complex of the East, the agricultural exporting South and the food producing Mid-West—that gave the U.S. economic system its extraordinary dynamism. None the less, the expansion of the U.S. agricultural frontier, creating large exportable surpluses, had the same stimulating effect on the European economy as the settlement of other empty spaces in the temperate latitudes outside Europe.

31

controlled the transport infrastructure in international trade and was the major import market for primary products.

(b) the emergence of the system of international division of labour under the hegemony of this growth pole; the inducement to specialise favoured rapid settlement of vast empty spaces in temperate zones and the integration of other areas into the world market through the export of primary products.

(c) the creation of a network for transmitting technological progress as a subsidiary of the international division of labour; this network facilitated the export of capital and at the same time linked capital outflows to the system of international specialisation which it tended to consolidate; since production of capital goods was concentrated in the nucleus described above, new production techniques also remained geographically concentrated, benefiting those activities in which the dominant economy already had experience or in which it had more direct interest. Hence the evolution of technology was conditioned by the system of international division of labour that emerged with the Industrial Revolution.[1]

TYPOLOGY OF ECONOMIES EXPORTING RAW MATERIALS

The Latin American countries began to enter the channels of expanding international trade in the 1840s. The primary exporters involved in this process tended to fall into three groups: (a) countries exporting temperate agricultural commodities; (b) countries exporting tropical agricultural commodities; (c) countries exporting mineral products. In each case, foreign trade helped to establish a distinctive economic structure whose characteristic features should be borne in mind when studying its subsequent evolution.

The first group is composed essentially of Argentina and Uruguay. In this case, exportable agricultural production was based on the extensive use of land and was destined to compete with the domestic production of countries undergoing rapid industrialisation. Extensive use of good agricultural land made it possible to achieve high profitability from the start. On the other hand, the very extensiveness of the agriculture practised and the sheer volume of freight involved necessitated the creation of a widespread transportation network which indirectly led to the rapid unification of the domestic market, focusing on the major ports of shipment. This group of countries displays the characteristics of regions referred to

[1] For the relation between development and international trade in the nineteenth century see Ragnar Nurkse, 'Trade Theory and Development Policy', in H. S. Ellis (ed.), *Economic Development for Latin America*, London, 1961.

earlier as constituting an expanding frontier of the industrialising European economy. This frontier, to which European agricultural technology was transplanted in the early stages, soon became an important centre for developing new agricultural techniques of its own. Both the techniques of farming vast open spaces and of large-scale transportation, storage and shipment of cereals originated in the United States. In sum, the countries in this group, precisely because they competed with the domestic production of countries at a more advanced stage of development and with regions of recent European settlement enjoying a high standard of living, were from the start integrated into a productive sector of the world economy characterised by constant technological advance. Throughout the phase of expansion in their foreign trade, these countries achieved high rates of growth.

The second group, consisting of countries exporting tropical agricultural products, includes more than half the Latin American population. It includes Brazil, Colombia, Ecuador, Central America and the Caribbean, as well as certain regions of Mexico and Venezuela. Countries in this group entered international trade in competition with colonial areas and the southern region of the United States. Sugar and tobacco remained typically colonial products until the last years of the nineteenth century. It was the rapid expansion of the world demand for coffee and cacao from the mid-nineteenth century onwards that enabled tropical commodities to play a dynamic role in integrating the Latin American economy into world trade during the period under consideration. In this case, structural changes in the British economy had less direct impact, since the British market continued to be abundantly supplied by colonial regions where labour was plentiful and wages were low. The role of dynamic centre fell to the United States and, to a lesser extent, to the European countries. On the whole, tropical commodities were of little significance as a factor in development, although they did involve the opening up of large areas for settlement. On the one hand, their prices continued to be influenced by the low wages prevailing in colonial regions, which had long been traditional tropical commodity producers. On the other, they did not usually require the creation of a complex infrastructure; on the contrary, in many regions traditional means of transport continued to be used. Finally, since they were produced in areas lacking the capacity to develop new techniques for themselves, tropical products tended to remain within the framework of the traditional economies. None the less, in certain regions tropical export agriculture did manage to play an important role in development. The most notable instance is probably that of the coffee region of São Paulo, in Brazil. Here the physical and chemical qualities of the soil permitted extensive coffee planting over large areas. The relatively high productivity of labour and the vast size of the area planted favoured the creation of an infrastructure and promoted home market expansion. The special nature of this case becomes evident when we recall that at the end of the nineteenth century the São Paulo highlands supplied two-thirds of the total world coffee output.

The third group, consisting of countries exporting mineral products, includes Mexico, Chile, Peru and Bolivia. Venezuela entered this group in the 1920s as an exporter of petroleum. By creating a rapidly expanding market for industrial metals, the transport revolution of the mid-nineteenth century brought about a radical change in Latin American mining. In the first place, precious metals, notably silver, rapidly lost their importance. Secondly, small-scale mining operations of the artisan or quasi-artisan type were gradually replaced by large-scale production controlled by foreign capital and administered from abroad. The considerable rise in the world demand for non-ferrous metals coincided with major technological progress in production methods which permitted or required the concentration of production in large units. This process of concentration, carried out initially in the major producing country—the United States—soon spread to other areas, where local producers were marginalised by American organisations with heavy financial backing and the technical 'knowhow' required to handle low-grade ores. Thus, the development of the export mining industry entailed not only denationalisation but the establishment of a productive sector which, given its marked technological advance and high capital intensity, tended to become isolated and to behave as a separate economic system, or rather, as part of the economic system in which the decision centre controlling the production unit belonged. Foreign control of a highly capitalised activity, employing a small labour force, meant that the major share of the flow of income generated by this activity was deflected from the domestic economy. In these circumstances its value as a factor for inducing direct change in the domestic economy was practically nil. Moreover, since the infrastructure created to serve export mining industries is highly specialised, the resultant external economies are minimal or non-existent for the economic system as a whole. Finally, since this type of mining activity called for specialised imports and created a limited flow of wage income, it made no significant contribution to the creation of a domestic market. Its potential as a dynamic factor became evident only when the State intervened, obliging mining companies to acquire part of their inputs locally and collecting, in the form of tax revenue, a significant share of the flow of income traditionally remitted abroad.

CHAPTER 5

REORIENTATION OF THE INTERNATIONAL ECONOMY IN THE PRESENT CENTURY

EXPORT EXPANSION PHASE

The three decades preceding the First World War were a period of rapid economic development and intense social change for Latin America as a whole: in Mexico, where the Porfirio Díaz administration created the conditions for a large inflow of foreign capital directed mainly into mineral production; in Chile, whose victory in the War of the Pacific against Bolivia and Peru enabled her to monopolise the sources of nitrate; in Cuba, where, even before independence was attained in 1898, the country's increasing integration into the United States market had brought about a dramatic expansion in sugar production; in Brazil, where the spread of coffee over the São Paulo highlands and the influx of European immigrants hastened the collapse of the slave economy; finally, in Argentina, where economy and society underwent drastic changes under the impact of the great wave of immigration and the penetration of substantial foreign capital.

A closer look at the three largest countries reveals the importance of the changes that occurred during this period. In Mexico, the population increased from 9·4 million in 1877 to 15·2 million in 1910. In the last decade of the Porfirio Díaz administration (1900–10), the annual average growth rate of the real per capita product was 3·1 per cent. During this decade the production of minerals and petroleum, the country's basic export sector, grew at an annual rate of 7·2 per cent, that is, twice as fast as manufacturing production and nearly three times as fast as agricultural production.[1] In Brazil, the population increased from 10·1 million in 1872 to 17·3 million in 1900. In the last decade of the nineteenth century, the rate of population increase in São Paulo was over 5 per cent a year, while for the country as a whole it was under 2 per cent. Nearly all the 610,000 immigrants entering

[1] For basic data see Daniel Cosio Villegas, *História Moderna de México*, VII, *El Porfiriato: Vida Económica*, Mexico, 1965. See also Leopoldo M. Sólis, 'Hacia un Análisis General a Largo Plazo del Desarrollo Económico de México' in El Colégio de México, *Demografía y Economía*, I, no. 1, Mexico, 1967.

Brazil during this decade went to the State of São Paulo. Between 1880 and 1910, the total length of railways increased from 3·4 to 21·3 thousand kilometres. Coffee exports, which amounted to around 4 million 60-kilogram bags in 1880, rose to almost 10 million in 1900 and to over 16 million on the eve of the First World War, a total seldom surpassed in later years. In the same period, exports of cacao rose from 6,000 to 40,000 tons, and rubber exports from 7,000 to 40,000 tons.[1] However, it was in Argentina that the changes brought about in this phase were most marked. Between the periods 1890–1904 and 1910–14, Argentina's population doubled, increasing from 3·6 to 7·2 million; the country's railway network was extended from 12·7 to 31·1 thousand kilometres; cereal exports rose from 1,038,000 to 5,294,000 tons, and exports of frozen meat rose from 27,000 to 376,000 tons.[2]

In short, during the period under consideration, Latin America became an important component of world trade and a key source of raw materials for the industrialised countries. In 1913, the Latin American share in world commodity exports was as follows: cereals—17·9 per cent; livestock products—11·5 per cent; coffee, cocoa and tea—62·1 per cent; sugar—37·6 per cent; fruit and vegetables—14·2 per cent; vegetable fibres—6·3 per cent; rubber, furs, hides and leathers—25·1 per cent.[3]

NEW TRENDS IN THE INTERNATIONAL ECONOMY

After the First World War there were important changes in the long-term trends of the international economy. These changes were accentuated by the 1929 crisis. In the first place, there was a reversal of the upward trend in the external trade coefficient of the industrialised countries. In Britain, for instance, it fell from around 30 per cent (for the period 1910–13) to 25 per cent in 1927–9 and to 17 per cent in the 1930s. In the United States, Germany, France and Japan, the coefficient levelled off in the 1920s and declined in the 1930s.[4] This downward trend shifted again only after the Second World War, this time within a new international economic frame-

---

[1] Cf. Instituto Brasileiro de Geografia e Estatística, *Anuário Estatístico do Brasil, Quadros Retrospectivos, 1939–40*.
[2] See Aldo Ferrer, *La Economía Argentina*, Mexico, 1963 (translated by Marjorie M. Urquidi, *The Argentine Economy*, Berkeley, University of California Press, 1967). See also Roberto Cortés Conde, 'Problemas del Crecimiento Industrial (1870–1914)', Torcuato di Tella, Gino Germani and Jorge Graciarena (ed.), *Argentina, Sociedad de Masas*, Buenos Aires, 1965.
[3] Basic data from P. L. Yates, *Forty Years of Foreign Trade*, London, 1959.
[4] Cf. C. P. Kindleberger, *Foreign Trade and the National Economy*.

work in which the central feature of world trade had become the exchange of manufactured products between industrialised countries.

In the second place, there was a persistent deterioration in world market prices of primary products. This tendency, already discernible in the preceding period, became more pronounced after 1913. To the short-term inelasticity of supply of primary commodities and the structural rigidity of countries specialising in primary production for export, was added the effect of technological progress as a factor responsible for this downward trend in world prices of raw materials. After the First World War, synthetic nitrates progressively displaced Chilean nitrates. Synthetic fibres and synthetic rubber appeared shortly afterwards. Greater efficiency in the industrial use of mineral products was to have a similar effect.

The third tendency worth noting is the steady change in the composition of world trade, a tendency that became apparent only after the Second World War. In the three decades preceding World War I, the quantum of world trade in primary products increased at just about the same rate as the trade in manufactures. In the two decades following, as a result of the sharp rise in petroleum exports and the protectionism prevailing in the industrialised countries, the quantum of exports of primary products increased more than that of exports of manufactures. However, the most significant shifts in trend have occurred only since the 1950s. As Table 5.1 indicates, the situation in 1953 was already quite different from that of 1913 with regard to the share of foodstuffs and manufactures in the composition of world trade.[1]

The relative decline in natural fibres and the rise in petroleum are the main changes that took place in the period indicated. It was from the 1950s onwards that the new trends, which were to radically alter the composition of world trade in the course of a decade, became apparent. Between 1953 and 1967, the annual rate of growth of world exports of foodstuffs was 3·5 per cent, that of other primary products (excluding fuel) was also 3·5 per cent, of fuel, 7 per cent, of chemical products 15 per cent, and of other manufactures 8·5 per cent. As a result of these trends, exchanges between industrialised countries have become of growing significance in world trade. Thus, in 1966, the total exports of developed countries with a market economy amounted to 139 billion dollars, of which 106 billion were accounted for by their exports to each other.[2]

If we compare the overall pattern of development of the world economy

[1] Cf. P. L. Yates, *Forty Years of Foreign Trade.*
[2] For the basic data, see UN *Yearbook of International Trade Statistics, 1964,* and *Monthly Bulletin of Statistics, Dec. 1967* and *July 1968.*

TABLE 5.1. *World Trade Composition*

	1913	1953
	\% of total	
foodstuffs	29	23
agricultural raw materials	21	14
minerals	13	20
manufactures	37	43

in the half-century following the end of World War I with the half-century preceding it, significant differences become immediately apparent, particularly from the point of view of the underdeveloped countries. The earlier period was marked by the emergence of a system of international division of labour under the hegemony of the group of countries which had begun to industrialise during the first half of the nineteenth century. This system permitted the concentration in certain areas of production activities which benefited most from technological progress, as well as the fuller and more rational utilisation of abundant resources (labour and land) in other areas. The increased overall activity of an expanding world economy was accompanied by the establishment or accentuation of inter-dependence between its various parts. If we look more closely at this process, it becomes immediately apparent that it involved two forms of development. On the one hand, we have the development of industrial centres based on technological progress and a rapid accumulation of capital. This type of development entailed increasingly complicated pro-duction processes, which required both a change in the relative quantities of productive factors, with more capital per unit of labour, and a change in their quality, more particularly a progressive improvement in the human factor. On the other hand, we have the development of the so-called 'periphery', or outpost areas, induced by changes in overall demand and effected through the external sector. This second type of development was nearly always extensive in character; that is, it made it possible to increase the economic productivity of available factors without requiring signifi-cant changes in the forms of production. Thus, the substitution of a sub-sistence crop such as maize by an export crop such as coffee brought about an increase in overall output while requiring no major changes in produc-tion techniques. In other instances—the case of mining production—this peripheral development took the form of assimilating modern techniques and increasing the input of capital in a production sector strictly geared to exports and lacking the capacity to transmit its growth to the economy as a whole. In either case, peripheral development had little capacity to transform traditional techniques of production. Nevertheless, by requiring the modernisation of infrastructures and of part of the State apparatus, it set in motion an historical process which opened up important new possibilities.

THE 1929 CRISIS AND ITS IMPACT ON LATIN AMERICA

In the period which began with the First World War and assumed marked characteristics with the 1929 crisis, the traditional system of international division of labour played a progressively less important role. International demand for primary products lost its dynamism as a reflexion of the structural evolution that had taken place in the industrialised countries. Full realisation of the nature and magnitude of the problem and of its repercussions on the international economy was delayed by the Great Depression. The extent and severity of the depression obscured all other causal factors. It was not easy to perceive that the very magnitude of the crisis already reflected the important changes that were taking place in the world economy. The quantum of world exports fell by 25 per cent between 1929 and 1933, and the general level of export prices by 30 per cent, entailing a fall of over 50 per cent in the total value of world trade. Moreover, the change in flow of international capital movements greatly aggravated the situation of countries exporting primary products. Britain, the United States and France, who had exported an annual average of 3,300 million dollars in the form of short- and long-term capital in the period 1928–30, became net importers of 1,600 million dollars, on yearly average, in the period 1931–2. Britain, who in the period 1925–9 had paid for 22 per cent of her imports out of the income earned on British capital abroad, raised this proportion to 37 per cent in the period 1930–4. In Latin America, the crisis assumed catastrophic proportions, precisely because it was one of the underdeveloped regions which had been most closely integrated with the international system of division of labour. The entire modern sector of the Latin American economy was geared to external trade. In Mexico nearly 30 per cent of the country's reproducible capital was controlled by foreign groups, and in Argentina more than 40 per cent. The situation in the other countries was much the same. The external debt and its servicing conditioned not only the behaviour of the balance of payments but also that of public finance and the monetary system. Throughout the decade following the crisis, the capacity to import was

TABLE 5.2. *Latin America: Evolution of External Trade*

	quantum of exports	terms of trade	capacity to import
1930–4	− 8·8	− 24·3	− 31·3
1935–9	− 2·4	− 10·8	− 12·9

SOURCE: ECLA, *Economic Survey of Latin America, 1949*.

severely curtailed, not so much as a result of the decline of the quantum of exports but mainly as a reflexion of the adverse trend in the terms of trade, as Table 5.2 clearly indicates.

Taking into account the population increase, the capacity to import declined by 37 per cent in the period 1930–4 relatively to the pre-crisis period, and by 27 per cent in the five-year period following. The impact of the crisis was felt most violently in the public sector because of its dependence on revenue from foreign trade and also as a reflexion of the financial significance of the external public debt. With the exception of Argentina, all the Latin American countries suspended debt-service payments for more or less lengthy periods, which made it even more difficult to obtain foreign capital to pay for badly needed imports of equipment.

Although the whole region was hard hit, the consequences of the 1929 crisis varied in accordance with the degree of the country's integration into the system of international division of labour and the nature of this integration. Countries such as Argentina, exporting temperate-zone food products, were *relatively* less severely affected, in the first place because demand for these products has a low income elasticity, particularly in countries with high living levels and, secondly, because the supply of these commodities, nearly all annual crops, is relatively elastic, since it is possible to reduce the crop areas from one year to the next. Finally, since these products compete with surpluses produced in developed countries, markets are relatively better organised.

In the case of tropical products, demand is also relatively inelastic in terms of income. But, given the inelasticity of supply in the case of perennial crops, any decline in demand provokes catastrophic falls in prices, which tend to become even more accentuated in the absence of any possibility of financing surpluses and withdrawing them from the market. In the case of mineral products, we have a different picture: the curtailment

TABLE 5.3. *External Trade Indicators for Selected Latin American Countries* (*% variation from annual average for 1925–9*)

	quantum of exports	terms of trade	capacity to import	quantum of imports
Argentina				
1930–4	− 8	− 20	− 27	− 32
1935–9	− 11	0	− 11	− 23
Brazil				
1930–4	+ 10	− 40	− 35	− 48
1935–9	+ 52	− 55	− 32	− 27
Chile				
1930–4	− 33	− 38	− 58	− 60
1935–9	− 2	− 41	− 42	− 50
Mexico				
1930–4	− 25	− 43	− 55	− 45
1935–9	− 11	− 36	− 39	− 26

SOURCE: ECLA, *Economic Survey of Latin America, 1949.*

of industrial production in the importing countries led to the liquidation of stocks and the collapse of production in the exporting countries. The fall in the volume of exports tended to be considerable. The external trade statistics of Argentina, Brazil, Chile and Mexico for the decade following the crisis illustrate the different forms of reaction in underdeveloped structures. Given the extreme inelasticity of coffee production and other tropical commodities, Brazil attempted to offset the fall in commodity prices by increasing her quantum of exports, which rose by 10 per cent in the 1930–4 period, relatively to the period 1925–9. Argentina reduced hers by 8 per cent, Chile by 33 per cent and Mexico by 25 per cent. The deterioration in Brazil's terms of trade was twice as severe as in Argentina's, but not very different from that in Chile and Mexico. The hardest-hit countries were the mineral exporters, affected both by the fall in prices and the reduction in the quantum of exports. The countries in the least vulnerable position were those exporting commodities with annual crop cycles, whose production structure was more flexible. In the following five-year period (1935–9) Brazil continued to force the external markets, making a concerted effort to dispose of her enormous output of coffee, since the accumulation of stocks was proving a heavy financial burden. This effort was completely defeated by the deterioration in the terms of trade. In

Argentina, the reduction in the quantum of exports was accompanied by a significant improvement in the terms of trade. The Chilean economy, more closely integrated with the system of international division of labour than any of the other three economies mentioned, was easily the most severely affected. Its behaviour during this decade revealed the extreme vulnerability of primary-exporter economies within the framework of the international division of labour established in the nineteenth century.

CHAPTER 6

SOME INDICATORS
OF THE DEGREE OF DEVELOPMENT
REACHED IN
LATIN AMERICA

ECONOMIC INDICATORS

Whereas the period extending from the Wars of Independence to the 1870s was one of stagnation in nearly all the Latin American countries, in the century that followed the Latin American economies underwent relatively intense development, although the pattern varied from country to country. In the first half of the century—during which development was induced largely through the expansion of raw material exports—the regions with temperate climates and abundant empty lands received a large inflow of immigrants and capital from Europe. In these regions, economic development was particularly intense during this first phase and was accompanied by a precocious urbanisation process and other social changes. The old society, essentially rural, in which political power was monopolised by a small minority of landowners, was rapidly transformed as large urban centres came into being, with the growing participation of the middle social strata. The southern region of the South American continent—Argentina, Uruguay and, to a lesser extent, Chile—and the southern areas of Brazil which had received an influx of European immigrants, became rapidly urbanised and the subsistence economy was completely replaced by a money economy. An elastic food supply and the relatively high wage rates demanded by the European immigrants contributed to the establishment of much higher living standards than those prevailing in the areas settled much earlier. Today, the living conditions of the Latin American population as a whole are basically an outcome of the social structures that emerged during their first phase of modern development—from about 1870 to 1914—and of the intensity of this development from that period up to the present time. In fact, living conditions in the various areas of the region were probably not very different in the mid-nineteenth century. With the expansion of production for export, the evolution of social structures was conditioned by, for example, the

43

relative importance of the existing subsistence economy, the recently incorporated European contingent and the degree to which manpower was absorbed by the monetary sector.

A comparison between the two phases of coffee expansion in Brazil reveals the significance of these factors. In the first phase, involving the occupation of lands in the State of Rio and the southern part of the State of Minas Gerais, expansion benefited from the abundant manpower available in the latter State as a result of the decline in gold and diamond production in an earlier period. The abundance of labour permitted the expansion of coffee to proceed within the framework of the traditional plantation, in which the monetary flow was minimal and the level of real wages extremely low. In the second phase, during which coffee planting spread to the São Paulo highlands, the shortage of labour played a key role. The government sponsored and financed a large inflow of European immigrants, stipulating from the outset that wages were to be paid in money, and that living conditions should be sufficiently attractive to appeal to prospective immigrants from southern Europe. These social changes account for the more rapid tempo of urbanisation in the São Paulo highlands, the formation of a domestic market nucleus in this region, and its subsequent development. If the standard of living of the people in the São Paulo highlands failed to keep pace with the region's productivity in the period that followed, this was due to the overall pattern of the Brazilian economy, whose integration, in the present century, made it possible for the surplus manpower in the less-developed regions to exert pressure on the wages paid in the more-developed regions.

In Argentina, the manpower shortage and the intensity of development in the phase of expanding exports made it possible to create social conditions which placed Argentina, along with Uruguay, in an exceptional position among Latin American countries. In the industrialisation phase Argentina failed to achieve as high a growth rate as Mexico or Brazil. None the less, since industrialisation has not produced a change in the pattern of income distribution or led to a significant absorption of surplus manpower, Argentina and Uruguay, alone of the Latin American countries, have remained able to combine development with effective improvements in the living conditions of the bulk of the population.

Latin America accounts for nearly 7 per cent of the world population and at present contributes about 5 per cent to the overall world product and 7 per cent to world trade. Its per capita income is one-third lower than the world average, but about twice that of the so-called Third World countries. Estimates of per capita income, relative to the 1960–2 period,

Indicators of Development

TABLE 6.1. Share of Various Regions in World Population
and Gross World Product

	% of real product	% of world population	per capita real product (in 1960 dollars)
developed countries with a market economy	58·7	19·7	1,744
U.S.A.	29·4	6·2	2,790
Western Europe	22·0	8·7	1,472
socialist countries	23·7	34·6	401
U.S.S.R.	12·1	7·2	986
Eastern Europe	4·7	3·3	825
China	6·6	23·2	167
underdeveloped countries			
Africa	1·9	6·9	164
Middle East	1·7	3·5	254
Asia	6·9	26·1	154
Southern Europe	1·9	2·2	501
Latin America	4·9	6·8	431
world total	100·0	100·0	585

SOURCES: (1) ECLA, *The Economic Development of Latin America in the Post-War Period*, UN, 1964.   (2) *Economic Bulletin for Latin America*, Oct. 1967.

reproduced in Table 6.1, were calculated on the basis of rates of exchange adjusted for changes in the purchasing power of the different currencies.

The Latin American average obviously conceals wide disparities between the different countries. Thus, Argentina's per capita income approximates the average for the Eastern European countries, whereas that of Haiti or Bolivia is below the African average. Haiti's per capita income is only 11 per cent of that of Argentina, representing a far greater difference than that between the Latin American average and the per capita income of the United States. Besides Argentina, the other countries with incomes per capita well above the regional mean are Uruguay, Venezuela and Chile. Mexico, whose relative position has improved substantially since the 1940s, now ranks close to Chile. Brazil's per capita income is one-third below the regional mean and Colombia's one-fifth.

Data on food consumption, while confirming the situation of underdevelopment in Latin America, reveal the intermediate position occupied by the region. Intake of animal proteins is substantially higher than in other areas of the Third World.

TABLE 6.2. *Per Capita Income Estimates for 1960 (converted to U.S. dollars using various conversion factors)*

	per capita income (in dollars)				gross domestic product (in million dollars)[5]
	I[1]	II[2]	III[3]	IV[4]	
Argentina	561	1,045	721	868	17,947
Bolivia	102	201	135	165	609
Brazil	250	342	245	289	20,305
Colombia	259	396	289	336	5,203
Chile	606	809	536	658	5,128
Ecuador	216	352	264	304	1,312
Paraguay	160	296	220	255	450
Peru	207	389	295	338	3,387
Uruguay	477	1,012	722	853	2,124
Venezuela	1,043	871	763	809	5,933
Costa Rica	376	537	415	471	568
El Salvador	228	307	257	280	698
Guatemala	271	327	260	291	1,094
Haiti	72	105	84	94	390
Honduras	194	230	191	208	406
Mexico	346	582	464	518	18,688
Nicaragua	228	277	214	243	359
Panama	439	520	434	474	484
Dominican Republic	239	285	226	253	766

[1] official exchange rates; [2] equivalent purchasing power with weighting based on average relative prices in Latin America; [3] equivalent purchasing power with weighting based on relative U.S. prices; [4] weighted average of [2] and [3]; [5] using the exchange rate of column IV.

SOURCE: 'The Measurement of Latin American Real Income in US dollars' in ECLA, *Economic Bulletin for Latin America, Oct. 1967.*

In food consumption, too, there are considerable disparities between the different Latin American countries. Thus, Argentina with an average daily per capita intake of 3,090 calories and 57 grammes of animal protein has a diet similar to that of the higher-income countries. On the other hand, many countries have intakes below 2,000 calories and 15 grammes of animal proteins. Disparities within nearly all the countries are equally significant, and are particularly marked in countries that have large indigenous populations and are still culturally heterogeneous. In Brazil the sheer size of the country, and the restricted mobility of labour prevailing until the beginning of the present century, gave rise to marked regional disparities in living conditions.

Indicators of Development

TABLE 6.3. *World Food Consumption, by Region*
(per capita per day, in recent years)

	calories	proteins (grammes) total	proteins (grammes) animal	fats (grammes)
North America	3,100	93	66	142
Europe	3,000	88	36	94
Latin America	2,450	67	25	61
Middle East	2,450	76	14	45
Africa	2,350	61	11	56
Far East	2,050	56	8	28
World	2,400	68	20	56

SOURCE: ECLA, *The Economic Development of Latin America in the Post-War Period*, 1964.

SOCIAL INDICATORS

Social indicators confirm the region's extremely irregular pattern, with Argentina at one end of the scale and Haiti at the other, and Mexico and Brazil, which together account for half the total Latin American population, in the middle.

TABLE 6.4. *Health Indicators (about 1960) for Selected Countries*

	death rate per 1,000 inhabitants	life expectancy at birth	no. of hospital beds per 1,000 inhabitants	no. of physicians per 10,000 inhabitants
Argentina	8–9	64–6	6·4	13·0
Chile	12–13	53–6	5·0	6·2
Mexico	13–16	51–5	1·4	5·8
Brazil	11–16	50–8	3·4	4·0
Colombia	14–17	48–53	3·2	4·3
Peru	13–18	48–55	2·2	4·7
Bolivia	20–5	40–5	1·8	1·9
Haiti	20–8	36–45	0·7	—
France	11·8	68·0	8·3	10·6
United States	9·4	69·5	9·1	13·4

SOURCE: ECLA, *The Economic Development of Latin America in the Post-War Period*, 1964.

TABLE 6.5. *Education Indicators (about 1950) for Latin American Countries*

	illiterates as % of persons 15 years and older	% of 5–14-year-olds enrolled in primary schools	% of 15–19-year-olds enrolled in secondary schools	higher education per 100,000 persons
Argentina	14	66	21	480
Bolivia	68	24	7	166
Brazil	51	26	10	98
Chile	20	66	18	290
Colombia	43	28	7	94
Costa Rica	21	49	7	192
Cuba	22	49	—	—
Dominican Republic	57	40	7	106
Ecuador	44	41	9	127
El Salvador	61	31	4	65
Guatemala	71	22	7	84
Haiti	89	15	—	28
Honduras	65	22	3	57
Mexico	43	39	4	111
Nicaragua	62	23	3	81
Panama	30	54	24	190
Paraguay	34	51	9	121
Peru	58	44	—	193
Uruguay	15	62	17	484
Venezuela	48	40	6	137
Italy	14	54	29	520
United States	3	88	60	1,511

SOURCE: ECLA, *The Economic Development of Latin America in the Post-War Period*, 1964.

Indicators of levels of education show a similar pattern. The illiteracy rate among the population aged 15 years and over varies from 14 per cent in Argentina to 89 per cent in Haiti, with Mexico and Brazil falling midway between these extremes with rates of 43 per cent and 51 per cent respectively. However, disparities are even greater than these percentages indicate, since the *quality* of literacy varies greatly between countries. Of all pupils entering primary school, 50 per cent reached the fifth grade in Argentina as against 4 per cent in Haiti. In Chile this proportion is around 30 per cent, in Mexico 19 per cent, in Brazil 17 per cent and in Colombia

12 per cent. The average length of stay at primary school in Latin America is only 2·2 years and, as is only to be expected, this average conceals wide differences.

The analysis of social indicators reveals that in countries where national product increased from the mid-nineteenth century onwards in conditions of manpower shortage—Argentina, Uruguay and, to a lesser extent, Chile—the gains from development have been fairly widespread. Comparison between Venezuela and Uruguay is illustrative in this respect. Measured in dollars of comparable purchasing power, the per capita incomes of the two countries are almost the same. None the less, nutrition levels in Venezuela are close to the Latin American average, whereas in Uruguay they are well above. The same differences exist with regard to the average life expectancy at birth which, in Venezuela, is between 53 and 57 years (close to the Latin American average) while in Uruguay average life expectancy is as much as 65–8 years.

The data on educational levels are equally conclusive: of 1,000 children starting primary school, 488 reach the fifth grade in Uruguay as against only 214 in Venezuela; 144 complete secondary education in Uruguay as compared with only 15 in Venezuela; finally, 7 complete a higher course in Uruguay as against 0·6 in Venezuela. In other words, a Uruguayan child starting primary school has a 10 times greater chance of taking a higher degree than his Venezuelan counterpart. It should be added that the Paraguayan child also has a 50 per cent greater chance than the Venezuelan child of starting school at all.

III. THE TRADITIONAL STRUCTURAL PATTERN

CHAPTER 7

CHARACTERISTICS OF AGRARIAN STRUCTURES

LARGE ESTATES AND SOCIAL ORGANISATION

In Latin America, agrarian structures are not only an element of the production system but also the basic feature of the entire social organisation. We have seen, in chapter 2, that both in the economies whose point of departure was export agriculture and in those initially organised around mining production, the large estate tended to become the basic element of social organisation. From the outset, the principle governing grants of land was that grantees should have the necessary means to exploit their lands in order to produce a surplus which could be converted into cash and partially transferred to the Crown. After Independence, several countries sought to modify this principle by promoting *colonisation* schemes under which lands were granted as family holdings to settler families who undertook to work the land themselves. This policy was nearly always bound up with the encouragement of European immigration and achieved some success in Southern Brazil, Argentina and Chile.

The family farm system made headway in regions which remained relatively isolated and were characterised by the prevalence of recent settlement of European origin. Thus, in the southern regions of Brazil, where there was no profitable export crop, the pioneer European 'colonies' were forced to turn to a subsistence economy, producing marginal surpluses for sale in the home market, particularly in the rapidly expanding coffee areas. Given the abundance of land and the farming techniques which settlers brought from Europe, subsistence levels were relatively high, although the proportion of the crop marketed was low. In the phase that followed, stimulated by the growth of the home market, these regions developed within a social framework which offered much greater scope for individual advancement than that of other areas in the country.

Consolidation of the family farm system in regions where rapid agricultural expansion was based on production for export would have required conditions which did not exist in Latin America. The highly specialised nature of export agriculture meant that it was subject to a high degree of natural risk. A bad harvest could give rise to an irreversible process of debt. On the other hand, since world prices were subject to wide fluctuations, the financial risks were equally considerable. Survival thus depended mainly on financial capacity which nearly always increased more than proportionally with the size of the enterprise. But the problem is not confined to its microeconomic aspects. Other factors, relating to broader questions of economic structure, may be decisive in determining the predominant type of agricultural organisation. Thus, the growing importance of cattle-raising, and the possibility of cutting production costs in cereal farming by using the land in rotation with grazing, favoured the development of extensive farming in Argentina. Control of land remained in the hands of financially powerful groups who speculated in land and invested in cattle, leaving agricultural production to be organised, wherever possible, on rented lands. The experience of the American Mid-West, where the powerful groups controlling marketing clashed with small farmers, reveals the importance of the broad factors determining the structure of the economic framework in conditioning the methods of production. The development of transport systems had enabled railroad companies to introduce a differential tariff policy, which permitted the overall cost of transporting cereals to be reduced and facilitated their regular flow, so enhancing their competitive position in the world market. However, this policy tended to centralise all tertiary activities in Chicago, ruining local development prospects and transforming the interior into little more than a zone of agricultural production. The reaction of the local populace, voiced in the demand for a change in the rail tariff policy and leading to the enactment of State laws in matters normally coming within Federal jurisdiction, must be regarded as a virtual revolution in which social values prevailed over economic criteria. Had the Federal Government come down on the side of the interests vested in Chicago, backed not only by the written law but by economic arguments which were, at that time, irrefutable, the social framework which permitted the consolidation of the system of family holdings would probably have evolved very differently.

The type of agrarian structure which had prevailed in Latin America since colonial times, and which provided the framework for the region's social pattern, is characterised, as we have seen, by the dual pattern of *latifundio*–Indian community and *latifundio–minifundio*. Since the indigenous communities were simply transformed into instruments of social control, becoming from the economic viewpoint a constellation of *minifundios*, it is in the type of relationship established between *latifundio* and *minifundio* that we must seek the characteristic features of the region's agrarian structure. The *latifundio* system had its origin in the fact that large grants of land were originally distributed among a small number of persons who came to control, limit and block access to the ownership of land. Control was made easier by the fact that the best lands were those able to reap the external economies resulting from investments in the infrastructure which, even when financed by the State, were made for the benefit of the landowning class. Anyone lacking the financial means to buy land and either unwilling or unable to find work on the large estate had to establish himself on lands with poorer quality soil or badly situated from the economic viewpoint, becoming of necessity a smallholder.

In many regions of Latin America, land ownership is less a basis for the economic organisation of agricultural production than a means of extracting a surplus from an economy with an extremely low level of productivity. Where there is little likelihood of a profitable cash crop, small plots of land are granted to families undertaking to produce enough for their own subsistence needs. This subsistence economy is combined with a second type of activity, organised along commercial lines, either in lands set aside for this purpose, in which case the worker contributes his labour free for a certain number of days, or in the family plots, in which case he contributes part of the cash crop, thus paying an indirect rent, which is nearly always high, for the land he uses to grow his subsistence crops. This type of organisation makes it possible to expropriate a relatively large surplus from a labour force with extremely low productivity. Moreover, the natural and financial risks involved in all agricultural production are shared by the workers. On the other hand this type of organisation makes it possible to invest in agriculture regardless of its low profitability in terms of the cash return. The families working a subsistence plot on the large estate can be employed, in return for a supplementary wage, to open up new lands, to build access roads, to plant permanent crops or to carry out other capital improvements. By these means the large estates are constantly incorporating new lands although, by and large, they utilise only a fraction of the lands appropriated earlier.

TABLE 7.1. *Minifundios and Latifundios in the Agrarian Structure of Selected Latin American Countries*

| | minifundios | | latifundios | |
	% of farms	% of occupied land	% of farms	% of occupied land
Argentina	43·2	3·4	0·8	36·9
Brazil	22·5	0·5	4·7	59·5
Colombia	64·0	4·9	1·3	49·5
Chile	36·9	0·2	6·9	81·3
Ecuador	89·9	16·6	0·4	45·1
Guatemala	88·4	14·3	0·1	40·8
Peru	88·0	7·4	1·1	82·4

SOURCE: Inter-American Committee for Agricultural Development (CIDA), *Posse e Uso da Terra e Desenvolvimento Sócio-Económico do Sétor Agrícola à Brasil*, Washington, 1966.

LATIFUNDIO–MINIFUNDIO PATTERN AND UNDER-UTILISATION OF RESOURCES

If we exclude those countries that have carried out drastic land reforms— Mexico, Bolivia and Cuba—Latin America's agrarian structure follows a relatively uniform pattern. Throughout the region a small number of *latifundios* control about half the agricultural land, while a vast number of *minifundios* must content themselves with a meagre fraction and be ready to provide seasonal labour for the *latifundios*. Table 7.1 gives figures which provide a clear picture of the situation.

The definition of *minifundio* used here embodies an economic and a social criterion: it is taken to mean a plot of land which is too small to provide full employment for one family (two man-years) and cannot yield an income sufficient to sustain a standard of living considered to be the adequate minimum for the region concerned. A *latifundio* is defined as an estate employing more than 12 workers in a permanent capacity.[1] It should be pointed out that the *minifundio* is more widespread in countries with dense indigenous populations—Ecuador, Guatemala and Peru. The average size of the *latifundios* in Argentina is 270 times that of the *minifundios*; in Guatemala the *latifundio* may be as much as 1,732 times the size of the *minifundio*. In the latter country, as in other countries where the

[1] See Solon L. Barraclough and Arthur L. Domike, 'La Estructura Agrária en Siete Paises de América Latina', *El Trimestre Económico*, April–June 1966.

Agrarian Structures

TABLE 7.2. *Agrarian Structure Indicators in Selected Latin American Countries*

	minifundios	family farms	medium sized farms	latifundios
Argentina				
% of total farmland	3	46	15	36
% value of agricultural product	12	47	26	15
% of labour employed	30	49	15	6
Brazil				
% of total farmland	—	6	34	60
% value of agricultural product	3	18	43	36
% of labour employed	11	26	42	21
Chile				
% of total farmland	—	8	13	79
% value of agricultural product	4	16	23	57
% of labour employed	13	28	21	38
Colombia				
% of total farmland	5	25	25	45
% value of agricultural product	21	45	19	15
% of labour employed	58	31	7	4
Guatemala				
% of total farmland	14	13	32	41
% value of agricultural product	30	13	36	21
% of labour employed	68	13	12	7

SOURCE: CIDA, *Posse e Uso da Terra*, 1966.

indigenous populations are crowded on to constantly shrinking areas of impoverished land, the so-called '*microfundio*' or '*microfinca*' is the main form of landholding. The 74,300 *microfincas* in Guatemala yield an average income only one-third of that provided by its *minifundios* and about one-thousandth of the average income provided by its *latifundios*.

Apart from the *latifundios* and *minifundios*, Latin American agriculture is carried on in family farms and medium-sized farms. Family farms provide work for two to four people, medium-sized or 'multi-family' farms employ four to twelve workers. In Argentina, Brazil and Colombia, these

TABLE 7.3. *Farm Efficiency Indicators* (*Index: minifundios* = 100)

country and type of farm	value of output per hectare of total farmland	value of output per hectare of area under cultivation	value of output per agricultural worker
Argentina			
family farms	30	50	250
medium-sized farms	50	62	470
latifundios	12	49	620
Brazil			
family farms	59	80	290
medium-sized farms	24	53	420
latifundios	11	42	690
Colombia			
family farms	48	90	418
medium-sized farms	19	84	753
latifundios	9	80	995
Chile			
family farms	14	32	170
medium-sized farms	12	25	310
latifundios	5	21	440
Guatemala			
family farms	56	80	220
medium-sized farms	54	122	670
latifundios	25	83	710

SOURCE: CIDA, *Posse e Uso da Terra*, 1966.

intermediate forms of farm organisation account for 60 per cent or more of the total agricultural output.

In Chile, the only one of the countries mentioned above currently in the process of carrying out an agrarian reform programme, the *latifundio* occupies a major position both as a form of land tenure and as a form of organising production and providing a source of employment. The average size of the Chilean *latifundio* is more than 1,500 times that of the *minifundio*, but its average income is only 72 times greater. Comparing these figures with those for other countries in the region, we are led to conclude that the Chilean agrarian structure constitutes an extreme case both of the under-utilisation of land on the *latifundios* and its over-utilisation on the *minifundios*. In fact, if we relate the average size of the

TABLE 7.4. *Brazil: Investment per Farm in relation to Class of Farm Tenure*

class of farm tenure	average size	investment per farm (excluding cattle)	crop land per farm	investment per hectare of crop land
family farms	100	100	100	100
medium-sized farms	290	430	200	200
latifundios	3,660	1,100	1,150	100

SOURCE: CIDA, *Posse e Uso da Terra*, 1966.

latifundio to that of the *minifundio*, we find that the concentration ratio in Chile is three times as high as in Brazil and Colombia and five times as high as in Argentina. On the other hand, if we relate average incomes of *latifundios* and *minifundios*, we find that the Chilean ratio is only 10 per cent higher than the Argentine and Brazilian ratios and 50 per cent higher than the Colombian ratio. Table 7.3 enables us to compare the degree of efficiency in the utilisation of resources by the various types of farm. The figures for the *minifundios* are taken as the base.

The figures given indicate the extreme under-utilisation of the land held by latifundists. In Chile, the value of output per unit of land in the *latifundios* is 20 times lower than in the *minifundios*. In Argentina and Brazil it is around 10 times lower. It should be borne in mind, however, that the *latifundios* include lands of different types and hence they use only a fraction of their total areas. The index of yield per unit of land actually under cultivation is thus more significant. And on this measure of productivity too, the *latifundios* are below not only the *minifundios* but also the medium-sized family farms. The figures for the output per worker are equally interesting. The high labour productivity of the *latifundios* is largely the result of the extensive way in which the land is used, bearing in mind that the land used for farming is invariably of good quality since it is selected from among the abundant lands available on the large estates.

A sample survey carried out in eleven different regions of Brazil provides data which enable us to complete the picture outlined above, revealing other aspects of the typical Latin American agrarian structure.[1] The family farm is taken as the point of reference since the *minifundio* is a notoriously inefficient form of farming.

[1] For basic data and a detailed analysis of the Brazilian case, see Inter-American Committee for Agricultural Development, *Posse e Uso da Terra e Desenvolvimento Sócio-Econômico do Sétor Agrícola à Brasil*, Washington, 1966.

The *latifundio*, with an average area 31·6 times larger than that of the family farm, invested only eleven times as much. Investment per unit of crop land was no larger than on family farms. The *latifundio* is thus not justified by a greater propensity to invest, even if we exclude the investment represented by the lands left idle. If we compare the figures given for Brazil in the two tables above, we see that although investment per unit of crop land is the same for the *latifundio* and the family farm, the value of the *latifundio*'s output per unit of crop land is only half that of the family farm, whereas its labour productivity is twice as high. This is obviously accounted for by the fact that the *latifundios*, with their abundant sources of unused land, adopt extensive farming methods and invest in labour-saving equipment. In theory, the same amount of investment could produce twice the output on the family farms. We must thus conclude that investment in the *latifundios* is directed towards raising labour productivity, since they include large areas of unusable land. On the other hand, the productivity of labour is extremely low in the *minifundios* because the land must be more intensively worked in view of the small areas available. Since the productivity of labour is three times higher on the family farm than in the *minifundio*, and the investment yield per unit of crop land is twice as high on the family farm as in the *latifundio*, it seems obvious that a simple reorganisation of Brazil's agricultural structure would result in a substantial increase in the productivity of the factors employed. The present agrarian structure in Brazil does not act as a complete brake on the increase of production because there is still an abundant supply of land. But growth through the spread of *latifundios* condemns tracts of land to lie idle, thus raising transport costs and failing to create enough employment opportunities in the expanding areas at a time when there is increasing pressure on the land in the *minifundio* areas. Between 1950 and 1960 the average size of the Brazilian *minifundio* decreased from 2·6 to 2·4 hectares.

In the Latin American countries where the settlement of new land advanced more rapidly than in Brazil, the obstacles to development imposed by the agrarian structure were obvious sooner, setting in motion the land reform process analysed in a later chapter.

CHAPTER 8

DISTRIBUTION AND UTILISATION
OF THE SOCIAL INCOME

PATTERN OF DEMAND IN UNDERDEVELOPED STRUCTURES

The way in which a community distributes the social product is undoubtedly one of the most significant features of an economic structure. This aspect is particularly important in the case of underdeveloped economies. Exogenous forces, such as the external demand for a few primary products subject to short-run fluctuations in price, have a marked effect on the performance of the economy; there is often a considerable disparity between the remuneration of factors of production and their opportunity costs in productive use, both in the export sector and in the sectors most affected by modern technology; and such things tend to isolate the effects of one from another economic decision. This situation can give rise to demand schedules with characteristic discontinuities, each segment displaying different behaviour patterns or trends. Thus, in a given phase of expansion of the domestic product, one group of consumers may show a rapid advance in purchasing power while another remains stationary; or one group, benefiting from a rise in the real income of its members, may *diversify* its demand schedule through the inclusion of higher quality goods, while another grows through *extension*, that is, through the addition of new members of the group without any change in the demand schedule of existing members. Traditional economic analysis blurred the perception of these problems, based as it was on assumptions of homogeneous factors and of an identical technological horizon for all decision-making agents related to production. An understanding of the problems of underdevelopment requires the adoption of hypotheses based on different concepts, such as the absence of a unified labour market in the production of the same good, and the simultaneity of different production functions. Consequently, the demand schedule or the way in which the social income is distributed must be carefully studied, since it provides the key for determining the degree of non-integration of the economy in question or, put in another way, of the characteristics of its underdevelopment.

The pressure of the structural manpower surplus is undoubtedly the most important aspect of this problem, but by no means exhausts it. Another structural aspect to be considered is the extent of foreign control in the export sector or in any other sector acting as the dynamic pole of the economy and, as a rule, displaying a high level of profitability. In this case a rise in profits may signify no more than an increase in the flow of profit remittances abroad. Associated with this is the question of fiscal policy, which may become the determining factor for linking productivity increases in the foreign-controlled dynamic sector to the national economy.

COMPARATIVE ANALYSIS OF THE ARGENTINE, BRAZILIAN AND MEXICAN CASES

In Latin America, studies of income distribution are very recent. Income distribution curves have been established for a limited number of countries but systematic research into the non-economic factors responsible for the particular shape of the individual curves and their variations in time is still at an early stage. Table 8.1 reproduces data on income distribution for the three most highly populated countries.

Argentina has the least uneven distribution pattern, easily explicable by the fact that there is less disparity here in the living standards of urban and rural populations. Comparing the income distribution curve for Argentina with the curves established for the more highly industrialised countries, we see that the significant difference is the relatively greater weight of the higher income groups. In England, for instance, the richest 10 per cent account for 30 per cent, and in the United States for 31 per cent, of the total income, whereas in Argentina this decile accounts for as much as 39·1 per cent of the total, a percentage similar to that found in Brazil, a country burdened with a large structural manpower surplus. In England, the 50 per cent with the lowest incomes account for 25 per cent of the total income, and in the United States for 23 per cent, whereas in Argentina their share is 23 per cent, i.e. the same as in the United States. The concentration of income in the upper part of the curve, observed in the case of Argentina, is most probably related to the relative weight carried by the pattern of land ownership in this country, the greater prevalence of monopolies in the industrial sector and the high level of overall protection for the industrial activities vis-à-vis imports.

The most significant difference between Argentina, on the one hand, and Brazil and Mexico on the other is that in Argentina the standard of living of the 20 per cent of the population in the lower income brackets is more than three times as high as that of the corresponding group in

Distribution of Social Income

TABLE 8.1. *Income Distribution in Selected Countries*

	Argentina[1]	Brazil[2]	Mexico[1]
lowest decile	2·9	2·8	1·5
2nd	4·1	3·2	2·1
3rd	4·8	4·0	3·1
4th	5·5	4·4	3·8
5th	6·1	5·4	4·9
6th	7·1	6·4	6·0
7th	8·0	7·7	8·1
8th	9·6	9·8	12·0
9th	12·9	14·8	17·0
10th	39·1	41·5	41·5
Top 5 per cent	29·4	31·0	29·0
Top 1 per cent	14·5	19·0	12·0

[1] = households   [2] = individual earners

SOURCE: ECLA, *Estudio sobre la Distribución del Ingreso en América Latina*, UN, 1967.

Brazil and Mexico and, in the case of Brazil, is higher than that of the national mean. In other terms, the poorest fifth of the Argentine population has an average income of 300 dollars, whereas the income of the poorest half of the Brazilian and Mexican populations averages around 150 dollars, which means that this section of the population is only marginally integrated into the money economy. The half of the Argentine population ranked between the third and seventh deciles constitutes a fairly homogeneous group, the difference between the two deciles being 60 per cent, and has a relatively high standard of living, corresponding to 63 per cent of the national average. In Brazil, the half of the population ranked between the third and seventh deciles has an average income corresponding to 56 per cent of the national average, and the difference between the two extremes is 90 per cent.

The particular conditions under which Argentine agriculture developed, offering relatively high wages in order to attract European manpower whose access to ownership of the land was severely restricted, doubtless account for differences which still persist at present, although the disparities between the per capita income in Argentina and that of the other two countries, particularly Mexico, have been substantially reduced in the course of the last few decades. Average labour productivity in the Argentine agrarian sector is only 17 per cent lower than in the domestic economy

61

as a whole. In Brazil, it is 50 per cent below the national average and in Mexico two-thirds lower. Heavy population pressure on the land, which characterises the Mexican *Mesa Central*, accounts in part for this figure. In this region, where the population is organised in rural communities, land reform freed the rural worker from paying an open or disguised rent for his land, but also helped to reduce the mobility of labour. On the other hand, the development of farming in other regions benefiting from substantial public investments prevented prices of agricultural products from rising in the more crowded areas.

Since data on income distribution in Mexico are more readily available than for the other Latin American countries, they provide a basis for a more detailed analysis of the way in which gains from development are distributed in an underdeveloped economy.[1] Of all the countries in the region, Mexico undoubtedly holds the record for steady growth of the national product over the last three decades. Between 1940 and 1950 the accumulated rate of growth of the per capita product was 3·9 per cent a year, and in the decade following it was 2·7 per cent. During this period there were significant changes in the country's economic structure. In 1940, agriculture accounted for 24·3 per cent of the gross domestic product and manufacturing for 18 per cent; in 1950, the share of agriculture had declined to 22·5 per cent, while manufacturing had increased its share to 20·5 per cent; in 1960 these percentages had changed to 18·9 per cent and 23 per cent respectively.

The figures for the decade 1940–50 show that the average annual wage increased by 33 per cent in real terms, rising from 266 to 355 dollars at 1950 prices. However, a more detailed analysis of these figures shows that the average non-agricultural wage fell from 550 to 517 dollars, and the average agricultural wage from 95 to 85 dollars, corresponding to a decline of 6 per cent in the first case and 11 per cent in the second. Thus the average wage increased by only 33 per cent in a decade when average productivity increased by 44 per cent; but even more significantly, the rise in the average wage was simply the result of the transfer of labour from lower-wage sectors to sectors paying higher wages. The existence of a manpower surplus and the growth of the population exerted sufficient pressure on the labour market to bring about a decline in wage rates in both the rural areas and the towns. This transfer of income at the expense of wage-earners was facilitated by the inflationary process that occurred during this period. Differences between living conditions in the rural

[1] Cf. Ifigenia N. de Navarrette, *La Distribución del Ingreso en el Desarrollo Económico de México*, Mexico, 1960.

Distribution of Social Income

TABLE 8.2. *Mexico: Income Distribution in Selected Years*

	1950	1956–7	1963–4
lowest decile	2·7	1·7	1·5
2nd	3·4	2·7	2·1
3rd	3·8	3·1	3·1
4th	4·4	3·8	3·8
5th	4·8	4·3	4·9
6th	5·5	5·6	6·0
7th	7·0	7·4	8·1
8th	8·6	10·0	12·0
9th	10·8	14·7	17·0
10th	49·0	46·7	41·5
Top 5 per cent	40·0	36·5	29·0
Top 1 per cent	23·0	16·0	12·0

SOURCE: ECLA, *Estudio sobre la Distribución del Ingreso en América Latina*, 1967.

areas and the towns are so considerable that even under conditions of an overall decline in real wage rates there may be a marked increase in the overall consumption of wage-earners as a result of changes in the occupational structure.

The changes that have taken place between 1950 and 1963–4 are shown in Table 8.2.

These figures reveal other important aspects of the structural evolution of the Mexican economy. Four population groups can be clearly distinguished. The first group, composed of the 40 per cent of the population in the lowest income brackets, continues to be totally excluded from the benefits of development. The share of national income accruing to this group, which includes the bulk of the rural population and the poorest urban groups, was reduced from 14·3 to 10·5 per cent, showing that the average real wage of this section of the population remained stationary. The second group, composed of the 30 per cent of the population ranked between the fifth and seventh deciles, increased its average income at a rate 10 per cent above the national average. Since income per capita increased by around 47 per cent in the period under consideration, it can be inferred that the average real wage of this section of the population must have increased by slightly more than 60 per cent. The third group, comprising the population ranked in the eighth and ninth deciles and representing the skilled artisans and the middle brackets in general, increased its share from 19·4 to 29 per cent of the total income. The average wage of this group, which had corresponded to the national average in 1950, exceeded this average by 45 per cent in 1963–4, showing that this section of the population had practically doubled its standard of living. Finally, the fourth group, composed of the upper middle class and higher-income brackets—i.e. the top decile—decreased its share from 49 per cent to 41·5 per cent of the total income. A more detailed examination of the figures for this last group reveals that significant changes had taken place within the group. The first half, composed of the middle-income brackets and small entrepreneurs (including farmers using modern agricultural techniques), increased its average income at a faster rate than the national average, the rise in its real income averaging more than 80 per cent. The share of national income accruing to the 40 per cent ranking immediately above this subgroup, and including the upper income brackets, remained unchanged, which means that the rise in average real incomes was identical to the rise in national per capita income. Finally, the top 10 per cent—corresponding to only 1 per cent of the country's population—consisting of the top income brackets, decreased its share of the national income from 23 to 12 per cent, which signifies a decline in average real income.

The data analysed above reveal the importance of institutional factors in determining the pattern of income distribution in underdeveloped structures in the process of modernisation. The existence of a manpower surplus concentrated in the rural sector is the most important single factor. A quarter of a century of rapid development, which has enabled Mexico to more than double its per capita income, has not prevented stagnation and even decline in the living conditions of a large section of the population, representing certainly not less than one-third of the total. The second determining factor seems to be the growing organisation of the urban groups. From the fifth decile upwards, all groups have increased their share of the social product, which indicates that urban wage-earners have enjoyed greater participation in the benefits of development than they did in the 1940–50 period. The third salient feature is the upward social mobility of the higher income brackets: the average real income accruing to the ninth decile rose by 135 per cent in the period after 1950. Finally, it seems clear that fiscal policy has had a strong influence in breaking down income concentration in the top group. Although the 20 per cent with the highest incomes, accounting for 59·8 per cent of the national income in 1950, increased their share to 64·5 per cent in 1963–4, there has been a considerable change in the distribution pattern within this top group, largely in favour of the middle-class groups.

Distribution of Social Income

The action of the State affects the flow of income accruing to the community in a number of ways. Part of this income is transferred from the private recipient to the State and the structure of the tax system may be an important factor in determining the final pattern of demand. On the other hand, the way in which the government uses the resources it appropriates operates in the final analysis as a mechanism for redistributing income in favour of one or another group. The data available for Latin America do not permit us to undertake a detailed analysis. However, the available statistical information does provide an overall picture. In its study *The Economic Development of Latin America in the Post-War Period*,[1] the Economic Commission for Latin America outlined a scheme exemplifying the utilisation of personal income in the region as a whole. Since the data for Venezuela and Mexico—countries in which income is particularly highly concentrated—carried considerable weight in the preparation of this scheme and since data for Argentina were not available at the time, the figures must be taken as representing the Latin American mode rather than the Latin American average. For the purpose of constructing this representative model, the population was grouped into four categories. Group I, comprising 50 per cent of the total, with an average yearly income of 120 dollars, included the mass of rural workers. Group II, comprising 45 per cent of the total, with an average yearly income of 400 dollars, included the mass or urban wage-earners. Group III, comprising 3 per cent of the total, with an average yearly income of 1,750 dollars, included higher income brackets and small entrepreneurs. Finally, Group IV, comprising 2 per cent of the population, with an average yearly income of around 3,500 dollars, including the big landowners and entrepreneurs. Table 8.3 shows how these groups used their personal incomes.

Given the existing structure of the tax system, with its broad emphasis on indirect taxation, the proportion of personal income contributed to the State by the mass of urban wage-earners was equal to that of the small minority earning high incomes, who spend 6·5 times as much on consumption per head. The upper middle class, whose consumption spending per capita is four times that of the urban wage-earners, pays out relatively less in taxes. This is explained by the ease with which direct taxes can be avoided, particularly in the case of professionally earned income. Group II

[1] ECLA, *The Economic Development of Latin America in the Post-War Period*, 1964.

TABLE 8.3. *Allocation of Personal Income*

	taxes and social insurance contributions	savings	consumption	*total*
	% figures			
Group I	13·0	−3·0	90·0	100
II	20·0	3·5	76·5	100
III	16·5	9·5	74·0	100
IV	21·0	21·0	58·0	100
total population	18·4	6·6	75·0	100

TABLE 8.4. *Allocation of Public Expenditure*

	total	I	II	III	IV
			(% of GDP)		
A. taxes	15·2	1·7	8·4	1·9	3·2
B. government services					
education	1·8	0·2	1·1	0·3	0·2
health	1·2	0·7	0·5	0	0
other	2·4	0·8	1·6	0	0
total	5·4	1·7	3·2	0·3	0·2
A minus B	9·8	0	5·2	1·6	3·0

has a low savings coefficient, not so much because of a high propensity to consume—which, given its low income, would be normal—but because the tax burden weighs more heavily on this group. The propensity to consume appears to be higher for Group III, whose status requires competitive spending on 'prestige' forms of consumption.

The funds collected by the State are used to finance investments and collective forms of consumption which benefit the various sectors of the population in different ways. The figures given in Table 8.4 show how the State allocates its resources among the four groups indicated.

Group I, composed of the poorest half of the population, whose consumption is hardly diversified and only marginally enters the monetary flows, receives services from the State corresponding to only 1·7 per cent of the product, i.e. a sum practically equal to the total it pays out in taxes. It should be noted that the State's expenditure on education is the same for this half of the population as for the wealthiest 2 per cent of the population. Group II receives services from the State corresponding to 3·2 per cent of the product but contributes 8·4 per cent in taxes. Thus, this group contributes more than half the funds made available to the State mainly for allocation to investment. Since public investment is largely intended to create external economies for private investment and since the latter is in the hands of the 2 per cent minority whose savings represent a significant proportion of its income, it may be deduced that both in the way it finances its expenditures and in the way it allocates its resources, the action of the State serves not only to consolidate the existing pattern of wealth and income distribution but to foster an even more concentrated one.

CHAPTER 9

MONETARY AND FOREIGN EXCHANGE SYSTEMS

FAILURE TO ADJUST TO THE RULES OF THE GOLD STANDARD

In an earlier chapter it was pointed out that the world economic crisis of 1929 dramatically revealed structural changes that had been taking place in the world economy for some time. Among such changes we must mention the tapering off in world demand for most primary products. The crisis emphasised the magnitude of the 'external vulnerability' of economies specialising in the production of raw materials, among which the Latin American economies were prominent.

The financial movements involved in the international system of division of labour, based on so-called comparative advantage, were regulated by the Gold Exchange Standard, which assumed the definition of all currencies in terms of their gold value, free convertibility on the basis of a fixed rate of exchange (at least in so far as foreign transactions were concerned) and the free transfer of funds on the basis of 'foreign exchange reserves' held by the monetary authorities of each country. In countries with a diversified economy, characterised by some degree of substitutability between imports and home-produced goods, any sharp fall in exports due to external factors could be offset, to some extent, by an increase in domestic supply. Proper management of monetary reserves and foreign credits, in conjunction with a judicious policy of domestic expansion, could be sufficient to divert productive activity towards new types of export and towards the satisfaction of domestic demand formerly supplied by imports. In other words, the mechanisms of the Gold Exchange Standard could be adjusted to offset its more serious internal depressive effects without completely abandoning its rules. In economies specialising in the exportation of raw materials, however, the problem took a different form because of the rigidity of supply in the export sector and the incompressibility of demand for imports.[1]

[1] Cf. C. Furtado, *Teoria e Política do Desenvolvimento Econômico*, São Paulo, 1967, particularly chapter 20, 'A Tendência ao Desequilibrio Externo'. See also Victor L. Urquidi, *Viabilidad Económica de América Latina*, Mexico, 1962, chapter 3, 'Los Embrollos Monetários y Financieros'.

68

Latin American countries were characterised at the time by relatively high import coefficients. The share of imports in the domestic supply of manufactured goods was never less than one-third of the total and in some cases more than two-thirds. However, these figures reveal only one aspect of the real situation. In most of the countries, a large proportion of the product was excluded from the monetary flow, which suggests that if we take into account only the monetary sector of the economy, the import coefficient was in fact much higher. On the other hand, domestically produced goods could not be substituted for imports in the short or medium term, even if they could in the long run. Consequently, a temporary reduction in exports could provoke a serious internal depression unless the country had sufficient monetary reserves to tide it over a transition period during which it would attempt to recover its former export levels in traditional or other lines of export. In other words, the situation required an extremely able compensatory policy and careful orientation of investments in the export sector to make sure that the export sector achieved the flexibility which the sector producing for the home market lacked. One need only remember the wide fluctuations in world prices of primary products and the long gestation period of the cash crops involved (coffee trees, for instance, take four to six years to grow to bearing age and have a long productive life) to realise that an economy with a high import coefficient specialising in exports of one or two primary products would find it difficult to submit to the discipline of the Gold Standard. This would have required not only large monetary reserves—which would have meant freezing a considerable proportion of domestic savings—but also a policy of controlling the level of domestic activity, which was not feasible in countries lacking a developed capital market and a sufficiently flexible fiscal system.

Moreover, the problem was not confined to the short-run instability of world prices of primary products—a consequence of climatic factors and the structural inflexibility of supply in underdeveloped countries. No less serious was the disruption of markets during world-wide depressions, when Latin American countries found it impossible to take counter-action by reorientating their exports. Cyclical crises entailed not only falls in the value of exports but also flights of capital, which precipitated the liquidation of monetary reserves, with a subsequent loss of credit abroad. The situation was particularly serious in view of the heavy external debts accumulated by Latin American countries in the course of the nineteenth century. Whatever the origin of these debts—wars during the phase of consolidating the nation-states, speculation by groups dominating the state apparatus, or investments in infrastructure, mainly in railroads and ports—it is certain that temporary payments difficulties led to the negotiation of fresh loans and burdensome refinancing arrangements, making external debt service one of the major items in public budgets.

Given the sharp fall in the value of exports and the extent to which government revenues depended on the export trade, it is understandable that, faced with a major crisis, Latin American countries should have begun almost automatically to finance part of their public expenditures by expanding the money supply. This led to immediate expansion of imports, precipitating liquidation of the monetary reserves and the devaluation of the exchange rate. In fact, anticipatory measures, reflecting falls in prices of raw materials in the major importing markets, were enough to spark off capital flights and devaluations of the exchange rate. The strains of devaluation forced governments to make greater financial efforts to meet debt service claims at precisely the time when public receipts were declining. A deficit in the public sector was thus inevitable and monetary expansion to finance the deficit became virtually an automatic necessity. In practice, the domestic effects of the external crisis were attenuated by the simple fact that the rules of the Gold Standard were not obeyed, or were jettisoned at the first sound of the alarm bell. During the lulls, governments created 'stabilization' or 'equalization' funds for the purpose of intervening in the exchange market in an attempt to stabilise it. But these experiments all ended in a return to inconvertibility or floating exchange rates which made it possible to penalise capital flights when crises occurred.

Experience proved that the system of floating exchange rates allowed the Latin American countries to protect themselves more easily against the impact of cyclical crises and generally against contractions in the capacity to import, inasmuch as the inflexibility of the productive structure tended to be partially offset by adjustments in the price structure. The consequent changes in income distribution were for a long time absorbed without creating major social tensions. After a time, however, and particularly in some countries, the emergence of a more clearly defined social structure provided an outlet for these social tensions and increasingly serious inflationary processes were set in motion.

The sudden and periodic monetary devaluations provoked by the cyclical crises in the Latin American economies had a number of consequences. Since devaluations coincided with falling export prices, they offset the decrease in the money income of the export sector, transferring a substantial proportion of the loss in real income to the economy as a whole, through the relative rise in import prices. In countries whose exports carried considerable weight in the world market—as was the case with Brazilian coffee, which accounted for over half the total world supply—this mechanism could aggravate the downward trend in world market prices. In most cases, however, the consequences were strictly internal, taking the form of a 'socialisation of losses' or of a mechanism for defending the leading sectors of the economy. In the phase that followed, an upward shift in external demand could lead to partial revaluation of the currency at the exchange level, the export sector thus restoring to the community as a whole part of the income it had appropriated during the depression. The flexibility of the price structure made it possible to cushion the impact of the external crisis and preserve the export sector's capacity to recover. But there can be no doubt that it also tended to open the way to a long-term deterioration in the terms of trade, inasmuch as it increased the price-inelasticity of the world market supply of primary products.

CENTRAL BANKS CREATION

In the classic age of the Gold Standard, Latin American monetary systems, with their floating exchange rates and chronic non-accelerating inflation, were regarded as textbook curiosities. A few descriptive studies published in Europe[1] drew attention to these peculiarities. But the theoretical assumptions of the time made it difficult to see in these features anything beyond the consequences of political instability and the absence of adequate institutions equipped to handle monetary systems properly. It was in this spirit that important internal financial groups, intent on maintaining the regularity of external debt service payments and interested in the transfer of dividends on the substantial direct investments beginning to be made in the region after the First World War, pressed Latin American governments to reform their monetary systems, offering technical assistance for this purpose. This ushered in the phase of reforms in the issue systems and the creation of central banks. Under the guidance of British and United States technicians, central banks were established in one Latin American country after another from 1925 onwards.[2] These banks, designed to

---

[1] Chilean inflation was the subject of two monographs published before the First World War, one written by Benjamin Subercaseaux and published in France, the other by Alfred Wagman, published in Germany.

[2] Uruguay, whose central bank was created in 1896, was the only country in the region with a centralised system of monetary authorities before the First World War. Mexico's central

function within the framework of the Gold Exchange Standard, were to have a monopoly of note issue, determine the bank rate, undertake open-market operations and act as 'lenders of last resort', that is, rediscount bills held by the commercial banks. It is not very likely that members of the technical missions imagined that the creation of a central bank would suffice to conjure up money and capital markets. What they essentially had in mind was the regulation of a government's discretionary powers of currency issue. It was hoped, in this way, to put an end to the chronic budgetary deficits which were thought to be the root cause of inflationary pressures. Since control of the central bank was to be jointly in the hands of the private banks and the business community in general, political pressure would be minimised. The government would have to finance its expenditures from legitimate resources by collecting taxes or turning to the capital market. The power to issue legal tender was controlled by the level of gold and convertible foreign exchange reserves held and rediscount operations were limited to short-term commercial and agricultural paper.

Since the central banks lacked the requirements necessary to control interest rates by the classical means (attracting funds from abroad whenever necessary) and, on the other hand, since the commercial banks in the region were relatively conservative, the monetary reforms of the 1920s were in practice reduced to an attempt to control the power of note issue. The rigidity introduced into the monetary system by these reforms helped to aggravate the consequences of the 1929 crisis. Monetary reserves were more rapidly exhausted and capital flights were penalised far less. The public-sector deficit—which could not have been avoided without paralysing the state machine—tended to be financed by issuing government bonds rediscounted by the central banks.

The Central Bank of Argentina, created in 1935, was the first to depart from the conventional blueprint based implicitly on the working of the Gold Exchange Standard and to incorporate novel features in its statutes. It could intervene in the exchange market on behalf of the government and, under the supervision of the treasury, could engage in operations with government securities to provide short-term finance for State deficits. Experience had shown that these practices were needed and they were introduced in more than one country. What was new was the acceptance of the existing situation as the basis for the creation of a central banking system, which meant acknowledging the shortcomings and artificiality of

bank—the Banco de México—was founded in 1925, without the aid of the Anglo-American missions sent out in the twenties and thirties.

the orthodox approach. However, because it incorporated the accumulated experience of years of effort to adapt to fluctuations in the foreign trade sector, the new system was at the time regarded as an extraordinary innovation.[1]

EXPERIMENTS IN MONETARY AND FOREIGN EXCHANGE POLICY AND THE INFLUENCE OF THE IMF

In the absence of a sufficiently developed capital market and given the failure to control the process of currency issue—by using the rediscount mechanism the central bank could go on bolstering the total supply of money and credit—the main weapon of monetary policy in Latin America tended to be control of the reserves held by deposit banks. While the main aim of classical reserves policy was to assure the financial solvency of the commercial banks, Latin American practice gave rise to complicated reserves policies, which took into account not only the basic resources held by the commercial banks but also the expected increase in these resources, and which were carried out by the central banks with the specific aim of controlling the total supply of money and credit. Another significant innovation was the creation of a second line of reserves for the banking system—in point of fact, deposits held with the central bank—consisting of government securities offering interest rates far below the current bank rate.

Another field in which the Latin American experience has been extremely varied since the 1929 crisis is that of intervention in foreign exchange operations. In view of the severity of the Great Depression and the inflexibility of the fiscal systems, some countries began to manipulate their exchange rates in order to prevent the currency devaluation from aggravating the effects of a fall in export prices or sparking off an excessive rise in the prices of certain products such as fuels and wheat. In the past, sudden devaluation had been a mechanism for redistributing income, which operated in favour of certain groups. The purpose of manipulating

---

[1] The Banco Central de Argentina was created with British technical assistance. Raúl Prebisch, who was the Executive Director of the Argentine central bank from its foundation up to 1943, inspired by the empiricism with which the Bank of England had traditionally conducted its affairs, departed from the rigid patterns imposed on the newly created central banks. It should also be borne in mind that at that time Argentina already possessed a relatively developed capital market. During the 1938 crisis, Prebisch took masterly action to counter depressive domestic effects and the Argentine central bank was thenceforth regarded as a model in the region. For the Latin American experience in this field, see Miguel S. Wionczek, 'Central Banking', in Claudio Veliz (ed.), *Latin America and the Caribbean: A Handbook*, and Frank Tamagna, *Central Banking in Latin America*, Mexico, 1965.

the exchange rates was to control this mechanism so that devaluation would not unduly favour some groups while penalising others. The next step was to orientate the manipulation of exchange rates in order to build up reserve funds to absorb inflationary pressures. Finally, there was a move in the direction of using differential rates to direct the pattern of investments. The simple fact that capital formation is relatively more dependent on the capacity to import than on the level of aggregate expenditure means that devaluation will act as a curb on investment unless corrective measures are adopted by providing disguised subsidies in the form of multiple exchange rates.

In the last two decades, the influence of the Internal Monetary Fund (IMF) has made itself increasingly felt in Latin America. Innovations and experiments in the field of monetary and foreign exchange policies have not ceased completely but, as balance of payments difficulties become more serious, with a growing dependence on short- and medium-term foreign loans to finance deficits, the IMF blueprint has been more widely accepted. Under IMF regulations, exchange rates are fixed in terms of U.S. dollars. Balance of payments equilibrium presupposes internal stability, that is, the absence of uncontrollable inflationary pressures. The use of fiscal and monetary instruments to maintain this internal stability is the recommended IMF weapon. Since the fiscal structure in underdeveloped countries is not very flexible and, in many respects, totally inadequate, the responsibility falls mainly on monetary policy, i.e. on the control of credit. Thus we return by a different path to the conclusions underlying the policies of the orthodox central banks established in the 1920s. Where structural factors give rise to constant pressure on the balance of payments, monetary policy must create a permanent depression in order to keep the economy in equilibrium. This problem will be reconsidered when we come to analyse the pattern of Latin American inflation.

IV. CHARACTERISTICS OF
THE INDUSTRIALISATION PROCESS

THE INDUSTRIALISATION PROCESS.
1: THE INITIAL PHASE

INDUSTRIALISATION INDUCED BY EXPANSION OF EXPORTS

In countries specialising in primary production for export, that is, countries in which productivity was raised in response to the expanding world demand for raw materials, the change in the structure of production as development proceeds, particularly the industrialisation process, is characterised by a number of distinctive features which constitute one of the most interesting aspects of the economic theory of underdevelopment. The rise in productivity and the consequent increase in the purchasing power of the population led to diversification in the pattern of overall demand involving also a more than proportionate rise in the demand for manufactured products. It has been observed that in countries with a per capita income level below 500 U.S. dollars there is a high income-elasticity of demand for manufactured goods, the coefficient value being between 1·3 and 1·5. Hence any rise in the population's purchasing power will mean not only diversification of demand but diversification in a particular direction, requiring a more than proportionate increase in the supply of manufactures. Since specialisation in primary exports (almost invariably only one or two products) concentrates resources in a few lines of production, the evolution of the productive structure will be the inverse of that of the demand schedule. Thus, rapid growth of an export monoculture may be accompanied by an increase in imports of food, expansion of an export mining sector may lead to the substitution of imported manufactured goods for local craft products destined for the home market, etc. Considering the process as a whole, it becomes apparent that rising productivity is accompanied by a simplification in the supply structure of home-produced goods and diversification in the overall composition of demand.

In the Latin American countries, the process outlined above was the starting point for industrialisation. Specialised production permitted a rise in productivity and income, facilitating the formation of a domestic market nucleus for manufactured products and the creation of an infrastructure. Whereas the classical industrialisation experience was the result of innovations in productive processes which, by cutting prices, made possible substitution for craft manufactures and the creation of a home market for their own products, in the Latin American case the market was created as a result of the rise in productivity brought about by export specialisation and was at first supplied by imports. In this case, the competitor to be displaced by industrialisation was not the craftsman of low productivity but the highly efficient producer operating through the world market. None the less, growth of the domestic market was an inevitable accompaniment of export expansion. When the home market reached a certain size, a protectionist policy was enough to spark off an industrial upsurge, particularly since industrial investment could take advantage of the external economies provided by the existing infrastructure. The embryonic home market's capacity to induce industrialisation was, of course, dependent on a number of circumstances varying from one country to another. Where the export nucleus consisted of mining industries, the labour force directly absorbed was strictly limited; moreover, in such cases the capital was almost always predominantly foreign. There was thus little possibility of creating an adequate domestic market. The degree of concentration of land ownership and the relative size of the manpower surplus also played an important role in shaping the final pattern of demand, since both factors affected the distribution of income. A high concentration of income meant that consumption of luxury goods would tend to predominate and, in the case of manufactured luxuries, that they would have to be imported. The size of the manpower surplus affected the creation of the domestic market nucleus even more than the system of land tenure. Given the abundance of land, the shortage of manpower led to intensive use of labour and extensive use of land, making it possible to reconcile concentration of income with relatively high wage rates. Under these conditions—and they fit the case of Argentina and Uruguay—concentration of income did not inhibit the growth of a large domestic market for manufactured products.

In sum, the transition towards an industrial economy depended on a number of factors, the most salient being:

(*a*) the nature of the export activity: this determined the relative amount of manpower to be absorbed by the expanding high-productivity sector;

(*b*) the type of infrastructure required by the export activity: temperate agriculture creating an extensive transportation network; tropical agriculture, concentrated in smaller areas and often in mountainous regions, being able to make do with a more modest infrastructure; mining production requiring a specialised infrastructure, in most cases scarcely producing external economies for other economic activities;

(c) ownership of the investments made in the export economy: foreign ownership reducing the proportion of the flow of income generated by the expanding sector that remains in the country; given the greater prevalence of foreign ownership in the export mining economies, their negative aspects were aggravated;

(d) the wage rates prevailing in the export sector during the initial phase, these being dependent largely on the relative size of the manpower surplus;

(e) the size of the expanding sector, in most cases reflecting the country's geographical area and population size.

Argentina offers the perfect example of a country in which a primary-product export economy gave rise to the rapid growth of a sizeable domestic market for manufactured goods, providing the basis for the emergence, with hardly any transitional phase, of an industrialisation process. The unprecedented growth of the population as a result of immigration, rapid urbanisation and the extensive infrastructure required by the type of export produced, provided a combination of circumstances that proved exceptionally favourable to industrialisation. The relatively high level of wages obtaining in the initial phase of expansion, and the population's advanced integration into the market economy are equally important factors in accounting for the impetus given to industrialisation in this country even before the First World War. We find a diametrically opposite example in the case of Bolivia which, despite an important export sector, took no steps towards industrialisation.[1] In this second case, the export mining economy absorbed an insignificant fraction of the country's labour force at low wage rates, while the infrastructure created for the mining economy was of little importance to the country's other economic activities. In short, the export sector followed the structural economic pattern prevailing in the traditional sectors and the bulk of the labour force was excluded from the benefits of gains in productivity.

[1] Bolivia's population at the time of Independence certainly exceeded that of Argentina. According to census data, Bolivia's population increased by only 60 per cent between 1831 and 1900, whereas in Argentina the population increased by 130 per cent between 1869 and 1895. Between 1900 and 1950, the Bolivian population grew from 1,696,400 to 3,019,000 while the Argentinian population grew from 3,954,911 to 15,897,127 between 1895 and 1947.

Economic Development of Latin America

In the group of countries exporting tropical agricultural products, Brazil enjoyed the set of conditions most favourable for the transition to industrialisation. In contrast with Colombia and Central America, coffee was produced in the São Paulo highlands with extensive farming methods under conditions favouring the creation of an important transportation network. Moreover, with the shortage of manpower in this region,[1] wage rates had to be high enough to attract settlers from other regions, particularly from Europe. On the other hand, given the abundant supply of foodstuffs, produced in the region itself or in the southern areas of European settlement which had accompanied the expansion of the coffee frontier or taken place in an earlier period, the capacity to import was not absorbed by food imports. Finally, exceptionally favourable conditions for the installation of hydro-electric power plants meant that the region could benefit from the electric energy available at extremely low rates from the start of industrialisation.

Of the countries exporting both agricultural and mineral products, Mexico deserves special attention because of the distinctive features of its early industrial development. The new phase of development of the export mining industry, based on the expansion of world demand for industrial metals, was centred in the northern part of the country. This once more raised the problem of connecting these areas with the central region, where the Mexican population was most concentrated. Historical experience provided a severe warning on the consequences of non-integration: the isolation of the northern areas undergoing rapid settlement had led to the loss of Texas and California. On the other hand, an agricultural export activity of great importance at the time was situated in the far south, in the Yucatán Peninsula, which was the centre of henequen production. Convinced that the country's survival depended on its integration, the Mexican government pursued a policy of building up a transportation network and eliminating the internal barriers that had traditionally fragmented the national market. Physical barriers, which made it difficult for foreign products entering the country by sea to reach the central plateau, had encouraged the establishment of a complex of textile industries since the

---

[1] The mobility of the rural labour force in Brazil was hampered by the slave system which lasted until 1888 and, later, by restrictions on population movements imposed by local authorities at the behest of the large estate owners. The population increase in the State of Ceará, stimulated by the penetration of cotton and the great drought of 1877, led to the first significant migrations in the Northeastern region. At first migration was directed towards the Amazon region where rubber production was undergoing rapid expansion in the last two decades of the nineteenth century and the first two decades of the twentieth. C. Furtado, *Formação Económico do Brasil*, chapters 21 to 24.

first half of the nineteenth century. However, internal tariff barriers had inhibited their development, permitting the survival of local weaving, one of the oldest traditional crafts of the Mexican people. The integration of the domestic market brought about by the building of railroads and the elimination of local tariff barriers led to the rapid expansion of the existing manufacturing nucleus. Thus, in contrast with Argentina and Brazil, the first phase of Mexican industrialisation is closer to the classic model: local artisan production is displaced by the introduction of new techniques, and industrial products serve markets previously satisfied largely by the supply of local craft manufactures. It is important to bear this aspect in mind when considering Mexico's subsequent evolution. The nature of exports—mainly mineral products—and the abundance of manpower, which made it possible to keep wages at extremely low levels, could have hampered the country's development. There was a strong likelihood that, as the capacity to export grew, increasing quantities of foreign manufactured goods would enter the country, ruining the local craft industries without creating alternative forms of employment for the population. This problem hardly arose in countries such as Argentina and Brazil, with their relatively sparse populations, traditionally supplied by imported manufactures. In Mexico, a relatively dense population was traditionally supplied by local artisan production, whose displacement by imports would have been all the more serious as the expanding export sector's capacity to absorb labour was limited.

Like Chile, Mexico benefited from a protectionist policy in the first half of the nineteenth century, that is, before liberal ideology had come to be widely accepted. Unlike Chile, however, the country went through a phase of great political instability accompanied by economic stagnation or retrogression. But this did not prevent the emergence of a nucleus of manufacturing activity, which was to be of decisive importance in the period that has come to be known as the 'Porfiriato',[1] an era of political stability and expanding export activities. In fact, despite the predominance of liberal ideas in this period, the industrial nucleus managed to consolidate itself and expand under the stimulus provided by the integration of the domestic market promoted by the government and the natural protection afforded by the concentration of population in the central plateau.

[1] From the name of Porfirio Diáz, the dictator who ruled Mexico from 1876 to 1910. The term *Porfiriato* appears in the monumental work edited by Cosío Villegas, *História Moderna de México*, of which vol. VII, *El Porfiriato: Vida Económica*, was published in Mexico in 1965.

DIFFERENCES BETWEEN THE ARGENTINE AND MEXICAN CASES

Mexico and Argentina, the two Latin American countries to attain a significant degree of industrialisation before the First World War, represent totally different historical experiences. In the case of Mexico, industrialisation began in the period before the rapid expansion of exports in the second half of the nineteenth century and was fostered by the existence of a market previously supplied by local craft manufactures. Whereas in Argentina export activities were directly responsible for the rise in the purchasing power of large sections of the population, in Mexico the flow of income directly generated by exports was strictly limited. Nevertheless, expansion of the foreign trade sector created conditions for the establishment of an infrastructure which unified the home market to the advantage of an existing manufacturing nucleus. Around 1900–5, the industrial sector in Argentina already contributed 18 per cent to the domestic product, and in Mexico it contributed 14 per cent.[1] In both cases, the dynamic centre of economic development during this period was the expanding export sector. In other words, development was a reflexion of the national economy's integration into the international system of division of labour. However, while in Argentina the expansion of exports led to the vigorous growth of the home market, which in turn induced industrialisation, in Mexico the home market grew much more slowly. In Argentina infrastructure investments were a product of the nature and location of the export activity. In Mexico, the creation of an infrastructure was largely a reflexion of the government's unification policy designed to counteract the centrifugal forces at work in the country, which had been aggravated by long civil wars and the presence of a powerful neighbour openly professing an imperialist doctrine. One further point must be made. In countries exporting primary products, the initial phase of industrialisation was influenced by the nature of the products exported, inasmuch as the processing of such products, whether for export or for meeting home market requirements, amounted to an industrial activity. Thus, the processing of agricultural and livestock products for both export and home markets was the original nucleus of modern Argentine industry, and the processing of minerals was an important sector of Mexican industry. This explains how Mexico gained the metallurgical experience that was to play a key role in the country's industrial development, particularly in the later

[1] Earlier statistics of industrial production and the industrial sector's contribution to the gross domestic product in Latin American countries can be found in ECLA, *El Proceso de Industrialización en América Latina, Anexo Estadístico,* 1966.

period when the export sector was hit by the world crisis. Finally, it should be recalled that, although both countries were under the influence of liberal ideas during the phase of growth stimulated by a dynamic export sector, State action in Mexico could not ignore the existence of an industrial nucleus dating from an earlier period, since its displacement would entail social repercussions exacerbated by the export sector's limited capacity to absorb manpower. The problem was complicated still further by the fact that the penetration of capitalist forms of production in the agricultural sector was causing widespread movements of population. Whereas Argentine development was accompanied by a rise in the population's overall standard of living, in Mexico there was increasing marginalisation of large groups of the population and an aggravation of social tensions that exploded in the revolutionary phase that seized the country from 1910 onwards. In the next phase of industrialisation, when more far-reaching action by the government became indispensable, the Mexican State showed a greater aptitude for action in the industrial field, which would be difficult to explain if we did not take into account the experience of the previous period.

CHAPTER II

THE INDUSTRIALISATION PROCESS.
2: IMPORT SUBSTITUTION

INTRINSIC LIMITATIONS OF THE FIRST PHASE
OF INDUSTRIALISATION

The industrialisation process that had started in some Latin American countries was profoundly affected by the 1929 crisis. This does not mean that the crisis represents a watershed between a period of prosperity and a period of depression. Indeed, some countries had already shown symptoms of a decline in the export sector in the period immediately preceding the crisis. In Brazil, for instance, there had been recurrent crises of over-production in coffee since before the First World War, and rubber had lost its privileged position in world trade in the decade following the war. In Chile, the nitrate crisis sparked off by competition from the synthetic product had been a burden on the country's economy for more than a decade. None the less, with the exception of Brazil, in all the region's most economically significant countries the quantum of exports was 50 to 100 per cent higher in the 1925–9 period than in the first decade of the century. It was in connexion with the industrialisation process that the 1929 crisis constituted a landmark. Until then, the development of the industrial sector had been a reflexion of export expansion; from then on, industrialisation was induced largely through the structural tensions provoked by the decline or inadequate growth of the export sector. The exception to this rule is represented by countries that were to experience a phase of vigorous export growth in a later period: Venezuela, Peru and the Central American countries.

In the countries in process of industrialisation, the industrial sector's contribution to the product in 1929 was as shown on p. 83.[1]

Before considering the features of the new phase in industrialization, the following question must be tackled: what possibilities were there for industrialisation in Latin America within the framework that prevailed

[1] The basic data on industrial production trends and the share of the industrial sector and imports in GDP are taken from ECLA, *El Proceso de Industrialización en América Latina, Anexo Estadístico.*

Industrialisation Process II

before 1929? In other words: to what extent did the sudden disruption of world trade frustrate an industrialisation process already making rapid headway?

	industrial sector as % of GDP
Argentina	22·8
Mexico	14·2
Brazil	11·7
Chile	7·9
Colombia	6·2

A careful scrutiny of the data available for Argentina, Brazil and Mexico shows that the industrialisation process stimulated by the expansion of exports was already showing clear symptoms of exhaustion before the 1929 crisis. Thus, structural changes in the Argentine economy had been of little significance since 1910. In that year, industrial output contributed 20 per cent to the gross domestic product, a proportion that remained virtually unchanged until 1920. In 1920 it rose to 23·6 per cent, but declined to 22·8 per cent in 1929. This structural immutability coincided with the vigorous growth of the Argentine economy. In the course of the two decades mentioned, the volume of industrial output increased by 120 per cent and the quantum of exports by 140 per cent. In Mexico, the coefficient of industrialisation (share of industrial output in gross domestic product) began to decline in the first decade of the twentieth century, before the revolutionary period. In the period 1900–10, the average yearly rate of growth of the gross domestic product was 4·2 per cent, whereas that of industrial output was only 3·6 per cent. In Brazil, where the industrialisation process lagged behind that of the other two countries, the index of industrial output rose by 150 per cent between 1914 and 1922, but between the latter year and 1929 it remained practically stationary.

To grasp the intrinsic limitations of this initial phase of industrialisation in the Latin American countries, some of its basic features should be borne in mind. It consisted essentially of the establishment of a nucleus of industries producing non-durable consumer goods—textiles, leather goods, processed foodstuffs, clothing—which had become a feasible proposition as a result of the increased income made available for consumption with the expansion of exports. Moreover, the urbanisation process that was taking place at the same time created new demands in the building sector, opening up prospects for manufacturing building materials, which largely replaced the traditional materials produced by local craftsmen. But these industries—non-durable consumer goods and building materials—had little power to generate sustained growth. In the case of consumer goods of a non-durable nature, the vigorously upward shifting trend of the growth curve in the early stages was due simply to the fact that they were replacing goods hitherto imported. Thus, the output of textiles in Brazil increased from 22 million metres in 1882 to 242 million in 1905 and 470 million in 1915.[1] After 1915, however, the growth of the textile industry was extremely weak since import substitution had exhausted its possibilities and the growth of the export sector had slowed down or levelled off.

Given an elastic supply of labour—even when largely recruited abroad, as in the case of Argentina—the growth of the industrial sector will proceed under conditions of steady wage rates as will the expansion of the export sector in an economy with a sizeable subsistence sector. Increased industrial output is due largely to the addition of new units of production similar to those already in existence, and is dependent on imported equipment. There is no question of creating a system of industrial production by steadily diversifying production. What is involved is simply the addition of similar units in certain sectors of industrial activity. The labour force absorbed, benefiting from a wage rate above the national average, provides reinforcement for the domestic market in the same way that growth of the export sector, by absorbing part of the surplus manpower, contributes to the expansion of the home market. Thus there was no essential difference between industrial expansion in this initial phase and the growth of export agriculture. The main difference was that the latter, dependent on overseas demand, acted as an exogenous variable, whereas investment in the industrial sector was dependent on the growth of a market created by the expansion of exports. In fact, the export sector acted as a multiplier of employment in the industrial sector. The industrial sector could overcome this dependence only if it became sufficiently diversified to generate its own demand. In other words, it required the establishment of machine-making and other industries whose output could be absorbed by the industrial sector itself and by other productive activities. But the facilities available abroad for financing investments in infrastructure and even industrial investments were tied to the acquisition of equipment and technology in foreign centres. Financial dependence made it necessary to buy equipment from foreign suppliers, with the result that industrial activity was limited to the processing of local raw materials or to the finishing of imported semi-manufactured consumer goods, the equipment used being invariably purchased abroad. With an industrial complex geared to the

[1] For data on the evolution of the Brazilian cotton textile industry see Stanley J. Stein, *The Brazilian Cotton Manufacture: Textile Enterprise in an Underdeveloped Area, 1850–1950*, Harvard Univ. Press, 1957.

processing of consumer goods, there was little need to assimilate modern technology. The only technical assistance given to existing industries was the replacement of worn-out equipment, which could be handled by agents acting for the import houses. This apparent initial advantage turned out to be negative in the next phase, since industries could be established without the emergence of a genuine industrial outlook, which presupposes not only the encouragement of managerial skills but the training of skilled personnel equipped with a thorough knowledge of technical processes.

STRUCTURAL CHANGES INDUCED BY THE CRISIS OF THE EXPORT SECTOR

The sudden collapse of the capacity to import, the contraction of the export sector and the ensuing fall in export profits, the blocking of international channels of finance, all provoked by the 1929 crisis, profoundly altered the course of development of the Latin American economies, particularly of those that had already begun to industrialise. The contraction of the export sector led to two types of reaction, depending on the degree of diversification attained by the economy concerned: (*a*) factors of production were shifted back into the pre-capitalist sector—subsistence agriculture and craft manufactures—as the money economy shrank; (*b*) the industrial sector geared to the home market was expanded in an effort to replace, wholly or in part, goods previously purchased abroad. The second case constitutes what has been called the import-substitution process, defined as the increase in the share of industrial output destined for the home market (*E*) in the gross domestic product (*P*) under conditions in which the share of imports (*M*) in the product is on the decline. In terms of growth rates we have:

$$\frac{dE}{dt} > \frac{dP}{dt} > \frac{dM}{dt}. \tag{1}$$

To measure the extent of import substitution (*SM*) the following formula may be applied:

$$SM = \frac{Mt - 1}{Pt - 1} - \frac{Mt}{Pt}. \tag{2}$$

The evolution of the import coefficient from 1929 onwards in the Latin American countries with the longest-established industries is indicated in Table 11.1. Estimates are based on GDP and imports series, both at constant prices, taking 1960 as the base year.

In the decade following the crisis, there was a substantial decline in the

TABLE 11.1. *Evolution of Import Coefficient in Selected Countries*
(*imports as % of GDP*)

	Argentina	Mexico	Brazil	Chile	Colombia
1929	17·8	14·2	11·3	31·2	18·0
1937	13·0	8·5	6·9	13·8	12·9
1947	11·7	10·6	8·7	12·6	13·8
1957	5·9	8·2	6·1	10·1	8·9

TABLE 11.2. *Evolution of Industrialisation Coefficient in Selected Countries*
(*industrial output as % of GDP*)

	Argentina	Mexico	Brazil	Chile	Colombia
1929	22·8	14·2	11·7	7·9	6·2
1937	25·6	16·7	13·1	11·3	7·5
1947	31·1	19·8	17·3	17·3	11·5
1957	32·4	21·7	23·1	19·7	16·2

import coefficient in all the countries mentioned and in the case of Chile it fell dramatically. Of the countries included in the table, Chile is the only one in which the domestic product had not recovered its 1929 level in absolute terms by 1937. The extremely high degree of its integration into the pattern of world trade—for a country exporting raw materials—and its dependence on imports of food products which would be difficult to replace (tropical commodities and sugar, for instance) made Chile not only the country most violently affected by the crisis but also the one in which the import-substitution process faced the greatest obstacles. The reduction in the import coefficient was made possible by the more than proportional growth of the industrial sector, i.e. the increase in the industrialisation coefficient. Table 11.2 shows the evolution of the industrialisation coefficient based on the GDP and industrial output series, calculated in 1960 prices.

Chile shows the most significant rise in the industrialisation coefficient in the course of the 1930s. Even so, the rise in industrial output would not be sufficient to account for the considerable decline observed in this country's import coefficient, which also reflects substitution for imports in the agricultural sector, a substantial reduction of investments and their reorientation with a view to cutting down on their import content. By

Industrialisation Process II

TABLE 11.3. *Evolution of Import Substitution in Selected Countries*

	1929–37	1937–47	1947–57	1929–57
Argentina	4·8	1·3	5·8	11·9
Mexico	5·7	−2·1	2·4	6·0
Brazil	4·4	−1·8	2·6	5·2
Chile	17·4	1·2	2·5	21·1
Colombia	5·1	−0·9	4·9	9·1

applying formula (2) and on the basis of the data presented above, we can measure the intensity of the substitution process in different periods.

If we exclude Chile, the substition process proceeded at the same rate of intensity in the four remaining countries during the first period under consideration. In the following decade, which was influenced by the recovery of raw materials in world trade in the immediate post-war period, the substitution process lost momentum or even suffered a setback in countries registering the lowest import coefficient, i.e. Brazil and Mexico. In the period after 1947 the substitution process went ahead once more, but with diminished intensity. It is interesting to note that in Argentina, which provides the exception to the rule, industrialisation lagged behind in the period under consideration. Given the particular circumstances of each country and the fact that they were all at different stages of industrialisation, it would be wrong to expect any clear positive correlation between the rate of substitution and the growth of industrial output. None the less, if we compare the data for the two countries with the most similar degrees of development—Brazil and Mexico—we find they follow a clearly parallel trend in their substitution and industrialisation processes in the three decades considered.

Table 11.4 indicates the percentage increases in industrial output in the periods under consideration.

We have already referred to the special features of the Chilean case. Being a mineral-exporting country, Chile's industrial activity was partly integrated with the export sector whether through the processing of ores or the development of by-products. As a result of the sharp decline in these activities during the 1930s, the overall index does not reflect the substitution process that really took place in the manufacturing sector. For example, between 1929 and 1937 the output of cotton textiles was more than quadrupled, that of clothing more than doubled and that of paper more than tripled. However, the impossibility of curtailing food

TABLE 11.4. *Intensity of Industrialisation Process in Selected Countries*

	1929–37	1937–47	1947–57	1929–57
Argentina	23	73	50	220
Mexico	46	86	98	407
Brazil	42	82	123	475
Chile	16	9	58	100
Colombia	90	110	130	830

imports and the need to increase imports of fuels and raw materials, such as cotton, in a phase when the import capacity had been reduced by one-half, account for the slow rate of Chilean industrialisation in the 1930s. It was no doubt partly as a result of these difficulties that the country became aware of the urgent need for State action, designed to introduce changes into the economic structure and to foster the development of the industrialisation process. The creation of the Corporación de Fomento de la Producción (CORFO) in 1939, a government agency that was to provide a model for other Latin American countries ten years later, was the point of departure for the second phase of Chile's industrial development. CORFO was responsible for devising and carrying out an electrification plan, for creating the basis for petroleum production and refining, for establishing a modern steelworks at Huachipato, for developing sugar beet production and fostering the paper industry and for several other initiatives in the industrial field. Chile is thus less a case of industrialisation based on spontaneous import substitution than of industrialisation fostered by State action designed to surmount the obstacles to the country's economic development created by the disruption of the foreign trade sector.

In the case of Colombia, the fact that industrial development was still at an early stage in 1929 permitted the two phases of the industrialisation process in some ways to overlap. The nature of the export sector, dominated by coffee grown mostly on family holdings, fostered the growth of the home market, leading to the establishment of non-durable consumer goods industries as early as the 1920s. The crisis, acting as an additional protection mechanism, speeded up this process. An elastic domestic supply of foodstuffs, agricultural raw materials and fuel was another favourable factor. None the less, Colombia's industrialisation coefficient in 1947 still lagged behind the coefficient registered in Argentina, Mexico and Brazil in 1929. It was in the three latter countries that the import-substitution process revealed its full potential as a factor for stimulating industrialisation.

The 1929 crisis, by initially taking the form of a contraction in the capacity to import, provoked exchange depreciations in these countries, which unleashed the inflationary processes mentioned in earlier chapters. Both these factors (exchange depreciation and inflation) had the effect of raising the profitability of the industrial nucleus geared to the domestic market. The process can be clearly observed in the case of the Brazilian textile industry. This industry, which had undergone remarkable expansion before the First World War, continued to increase its productive capacity in the 1920s. Between 1915 and 1929, the number of spindles in operation increased from 1·5 to 2·7 million and the number of looms from 51,000 to 80,000, an increase reflected in the creation of a relatively large margin of idle capacity.[1] As indicated in the preceding chapter, once the first phase of import substitution had run its course, the expansion of this sector became dependent on the growth of overall demand which, in the period that came to an end with the crisis, was closely bound up with the behaviour of the export sector. The existence of unused capacity in the Brazilian textile industry, and the fact that the industry was only very marginally dependent on imported raw materials, enabled it to expand its output rapidly in the period that followed. Thus, between 1929 and 1932 output increased by one-third, and between 1929 and 1939 by two-thirds. This vigorous growth is accounted for by the fact that certain sectors of the market, formerly supplied by imports—particularly of better-quality articles—were now supplied by domestically produced goods. A second factor was the enlargement of the existing market brought about by industrial expansion itself, which raised the level of overall demand. We see here the twin aspects of the substitution process. On the one hand, domestic production improves its competitive position and supplies a wider section of the market; this becomes possible because the level of money demand remains constant while relative prices of imports rise, and because domestic supply has a certain degree of elasticity—otherwise marginal costs would rise, offsetting the favourable effect for the domestic product of the price increase in imports. On the other hand, the development of industrial production creates an additional flow of income which enlarges the domestic market.

[1] In the latter half of the twenties, Brazilian textile manufacturers conducted a vigorous campaign aimed at persuading the government to prohibit imports of equipment. This clearly indicates the impasse reached at the end of the stage in which the growth of the industrial sector failed to effect any significant structural changes in the economy.

SUBSTITUTION PROCESS AND STATE ACTION

Import substitution took place only in countries that had already completed the initial stage of industrialisation, i.e. countries that already possessed a significant nucleus of non-durable consumer goods industries. By and large, these industries could make more intensive use of equipment and plant by introducing one or more extra shifts. This made it possible to increase output without further fixed capital investment, that is, without importing additional equipment. In conjunction with this elasticity of supply, the other essential condition for embarking on import substitution is the expansion of money income, which should be sufficient to offset the depressive effects of the contraction in export activities on the level of employment. This additional condition was more easily met in countries with a perennial cash crop, such as Brazil, where the government began to buy up coffee stocks, financing this operation with credits provided by the monetary authorities. Where these conditions were met, industrial production expanded rapidly and its profitability increased even faster. Bearing in mind the acute depression of the export sector, it is easy to understand why not only available financial resources but entrepreneurial capacity should have been attracted by industrial activities.

The increase in the output of manufactured non-durable consumer goods that took place at the beginning of the import-substitution process was matched by a rising demand for intermediate products and equipment in general. Given the limited import capacity, costs of industrial inputs tended to rise, opening up new sectors to investment. In countries with considerable metallurgical experience, such as Mexico, or in those where the government's action in promoting basic industries had proved most effective, the import-substitution process was able to continue and extend its range. Comparison of the Argentine, Brazilian and Mexican experiences illustrates this point. In Argentina, a considerable effort was made, during the 1930s, to maintain the country's credit-worthiness abroad. This required a policy of domestic restraint. Production of import substitutes in the agricultural sector—cotton and other agricultural raw materials—was encouraged, and industrialisation was orientated towards the manufacture of non-durable consumer goods. The concern to defend the level of domestic activity during phases of cyclical depression involved favouring industries with a less elastic demand, i.e. the non-durable consumer goods industries. It was assumed that the demand for consumer durables and equipment could be more easily curtailed as a means of coping with the sharp decline in the country's capacity to import. In

90

other words, Argentina's chief concern was to adapt itself to the unstable conditions prevailing in the world market for raw materials. Mexico's position differed in certain fundamental aspects. In contrast with Argentina, the export sector was controlled by foreigners in the 1920s, which tended to clarify the demarcation line between the interests of the Mexican State and those of the export groups. In the 1920s and early 1930s, the Mexican State was already preparing the ground for far-reaching action in the economic sector, with the creation of the central bank, a government development bank (*Nacional Financiera*) and the Federal Electricity Commission. The expropriation of the petroleum industry in the late 1930s marks the culmination of the crisis between the Mexican State and the powerful foreign groups controlling the country's export activities. Brazil's position was somewhere between that of Argentina and Mexico. In contrast with Argentina, where the exporting interests managed to strengthen their position in the State through the military coup of 1930, in Brazil the position of exporting interests was weakened.[1] However, there was nothing like the dichotomy noted in the Mexican case. The Vargas government, in spite of the defeat of the counter-revolution backed by traditionalist groups in 1932, pursued a policy of compromise with the coffee growers, buying up surplus coffee stocks even when these mostly had to be destroyed. None the less, the acuteness of the crisis in Brazil made it extremely difficult to foster any illusion that the export sector could be restored to its former role. Thus, during the 1930s, the Brazilian government tried to unify the home market by eliminating the surviving trade barriers between states; it created the National Steel Company, which was responsible for building the steel plant at Volta Redonda, and it promoted the training of industrial workers on a nationwide scale.

In the post-war period, the industrialisation process in the three countries under consideration came to depend far more on State action

---

[1] The 1929 crisis had far-reaching political repercussions in most Latin American countries, in many instances triggering off military takeovers and popular uprisings. However, these political disturbances did not always mean the same thing. In Argentina, for instance, the Unión Cívica Radical, a party essentially representing the middle classes and particularly the urban middle class, had been in power since the 1916 election; the 1929 crisis, by creating the conditions that led to the military *putsch* of 1930, smoothed the path for the restoration to power of conservative groups, bringing together interests connected with foreign trade, land speculation and stock-raising. A different process occurred in Brazil: with the 1930 revolution, more in the nature of a popular uprising than a military takeover, the coffee oligarchy was ousted from power under pressure from peripheral groups in the Northeast and the South (Vargas was Governor of the State of Rio Grande do Sul). Since the urban middle class was less influential than in Argentina, the displacement of the oligarchy led the Vargas government to move less in the direction of a formal democracy—as was the case in Argentina under the Unión Cívica Radical—than towards an enlightened authoritarianism.

designed to concentrate investment in the basic sectors, on the temporary recovery of the export sector and on the introduction of foreign capital and technology than on import substitution. However, it was still regarded as import substitution since industrial production was strictly geared to domestic demand and took over markets formerly supplied, albeit on a small scale, by imports. Strictly speaking, new markets were created by the expansion of overall demand that accompanies industrialisation. Since these economies reproduced forms of consumption that already existed in other countries, the supply of a particular commodity was bolstered by imports in the initial stage although this stage tended to become increasingly brief.

In the four countries under consideration—Argentina, Mexico, Brazil and Chile—industrialisation induced by import substitution is, strictly speaking, a phenomenon of the 1930s and the war period, that is, the period when the decline in the capacity to import permitted the intensive use of an industrial nucleus formed in an earlier period. The fact that industrialisation in these countries was intensified during the depression of the external sector is a clear indication that the process could have started sooner if these countries had had the benefit of appropriate policies. In other words, advance beyond the first stage of industrialisation required economic measures designed to change the structure of the industrial nucleus, and in default of such measures the industrial sectors found themselves in a relatively depressed situation. By creating the conditions for an intensive use of existing capacity and by broadening the demand for intermediate products and equipment, the crisis made it clear that the industrialisation process could only move one stage further if it extended its range. State action, leading to the creation of basic industries, was to open up a third stage in the process of industrialisation in Latin America.

CHAPTER 12

IMBALANCES CREATED BY IMPORT-SUBSTITUTING INDUSTRIALISATION: STRUCTURAL INFLATION

DEVELOPMENT AS A CONSEQUENCE OF STRUCTURAL CHANGE

The countries specialising in primary production for export, within the framework of the system of international division of labour that developed in the nineteenth century, created economic structures with a highly inflationary bias. We have seen that cyclical crises in these countries entailed not only a fall in the quantum of exports but also deterioration in the terms of trade, flights of capital and obstruction of foreign credit lines. Thus there was a more accentuated and more rapid reduction in the capacity to import than in the flow of the money income generated by the export sector, creating pressures on the balance of payments which could not be eased simply by mobilising gold and exchange reserves. The immediate alternative was a devaluation of currency, bringing about an expansion in the export sector's money income, an increase in the tax revenue derived from export income and a rise in the prices of imported goods. Inflation was thus a consequence of the economic system's effort to adapt itself to a combination of external pressures. Since it was not feasible to defend the currency by manipulating interest rates and mobilising gold and exchange reserves, and since the short-term capital movements aggravated the critical state of current-account balances, it was natural that flexible exchange-rate systems should have come to prevail. The disadvantage of these systems is that they make speculation easier and thus increase vulnerability to inflation.

Industrialisation based on import substitution started a new inflationary cycle in Latin America, which differed from the classical regional disequilibria engendered by the effort to adapt to pronounced fluctuations in the income of the foreign trade sector. We have seen that one of the requisites for starting the substitution process after the contraction in the capacity to import, was an expansion of money income. Although this expansion was in part absorbed by the increase in production destined for

93

the home market—and without this increase substitution could not have taken place—it sparked off a number of structural tensions which were translated into an inflationary process. The study of structural tensions is one of the most interesting aspects of recent Latin American development and its understanding was furthered only when the traditional theoretical framework for approaching inflation problems was called in question.

Considered simply in its broadest aspects, the problem can be stated as follows: structural economic change is inherent in any process of development and takes the form of sudden or gradual changes in the demand schedule and in the composition of supply. In fact, the study of development can be regarded as the identification and anticipation of such changes and of the interaction and possible causal relations between them. It is as though the development process were a chain of interdependent situations in which certain situations, while dependent on those preceding them, also possess the germinative capacity to modify the tendencies already shown. To say that development consists of structural change is practically a tautology. What matters is to identify the changes that condition further changes, the agents responsible for the decisions that engender these changes and the elements—situations or agents—that offer the greatest resistance to change. The degree of development depends on the effectiveness of the strategic decision centres and the flexibility of the structures themselves. In developed economies, the agents whose decisions are capable of provoking cumulative processes and hence of bringing about structural change act both on the supply side and on the demand side. In fact, there is a process of circular causation in which increased productivity and diversified demand are mutually reinforcing. How rapidly the agents will respond to the new situations will depend on the relative flexibility of the economic structure.

In the classical model of Latin American development—integration into the system of international division of labour—the dynamic sector, which was the supply of primary products, did not interact with domestic demand. Expansion of the export sector led to a rise in domestic income and diversification of a section of demand, indirectly provoking the growth and diversification of imports. Since imported goods were precisely those for which demand was most income-elastic, there could be no cumulative interaction between supply and demand in the direction of broadening any initial impulse to growth. On the other hand, as the export sector was limited to a few export products, it could not of itself offer many possibilities for innovation. Thus, neither the expansion of demand nor the growth of the export sector required structural changes of major significance. It can be said, therefore, that the development model in question was one that did not require much structural flexibility, or rather that it was compatible with structures having little capacity for change. In fact, by allowing development to proceed with the minimum of change, the export model that prevailed in Latin America created a climate of resistance to change on the social plane. By failing to make the ruling classes realise that structural change was an essential ingredient in development, it contributed towards the emergence of attitudes that were to become obstacles to the region's development in the period that followed.

FOCUSES OF BASIC INFLATIONARY PRESSURES

The significance of the observations made in the preceding paragraphs becomes apparent when we remember that industrialisation with a declining import coefficient, i.e. import-substituting industrialisation, is a form of development requiring rapid changes in economic structures. Imports, which had given flexibility to overall supply in the preceding period, enabling it to respond promptly to the evolution of the demand schedule, were now in relative or absolute decline and consisted increasingly of industrial inputs, that is, products for which demand could not be curtailed. In fact, imports now became the instrument to use in changing the production structure developed in connexion with the home market. Development had thus passed from the stage in which it took the form of changes in the composition of demand (and in the composition of imports) to a stage in which it could proceed only if the supply structure was rapidly transformed. Let us imagine a concrete situation. In response to tensions in the export sector, textile production is intensified by working extra shifts in order to replace imports. The level of overall income rises and with it the demand for a whole range of consumer goods. In some cases, domestic supply can respond immediately, even though indirectly and only in part, by setting in motion substitution processes. Pressure to increase imports of intermediate products and equipment will make itself felt, reducing the capacity to import consumer goods. There will be significant changes in relative prices and important transfers of income, reflecting the structural tensions needed to change the supply structure or rather to restore a balance between supply and demand. The time needed to bring about this balance largely reflects the structural flexibility of the country's system of production, taking into account the degree of differentiation it had achieved in the preceding period.

Structural tensions and the ensuing inflation were conditioned by local circumstances in each country. However, certain factors made their influence felt throughout the region, albeit in different degrees, and this makes it possible to attempt an overall interpretation of the inflation that accompanied import-substituting industrialisation in the Latin American countries. Among these factors, which should be considered as focuses of *basic* inflationary pressures, the following should be singled out:

(*a*) *The inelasticity of supply of agricultural products.* If Latin American agricultural structures had adapted to the growing demand for a few export commodities, they had failed to accommodate rising domestic demand. In fact, there was a substantial difference in the pattern of response. In the case of export agriculture we have a rigid system, almost invariably based on cultivation of a single crop, in which increased output is achieved by extensive farming methods, absorbing factors formerly employed in subsistence agriculture with a low economic productivity, even though the forms of production used are not essentially different. In the case of production for the home market, a highly diversified output was needed, with the capacity to accommodate changes in demand. This type of agriculture competed with the surpluses produced by the subsistence sector itself, which varied from year to year in accordance with climatic factors. Extensive growth in the case of production destined for the home market led to increasingly marginal prices, since the land brought under cultivation had to be further and further away from the markets or of poor quality. Given the rapid growth of the population employed in urban areas, a corresponding increase in agricultural productivity was required if output were to keep pace with rising demand. Unlike traditional export agriculture, whose growth could be extensive, agriculture producing for the home market had to develop by raising its technological level. Failure to do so resulted in a relative shortage of agricultural products in the urban areas, with a consequent rise in prices. As in the Ricardian model, the rise in agricultural prices was translated into an increase in the income accruing to landowners, thus consolidating the power of traditionalist groups and reducing the capacity of the supply structure to adapt itself to the new demand schedule.

(*b*) *Inadequacy of the infrastructure.* Transport and other basic services, originally geared to the needs of a few homogeneous export products, often displayed a considerable degree of inadequacy in relation to the requirements of the new production structure. Both in relation to agriculture, expanding into new areas, and in relation to industry, largely dependent on raw material supplies from the interior and requiring access to different areas of the country for domestic outlets for its products, the existing infrastructure revealed serious inadequacies. The problem was, of course, more serious in some countries than in others, but it arose in all of them to a significant degree. The existing network of warehouses and silos proved similarly inadequate in relation to production destined for home consumption. The financial infrastructure also called for considerable adaptation. The financing of homogeneous products of a standard type and with an assured demand in the great international centres is a relatively simple operation compared with the financing of a highly diversified agricultural production handicapped by precarious storage conditions. A substantial part of the investment made by Latin American governments in the last three decades was directed into the rehabilitation and improvement of transport systems and other public utilities.

(c) *Short-term inadequacy of labour.* Although there was an abundant supply of labour in most of the Latin American countries, it lacked skills suited to the demands of industrial activities. In many instances, even a tradition of handicraft industries was lacking, and the labour force had to move straight from technically backward agriculture to the factories. Even more important was the lack of an entrepreneurial tradition. With the exception of countries benefiting from recent European immigration, there was little entrepreneurial experience in the industrial sector. We have already remarked that the traditional export economy did not favour the development of a capacity for innovation. Apart from foreigners, the initial nucleus of industrial entrepreneurs was formed by national elements with experience in enterprises importing manufactured goods—almost invariably controlled by foreign groups. Given its isolation vis-à-vis the traditional ruling class and the professional middle class, this nucleus tended to grow slowly, constituting one of the main reasons for the lack of structural flexibility.

(d) *The inadequacy of fiscal systems.* We have seen that fiscal revenue was essentially dependent on foreign trade, particularly on imports. When this source of revenue was curtailed, a shift to an excise tax was tried, involving high collection costs. The regressive nature of this tax made it inelastic in relation to the rising level of domestic income. The income tax imposed in Argentina in the 1930s played no more than a complementary role. By and large, tax structures are extremely regressive and inelastic to the growth of income generated by activities connected with the home market. Thus, the State's capacity for collecting taxes involved heavier outlays and became more inelastic at a time when there was an increasing demand for investment of public funds. Since the possibilities of external financing had been sharply curtailed or had ceased to exist, and as there were no domestic financial markets to absorb public bond issues, governments throughout Latin America came to depend, to a greater or lesser extent, on credits from the banking system, with an automatic rediscount, to finance investment or even to cover part of current expenditure. Fiscal systems were only gradually brought up to date to cope with the new responsibilities assumed by governments and the new forms of economy that were emerging. Thus, the public sector itself became a factor in structural rigidity, even in areas where the government was seeking other means to promote development.

(e) *Increased financial commitments.* Given the fact that investment was being made under conditions of balance of payments difficulties, or even of a declining capacity to import, the costs of equipment (almost entirely imported) tended to rise in relative terms. The savings ratio therefore had to rise proportionally in order to keep pace with the real rate of investment. Enterprises had to take on additional financial investments and this became a factor exerting pressure for a rise in the price level.

The importance of the factors indicated varied from one country to another and, in the same country, from one period to another. Only when development was deliberately fostered did structural tensions become fully manifest. Thus, in the thirties, when the capacity to import was curtailed and money income expanded, investment shifted to industry, causing a minimum of tension in Argentina and a maximum in Chile. In the case of Argentina, export surpluses found an alternative market through the expansion of urban employment. In Chile, not only was there no possibility of domestic absorption of exportable production but the domestic supply of agricultural products proved extremely rigid. However, in the subsequent period, Argentine agriculture also became a focus of structural tension. Once the stage of extensive expansion in the region producing cereals and livestock had been exhausted, and agriculture found itself competing with other sectors of production in a market with a relatively inelastic labour supply, it became imperative to raise its technical level and increase capital inputs if economic structures were to retain the flexibility they had shown in earlier periods. In default of this development in depth of the agricultural sector, the supply of agricultural and livestock products tended to become inelastic and the home market began to compete with exports, aggravating the basic problem of the inadequacy of the country's capacity to import.

Structural tensions were often aggravated by the government policies pursued. In Brazil, for instance, the government continued its policy of buying up unsold coffee surpluses (which it proceeded to destroy) even

Imbalances: Structural Inflation

during the war years when the adverse trade balance and the budgetary deficit (Brazil had entered the war and partial mobilisation was taking place) gave rise to inflationary pressures. In Argentina, towards the end of the 1940s and in the early 1950s, the government's over-emphasis on industrial investment reduced the profitability of the agricultural sector, whose rigidity had already become manifest as the main focus of structural tension. By and large, by seeking to intensify investment, governments aggravated inflationary tensions. The achievement of a rate of growth that would make it possible to absorb the increase in the population of working age and to satisfy the expectations of groups that already had attained modern standards of living, turned into a difficult obstacle race for which the ruling groups and the administrative apparatus were ill equipped. The faster the pace aimed for, the more difficult, *ceteris paribus*, became the obstacles.

CIRCUMSTANTIAL FACTORS AND PROPAGATION MECHANISMS

In a structuralist analysis of inflation, attention is initially directed towards the focuses from which so-called basic inflationary pressures spread. These are the points in the economic structure that offer most resistance to the changes required by development.[1] The *basic* pressures act together with other factors which may be as much *circumstantial* as engendered by the inflationary process itself. Circumstantial factors often spark off a new inflationary wave. They could as easily be of an economic nature—a sharp rise or fall in export prices—as non-economic: the loss of a coffee crop through frost, a shortage of food supplies after a drought, government action of the kind instanced above. In fact, the inflationary process always starts with the action of some agent whose operations frustrate what may

[1] On the structuralist theory of inflation, the basic works are: Juan Noyola Vazquez, 'El Desarrollo Económico y la Inflación en México y Otros Paises Latinoamericanos', *Investigación Económica*, XVI, 4, Mexico, 1956; ECLA, *El Desequilibrio Externo en el Desarrollo Económico Latinoamericano: El Caso de México*, 1957; C. Furtado, 'The External Disequilibrium in the Underdeveloped Economies', *The Indian Journal of Economics*, April 1958; Osvaldo Sunkel, 'La Inflación Chilena—Un Enfoque Heterodoxo', *El Trimestre Económico*, Oct.–Dec. 1958; Aníbal Pinto Santa Cruz, 'Estabilidad y Desarrollo', *El Trimestre Económico*, Jan.–Mar. 1960; Julio Oliveira, 'La Teoria no Monetaria de la Inflación', *El Trimestre Económico*, Jan.–Mar. 1960; Raúl Prebisch, 'El Falso Dilema entre Desarrollo Económico y Estabilidad Monetaria', *Boletín Económico de América Latina*, March 1961; Dudley Seers, 'Inflación y Crecimiento: Resumen de la Experiencia Latinoamericana', *Boletín Económico de América Latina*, Feb. 1962. For an overall survey, see Rosa Olivia Villa Martinez, *Inflación y Desarrollo: el Enfoque Estructuralista*, thesis for the Universidad Nacional Autónoma de México, 1966. See also Werner Baer, 'The Inflation Controversy in Latin America: a Survey', *Latin American Research Review*, II, 2, 1967.

be called conventional expectations. Thus a rise in export prices, by providing additional public revenue, may prompt the government to launch a public works programme, changing conditions in the labour market, increasing urban employment, raising the demand for agricultural surpluses, provoking sudden shifts in the import schedule, etc. In this way, a number of expectations will be frustrated, causing resistance to the changes required in the allocation of resources. Once set in motion, the inflationary process tends to create situations that react upon the initial impulse and increase its inflationary impact. Thus the rise in money costs provoked by the inflation has repercussions on the export sector, reducing its competitive capacity abroad. The consequences may be a reduction in exports—which will affect the capacity to import and aggravate the inflation—or an exchange devaluation with a consequent rise in the price level of imported industrial inputs, which cannot but aggravate the inflation. Another example of where inflationary pressures are first derived from outside but then become autonomous is the behaviour of public services: cuts in utility rates may act as disincentives to investment in public facilities, increasing the structural rigidity of the economic system as a whole, or they may require compensatory public subsidies aggravating one of the focuses of basic inflationary pressure.

The most rigid points in the economic structure act like a barrier damming up the accumulated potential energy of a constantly rising level of water. In some circumstances, this energy can be diverted and the economic system will continue to operate as though it did not exist. It is far more likely, however, that the pressure will spread and affect other points of the economic structure, the course taken being dependent on the propagation mechanisms that it uses. Thus, the power to propagate the inflationary potential inherent in the need to finance a deficit in the public sector will depend on the method of financing adopted. A rise in agricultural prices will be reflected in falling real wages for the urban sectors or rising costs for the industrial sectors dependent on agricultural inputs. The speed at which inflationary pressures are propagated reflects the varying ability of the different social groups to defend their share in the social income and the effectiveness with which public and private sectors defend their respective positions in the process of appropriating available resources.

The *decision centres* able to intervene in the propagation of inflationary pressures are mainly those that intervene in credit, exchange and wages policies and in the method of financing deficits in the public sector. In other words, inflationary pressure tends to be propagated through the various monetary channels, and hence it can be said that these channels constitute its propagation mechanisms. Since these channels offer some resistance, the inflationary pressure may be partially absorbed. Thus, the credit system is not completely elastic, the decline in real wages may be gradual, the balance of payments deficit may be refinanced abroad, etc. If pressure is prolonged, however, or suddenly accentuated, the channels will offer decreasing resistance and may even come to act as automatic propagation mechanisms.

The difficulty in understanding the true nature of the inflationary processes that accompanied Latin America's development policies in the phase when the export sector lost its dynamism arose from the emphasis given to the propagation mechanisms. This led to the prevalence of the view that inflation reflected the poor functioning of money flows. Thus, the banking system's exaggeratedly lenient attitude towards the private sector or towards budgetary deficit abuses was blamed for the excess of demand over supply—and a *demand inflation* was diagnosed; in other instances, government complaisance was blamed for excessive wage increases and the existence of a *cost inflation* was recorded. There can be no question that both situations have occurred repeatedly in many Latin American countries in the course of the last three decades, particularly in the post-war years. However, they were nearly always *responses* to more deep-seated pressures, or rather they reflected an adaptation effort within the framework of a more complex process, whose main ingredients were structural inflexibility and the determination to press ahead with a development policy.

SIGNIFICANT CASES

Mexico, one of the industrially most advanced Latin American countries, is the only case in which inflationary pressures have been completely controlled. Since 1954, when the Mexican peso was devalued for the last time, the level of prices in the country has remained relatively stable, the increase being fairly close to that observed in the United States. To explain this singular situation, we must take into account several factors. First, there is a one-party political system which guarantees strict continuity in control of the Executive Power and subordinates the functions of the Legislative Power.[1] Since the trade union system is closely integrated into the government party, the likelihood of friction between those responsible for administering wages policy and trade union representatives is eliminated. On the other hand, the possibility that the export sector will exert

[1] An analysis of the present power structure in Mexico is given in Pablo González Casanova, *La Democracia en México*, Mexico, 1965.

strong pressure on the government to compensate for a fall in market prices abroad is practically ruled out. The propagation mechanisms are thus subject to control, which explains why changes in income distribution can be effected without altering the level of prices. Furthermore, the weakness of certain social groups creates conditions for a particular type of structural adaptation, and there have been times when the growth of the domestic product has been accompanied by a fall in the average real wages of these groups. But these considerations are not in themselves sufficient to explain the Mexican experience. An important aspect of this experience must be found in the greatly increased structural economic flexibility brought about by the social changes following the revolution and the determination shown by successive governments over the last three decades to promote the country's industrial development. Control of the petroleum industry not only created an important source of investment funds but also made it possible to carry out a policy of keeping down fuel prices, with favourable effects on industrial costs. Finally, the modernisation of the agricultural sector, involving large-scale irrigation works in the north and the introduction of improved cultivation techniques in the *Mesa Central*, eliminated one of the focuses of inflationary pressure most difficult to control. It should be added that the remarkable expansion of tourism in the last two decades has considerably eased Mexico's capacity to import. Thus, greater structural flexibility and stricter control of the propagation mechanisms created the conditions for achieving the monetary stability referred to above.

Both in Chile and in Argentina the situation is in many respects the opposite of that of Mexico. The power system reflects a compromise between powerfully structured groups and the propagation mechanisms are consequently in no position to resist inflationary pressures. In Argentina, the chronic inadequacy of the capacity to import, the failure to modernise agriculture and stock-raising, the intrinsic weakness of the State when faced with prolonged social tensions, the lack of a long-term industrialisation policy—all this in a precociously modernised country where popular expectations are constantly rising—have combined to produce one of the most complex inflationary processes on record.

The behaviour of the Brazilian inflation also displays individual features worth mentioning. In the decade following the Second World War, inflation played an important role in accelerating the country's development. The sharp rise in coffee prices after 1949, and in other export products after the Korean war, was reflected in the familiar favourable effects produced on the levels of income in both private and public sectors.

Imbalances: Structural Inflation

Nevertheless, given the structural inflexibility of the export sector, infrastructure, skilled labour market etc., the inflationary process dating from the war period tended to be aggravated. In order to curb any further propagation of inflationary impulses while at the same time defending coffee prices on the world market, the government maintained a stable exchange rate. As the domestic level of prices rose, there was a marked shift in income from the foreign trade sector (particularly the coffee sector) to the import sector. In this way, relative prices of imported equipment declined considerably, greatly increasing the profitability of the industrial sector. What was involved was a change in income distribution within the private sector, to the benefit of the most dynamic groups, giving rise to the extraordinary industrial growth of the 1950s. New investment in the coffee sector, already overburdened by structural surpluses, was discouraged, and diversification of the industrial sector was stepped up. With the introduction of an auction system for foreign exchange in 1954,[1] a substantial proportion of the increment in the export sector's income, which was being gradually absorbed by the industrial sector, was appropriated by the government, making it possible to reduce the inflationary potential created in the public sector largely as a result of heavy investment in infrastructure.

In the course of the present decade, the Brazilian inflation has come more and more to resemble the Argentine–Chilean model which has also been reproduced, in an acute form, in Uruguay. The propagation mechanisms are increasingly prompt to operate and the secondary focuses—created by the inflation itself—begin to act in increasingly autonomous ways. Banks, benefiting from the effects of interest regulations on holders of small and medium savings and from the cheap money available through the rediscount mechanism, tend to hold privileged positions. Firms reduce their own liquidity as much as possible and come to rely entirely on the banking system for their working capital. In consequence, the economic system becomes extremely sensitive to changes in credit policy. Any attempt to curb inflation by curtailing credit will cripple financially weak firms without affecting those who have connexions with the banks or are in a position to negotiate short-term loans abroad. Credit restrictions can thus paralyse certain businesses—not necessarily the least efficient—and raise money costs of others as a result of their increased financial commitments.

[1] The exchange reform introduced by Minister Osvaldo Aranha in 1954 established five categories of imported goods in accordance with their degree of *essentialness*. Since only a small amount of foreign exchange was made available for the category of goods considered less essential, quotations at exchange auctions for this category of imports rose, the consequent 'profit' reverting to the public coffers.

TABLE 12.1. *Consumer Price* (*Cost of Living*) *Indices in Selected Countries* (% *annual increases*)

	Argen-tina[1]	Brazil[2]	Bolivia[3]	Colom-bia[4]	Chile[5]	Mex-ico[6]	Peru[7]	Uru-guay[8]	Vene-zuela[9]
1956	+13·4	+21·1	+178·8	+5·1	+56·0	+5·0	+5·5	+6·7	+0·9
1957	+24·8	+15·9	+115·6	+15·0	+33·1	+5·8	+7·4	+14·7	−2·2
1958	+31·5	+14·7	+2·7	+13·1	+20·0	+11·4	+7·9	+17·5	+4·8
1959	+113·7	+39·2	+20·5	+8·5	+38·6	+2·5	+12·7	+39·5	+5·2
1960	+27·3	+29·4	+11·2	+6·1	+11·6	+5·0	+8·6	+38·8	+2·6
1961	+13·5	+33·3	+7·7	+7·8	+7·7	+1·7	+4·5	+22·5	−1·9
1962	+28·1	+48·8	+6·0	+5·6	+13·9	+1·0	+6·6	+10·9	−0·5
1963	+24·3	+72·4	−0·7	+24·5	+44·2	+0·6	+6·4	+20·6	+0·3
1964	+22·1	+93·0	+10·1	+15·7	+46·0	+2·3	+10·5	+43·2	+1·1
1965	+28·6	+65·8	+2·6	+5·5	+28·8	+3·6	+17·0	+56·5	+2·1
1966	+31·9	+41·3	+7·2	+20·4	+22·9	+4·2	+9·4	+73·5	−0·2
1967	+29·2	+30·7	—	+8·9	+18·1	+3·0	—	—	−0·9

[1] Federal capital. [2] Guanabara State. [3] La Paz (city). [4] National index for the average consumer. [5] Santiago (city). [6] Working class in Mexico City. [7] Working class in Lima and Callao. [8] Working class in Montevideo. [9] Caracas (city).

SOURCE: Interamerican Statistical Institute, *Statistical Bulletin*.

This is why the anti-inflationary policies prescribed by the International Monetary Fund, and followed by Chile towards the end of the 1950s and by Argentina and Brazil in the present decade, have provoked recessions in economic activity without achieving relative stability in the level of prices.

At a certain point, as we shall see in detail in a later chapter, structural inflexibilities begin to act not only as focuses of inflationary pressure but as a brake on development. At this stage, any development effort tends to be translated into acute inflationary pressures, which can be absorbed only by applying policies directly designed to induce structural change. In short, the problem of controlling inflation tended to become part and parcel of development policy, inasmuch as it had not proved feasible to achieve stability outside the framework of a concerted effort to promote structural reform.

V. GROWTH AND STAGNATION IN THE RECENT PERIOD

CHAPTER 13

EVOLUTION OF MACROECONOMIC STRUCTURES

DIVERSITY IN BEHAVIOUR PATTERNS

A comparative analysis of overall development trends in the recent period reveals wide differences in the stages at which the Latin American countries find themselves, and at the same time makes it possible to establish the broad outline of a representative model for the regional economy at the present time. For the purpose of this analysis we have used data covering the period starting in 1950 for the countries of greatest relative economic importance in the region:[1] Argentina, Brazil, Chile, Colombia, Mexico, Peru and Venezuela. All these countries have experienced significant structural economic change during the period under review, as can be seen from the figures given in Table 13.1. In all of them, the agricultural sector's share in the gross domestic product has decreased: between 1950 and 1965, it declined from 18·7 to 16·2 per cent in Argentina; from 22·5 to 15·7 per cent in Mexico; from 39·8 to 32·2 per cent in Colombia and from 27·4 to 22·5 per cent in Peru. However, structural changes did not always follow the same lines in the countries concerned. In Brazil, for instance, despite the relatively vigorous growth of the manufacturing sector, the agricultural sector continues to account for a large share of the domestic product, in view of the slow growth of the tertiary sector. In Mexico, the manufacturing sector grew relatively less than in Brazil, but there were more changes in the country's economic structure, reflecting

---

[1] Cuba, with a population similar in size to those of Chile and Venezuela and ranking fourth in regional per capita income for 1960 (after Argentina, Uruguay and Venezuela), is among the countries of greatest relative economic importance in Latin America. However, owing to the lack of data on this country, particularly data that can be compared with those available for the seven countries considered, the Cuban economy cannot be dealt with in an overall survey of the regional economy during the last decade. Cuba is thus excluded from the data on Latin America unless otherwise stated. The Cuban economy will be separately analysed in chapter 24.

TABLE 13.1. *Structural Evolution of GDP in Selected Countries* (% *of GDP*)

	agriculture	mining industry	manufacturing	building	basic services	other services	total
Argentina							
1950	18·7	0·7	28·9	4·9	9·4	37·4	100
1955	19·6	0·8	29·9	3·9	9·5	36·3	100
1960	16·9	1·4	31·4	4·1	9·4	37·8	100
1965	16·2	1·7	32·2	4·1	9·8	36·0	100
Brazil							
1950	31·3	0·3	16·5	1·1	7·1	43·7	100
1955	31·0	0·3	18·9	1·1	7·6	41·2	100
1960	28·3	0·5	23·4	1·2	8·6	38·0	100
1965	31·0	0·6	23·4	1·1	9·3	34·6	100
Mexico							
1950	22·5	5·7	20·6	3·1	5·8	42·3	100
1955	20·2	4·4	21·0	4·6	6·3	43·5	100
1960	17·4	4·3	23·0	5·0	6·1	44·2	100
1965	15·7	3·9	24·8	5·0	6·1	47·5	100
Chile							
1950	12·5	7·2	16·7	2·3	7·9	53·4	100
1955	12·8	6·9	18·8	3·1	8·7	49·7	100
1960	12·2	7·0	18·7	2·8	8·1	51·1	100
1965	10·9	6·8	19·9	2·7	8·7	51·0	100
Colombia							
1950	39·8	3·6	14·2	3·2	5·9	34·3	100
1955	35·2	3·5	15·4	4·5	7·6	33·8	100
1960	34·6	4·0	17·0	3·7	7·3	33·4	100
1965	32·2	4·0	17·3	3·4	7·7	35·4	100
Peru							
1950	27·4	5·4	14·6	3·5	4·7	44·4	100
1955	23·8	6·4	16·6	4·5	5·5	43·2	100
1960	22·9	9·0	17·7	3·2	5·5	41·7	100
1965	22·5	7·6	18·7	4·5	5·5	41·2	100
Venezuela							
1950	8·5	26·1	9·6	4·6	6·3	44·9	100
1955	7·3	27·0	9·4	5·0	6·0	45·3	100
1960	7·2	27·3	10·7	3·9	5·2	45·7	100
1965	7·7	25·2	12·9	4·4	5·9	43·9	100

SOURCE: ECLA, on the basis of figures taken from *Economic Survey of Latin America, 1963, 1965* and *1967*.

the greater dynamism of the tertiary sector—mainly as a result of the expansion of tourism—and a far more significant rise in the productivity of the agricultural sector. In Colombia and Peru, the expansion of the manufacturing sector was accompanied by a relative decline in the agricultural sector, whereas in Chile and Venezuela, countries dependent on imports for part of their food supply, the share of the agricultural sector remained fairly constant or decreased more slowly.

The decade 1950–60 was a period of relatively rapid growth in the region as a whole. Argentina and Chile excepted, the countries under consideration all showed relatively high rates of increase in the gross domestic product. Table 13.2 shows the evolution of the product by major economic sectors. From the figures in this table, taken together with those in Table 13.3, we can distinguish three types of behaviour.

(*a*) countries with a rising import coefficient displaying the structural flexibility consequent upon an open external sector. These countries show the characteristics of the classic Latin American model of development 'outwards', with an import-substitution process partly prompted by government action and due to the initiative of international corporations seeking to defend their position in local markets by taking anticipatory action. This was the case in Peru throughout the 1950s and in Venezuela during the latter half of the 1950s.

(*b*) countries whose import coefficient is declining but whose industrialisation has gained sufficient momentum to bring about structural changes and sustain development. This is the case in Brazil and Mexico, where industrialisation is proceeding as though the impetus provided by the structural tensions that arose in the 1930s had not yet spent its force. Colombia falls midway between this group and the first. Its import coefficient is beginning to decline, with the result that industrial development—both 'spontaneous' and government-fostered—has been intensified.

(*c*) countries that have already experienced a sharp fall in the import coefficient and have considerably expanded their industrial production, but in which the industrialisation process has lost momentum. This is the case in Argentina and Chile. The average annual percentage growth rate of the industrial sector in the fifties was 3·8 in Argentina and 4·3 in Chile, as against 9·9 in Venezuela, 9·2 in Brazil, 7·4 in Mexico, 7·0 in Peru and 6·5 in Colombia.

The 1960s saw a change in the overall picture. The data for the first half of the decade, whose major trends have persisted up to the present time, show an overall contraction in the growth rates of the domestic product. Among the countries in the first group, Venezuela's import cofficient has

TABLE 13.2. *GDP Sectoral Growth Rates in Post-War Period in Selected Countries* (% *annual rates*)

	Argen-tina	Brazil	Mexico	Chile	Colom-bia	Peru	Vene-zuela
agriculture							
1950–5	4·1	5·0	5·8	3·5	2·7	2·2	5·9
1955–60	−0·4	3·7	3·0	2·3	3·5	3·8	6·1
1960–5	2·1	6·9	3·9	3·1	3·0	5·9	6·6
mining industry							
1950–5	7·8	6·6	4·7	−2·9	4·3	8·8	8·7
1955–60	14·3	14·9	6·1	3·5	6·8	11·9	6·6
1960–5	7·8	11·1	4·2	5·0	4·4	2·6	3·7
manufacturing industry							
1950–5	3·8	8·1	6·6	5·4	6·9	7·8	11·6
1955–60	3·8	10·3	8·1	3·2	6·1	6·1	9·1
1960–5	4·1	4·9	8·0	6·7	5·9	7·4	9·4
building							
1950–5	1·5	6·4	6·4	3·9	12·4	10·7	10·6
1955–60	4·3	7·2	8·1	1·4	−0·2	−2·0	1·1
1960–5	2·0	2·8	5·9	4·6	1·9	13·5	7·9
basic services							
1950–5	6·2	4·4	9·6	6·0	9·6	—	18·0
1955–60	12·0	10·8	6·5	3·5	11·7	—	18·1
1960–5	9·9	9·7	10·0	7·4	9·2	—	12·0
Total GDP							
1950–5	3·2	5·7	6·1	3·1	5·3	5·1	8·7
1955–60	2·7	5·9	6·1	4·3	3·9	4·7	6·7
1960–5	2·8	4·9	5·9	3·5	4·5	6·3	5·4
GDP per capita							
1950–5	1·0	2·9	3·1	0·9	2·5	2·9	4·7
1955–60	0·9	2·9	3·1	1·9	0·9	2·1	2·8
1960–5	1·3	1·8	2·8	1·1	1·2	3·2	1·9

SOURCE: *Ibid.*

TABLE 13.3. *Structural Change Indicators in Selected Countries*
(*Index: 1950–5 = 100*)

	A	B	C	D	E
Argentina					
1955–60	88	99	75	100	84
1960–5	111	120	65	108	87
Brazil					
1955–60	66	95	108	127	104
1960–5	58	101	90	60	86
Mexico					
1955–60	89	114	82	123	100
1960–5	81	112	87	121	97
Chile					
1955–60	101	101	136	59	139
1960–5	138	131	85	124	113
Colombia					
1955–60	82	101	76	88	74
1960–5	75	111	74	86	85
Venezuela					
1955–60	109	89	85	78	77
1960–5	66	61	100	80	62

A: indices of the import coefficient. B: indices of the gross investment rates.
C: indices of the marginal productivity of investments. D: indices of the rate of
growth of the industrial product. E: indices of the rate of growth of the gross
product.

SOURCE: *Ibid.*

fallen, whereas that of Peru has continued to rise. In both countries the
industrial sector has continued to expand and its growth was accelerated
in the second half of the 1950s. The growth rate of the product declined
in Venezuela and rose in Peru. In Colombia, the import coefficient fell
slightly without any marked effect on the industrialisation process. In all
three countries an intensive import-substitution process is still in progress
and there are indications that substitution will reach saturation point by
the end of the present decade.

In the case of countries falling within group (*b*) there was a significant
slackening in the pace of the industrialisation process in Brazil, and the
country's import coefficient has continued to contract. In Mexico the
vigorous expansion of industry has continued and the growth rate of the

domestic product has remained high. A more detailed analysis of the figures shows that Brazil's import coefficient fell from 9·9 to 5·1 per cent between 1960 and 1965, whereas in Mexico the coefficient remained practically stable, changing only from 11·8 to 11·7 per cent.

In group (c) countries, significant changes have taken place in the 1960s. In the first place there has been a determined effort to recover the capacity to import. In Argentina the import coefficient index rose from 88 to 111, and in Chile from 101 to 138 (Table 13.3). The greater flexibility resulting from the recovery of the import capacity enabled the industrialisation process to be resumed although production has not sufficed to raise the rate of growth of the domestic product. The figures given in column C of Table 13.3 show that the productivity of investments declined in both countries, which could have been the result of a worsening in the terms of trade, which militated against the export drive, or of a drop in the capital-output ratio of the industrial sector, attributable to the inadequate size of the domestic market, errors in industrial planning and similar causes.

Taking the period as a whole, a number of general observations may be made. The first is the change in the behaviour of the external sector. Exports have expanded only where there has been a deliberate export-promotion policy. The export sector's traditional forms of extensive growth in response to expanding external demand have given way to other forms of growth based on the realisation that an inadequate capacity to import is a serious obstacle to development. In Chile, for instance, recovery in the growth of exports was the outcome of a deliberate policy designed to increase the country's share in the world copper market. Similarly, the record increase in Peru's fisheries exports is the result of a combination of deliberate measures taken in the country rather than a simple response to an expanding external market. In Argentina, a considerable effort has been made since the second half of the 1950s to reduce the relative prices of agricultural inputs, thus rechannelling resources to the export sector. In this way exports, once a factor in inducing development, have tended by and large to act as a brake on development because of their lack of dynamism.

The second point is that industrialisation of what we have called the first phase—directly induced by the growth of the export sector—has tended to proceed side by side with 'import-substituting' industrialisation, that is, industrialisation engendered by an inadequate capacity to import. Countries with a low level of industrialisation in 1950—an industrialisation coefficient of less than 15 per cent—sought to intensify the industrialisation process independently of the behaviour of the export sector.

Venezuela, in the first half of the 1950s, is the last example of a Latin American country in which the domestic product grew considerably without a corresponding increase in the share of the industrial sector. In actual fact, Venezuela's industrial sector was expanding but massive investment in the petroleum sector, whose inputs at that time were wholly imported, meant that the structure of the production system showed no appreciable change. In Peru, a country in which the import coefficient rose steadily throughout the entire period—from 13 per cent to 27 per cent between 1950 and 1965—the rapid growth of the industrial sector was matched by a steady structural transformation as indicated by the rise in the industrialisation coefficient (Table 13.1).

ANTICIPATION AND THE LOSS OF EFFECTIVENESS OF THE SUBSTITUTION PROCESS

Comparison of the experiences of Colombia, Peru and Venezuela with those of the group of countries whose industrialisation started in an earlier period—Argentina, Mexico, Brazil and Chile—shows that there has been an acceleration of the industrialisation process. This would appear to confirm the observation made above with respect to the second group of countries that the industrialisation associated with the crisis of the foreign trade sector corresponded to existing possibilities that had not been explored in an earlier period. In the 1950s a clearer perception of the problem enabled countries in the first group—the five Central American countries were to repeat this experience later as a result of their integration efforts—to *anticipate* their industrialisation process, not only by taking appropriate protectionist measures but by orientating investments in infrastructure so as to favour industrialisation and even by providing direct incentives to industry. It is significant, for instance, that in the mid-1950s government initiative in all three countries (Colombia, Peru and Venezuela) was responsible for sponsoring the installation of basic industries, including steel manufacturing. It should be pointed out, however, that this industrialisation was carried out with a much broader participation of international groups and directed towards integration with the import sector, whose fluctuations tended to have adverse effects on the level of domestic activity. Industrialisation seemed to proceed as if it were directed less towards the creation of an integrated system of production than towards the extension of the import sector. The experience of the sixties made it clear that these countries would find it difficult to reconcile the industrialisation process with a reduction in the import coefficient below

TABLE 13.4. *Gross Fixed Investment Rates in Selected Countries*
(% of GDP)

	1950–4	1955–9	1960–5
Argentina			
public investment	5·1	3·5	5·3
private investment	13·1	14·6	16·6
total:	18·2	18·1	21·9
Brazil			
public investment	—	—	4·7
private investment	—	—	8·7
total:	14·9	14·2	13·4
Mexico			
public investment	—	—	6·0
private investment	—	—	9·0
total:	13·4	16·3	15·0
Chile			
public investment	4·5	4·1	6·9
private investment	4·9	5·4	5·4
total:	9·4	9·5	12·3
Colombia			
public investment	—	—	3·3
private investment	—	—	14·0
total:	15·6	15·8	17·3
Venezuela			
public investment	9·6	11·1	5·5
private investment	17·8	13·4	11·2
total:	27·4	24·5	16·7
Peru			
public investment	—	—	4·7
private investment	—	—	18·7
total:	—	—	23·4

SOURCE: *Ibid.*

relatively high levels. On the other hand, the industrialisation coefficient tended to remain stable at a relatively low level. Contraction of the import coefficient to less than 15 per cent appears to create serious obstacles to development, a situation that seems to have arisen before the manufacturing sector managed to increase its share in the domestic product to 20 per cent. Among the countries whose industrialisation began earlier, Argentina, Mexico and Brazil have managed to continue their industrialisation with an import coefficient of around 10 per cent. Nevertheless, the

Macroeconomic Structures

Chilean experience has already demonstrated the difficulties of continuing to develop with an import coefficient below 15 per cent, which seems to indicate that the overall size of the market also acts as a restrictive factor. Thus, taking into account the foreign control of industrial investment, which seems to imply a high content of imported inputs, and the size of the domestic markets concerned, it can be deduced that import-substituting industrialisation is relatively ineffective as a factor for bringing about structural change in countries where it has been under way only since the fifties.

CHAPTER 14

AGRICULTURAL SECTOR

AGRICULTURAL PRODUCTION

The structural features of Latin American agriculture, described in detail in chapter 7, largely account for the behaviour of this sector in recent years. By and large we find a pattern of extensive farming, that is, agriculture geared to a utilisation of land and labour involving limited capital outlays. Moreover, the emphasis is on production of a few commodities, mainly those destined for export, enjoying a privileged position and monopolising available credit facilities and infrastructure. It is with this background in mind that we must analyse the evolution of the agricultural sector over the past few decades, a period characterised by the weakening of external demand and the expansion of the domestic market. The population explosion, rapid urbanisation and the rise in purchasing power of a part of the population failed to elicit the required response from the Latin American agrarian sector, since prevailing systems of extensive agriculture were no longer adequate methods for coping with the situation.

The figures given in Table 14.1 show that only in exceptional cases did agricultural and livestock production exceed population growth. It should be added that these figures underestimate the insufficiency of supply since, as a result of rapid urbanisation, demand for agricultural surpluses has grown much more rapidly than the population. Even if we assume that the food consumption patterns of the population that has emigrated from the countryside to the towns have remained the same, we would still have to consider the much higher wastage coefficient involved in transporting food, particularly in countries with a tropical climate, the inadequacy of means of transport and warehousing, the great distances involved, etc. Among the countries included in the table, only Mexico and Venezuela have significantly expanded the domestic supply of agricultural and livestock products. The low rates of growth for Argentina and Peru are mainly attributable to the slow growth or even decline of livestock production.

Increases in agricultural production depend not only on the extension of the area under cultivation but also on improvements in yield per unit of

Agricultural Sector

TABLE 14.1. *Growth of Agricultural Production and Population in Selected Countries, 1952–64 (% annual growth rates)*

	agricultural production	population
Argentina	1·8	1·8
Brazil	3·2	3·0
Colombia	2·4	2·8
Chile	1·8	2·5
Mexico	6·7	3·2
Peru	2·3	2·6
Venezuela	5·3	3·8

SOURCE: ECLA, *Economic Survey of Latin America, 1966*.

land used. It is significant that the expansion of Latin American agriculture continues to depend more on the incorporation of new lands than on increased yields. The figures for the region as a whole show that about two-thirds of the overall rise in agricultural production achieved between the years 1948–52 and 1964–5 is attributable to the increase in the area under cultivation. Over the same period, the unit yield for the production of cereals rose at an annual rate of 1·6 per cent, whereas in North America the rate was 2·9 per cent and in Europe 3·0 per cent. For the production of oil-seeds, the rise in the unit yield was 1·9 per cent in Latin America, 3·3 per cent in North America and 3·9 per cent in Europe.[1]

A comparative analysis shows that there were wide differences between the countries of the region, as regards both production trends and the levels of yield obtained. These differences are clearly illustrated by the figures given in Table 14.2. In Argentina there were substantial increases in wheat and rice yields, but maize and cotton yields showed no improvement. The pattern was similar in Venezuela, although the levels of yield obtained were much lower. In Mexico there was a striking rise in wheat and cotton yields, but little improvement in the yields of rice and maize, which is significant in view of the fact that maize is the staple food of the Mexican population. In Brazil, Colombia and Peru yields remained virtually at a standstill, the only exception being the production of cotton

---

[1] For an overall survey of the problem and comparative data for other regions see ECLA, *Economic Survey of Latin America, 1966*, part IV: Agriculture: Present Situation and Trends; see also Interamerican Development Bank, Montague Yudelman (ed.), *Agricultural Development in Latin America: Current Status and Prospects*, 1966, and ECLA/FAO/IDB, *El Uso de Fertilizantes en América Latina*, 1966.

5-2

TABLE 14.2. *Average Yields of Key Crops in Selected Countries*
(*100 kg per hectare*)

	wheat			maize			rice			cotton (fibre)		
	1948–52	1958–62	1964–65	1948–52	1958–62	1964–65	1948–52	1958–62	1964–65	1948–52	1958–62	1964–65
Argentina	11·5	12·8	18·6	14·8	18·2	16·8	30·5	33·2	48·6	2·4	2·2	2·5
Brazil	7·4	6·0	8·8	12·4	12·9	11·6[1]	15·7	16·6	15·2[1]	1·5	1·7	1·6
Colombia	7·2	9·0	9·6	10·7	11·3	9·1	20·4	20·0	19·9	2·2	4·3	4·9
Chile	11·9	13·4	13·6	13·8	20·4	27·8	29·0	26·5	27·3	—	—	—
Mexico	8·8	16·0	25·5	7·5	9·0	10·9	18·0	21·7	20·7	3·3	5·4	6·8
Peru	9·2	9·9	9·9	14·3	13·3	13·9	38·5	38·5	43·1[1]	5·0	5·4	—
Venezuela	4·7	6·0	5·5	11·4	11·3	10·1	11·4	15·2	18·3	2·8	2·1	3·3

[1] 1963–4.

SOURCE: ECLA, *Economic Survey of Latin America, 1966*.

in Colombia. The case of Brazil is particularly serious, since not only did yields fail to show any improvement but overall yield per hectare was one of the lowest in the region.

The level of yield obtained by Mexico for wheat and even that already obtained by Argentina is higher than in the United States and Canada and comparable with the European average, which is around 2 tons. In the case of maize, the yield obtained by Chile is close to the European average but much lower than that of the United States, which is around 4 tons. It should be pointed out, however, that the Chilean yield is more than double the Latin American average. In the case of rice, Argentina and Peru obtained yields approximating the European and U.S. averages. On the other hand, in Brazil, accounting for over three-quarters of overall rice production, the average yield was only about one-third of the European and U.S. averages. Average cotton yields were very high in Mexico and Peru, where cotton is grown on irrigated land.

Trends in agricultural yield are determined by a number of factors, whose relative importance varies from country to country. Among these factors must be mentioned the existence of an open agricultural frontier, that is, of land available for extending crop areas, the agrarian structure's capacity to raise the technical level of production, financial and technical support from the government and the intensity of the growth of demand for agricultural products. It seems obvious that in Mexico the land reform programme, the most significant part of which was carried out in the 1930s, and the determined efforts made by the government to invest in the agricultural infrastructure and promote an increase in the domestic supply of fertilisers, created a combination of circumstances favouring development of the agricultural sector. The Mexican experience is particularly striking since this country's basic natural resources were traditionally regarded in Latin America as being rather unfavourable to agricultural development. Even in 1948–52 its maize yield was the lowest in the region, although the population was heavily dependent on this staple food. The expansion of the irrigated area in Mexico, largely achieved in newly settled areas, raised substantially average levels of yield. The Venezuelan experience also provides an interesting example of government action designed to raise the technical level of agriculture. In this case, however, the problem is relatively much less serious since agriculture contributes less than one-tenth to the domestic product and the government is able to make use of the considerable resources derived from the petroleum sector.

One of the principal factors responsible for raising agricultural yields is the use of fertilisers. This factor, in conjunction with the use of improved

Economic Development of Latin America

TABLE 14.3. *Fertiliser* (*Nitrogen, Phosphorus and Potassium*)
Consumption in Selected Countries
(*annual averages in thousands of tons of plant nutrients*)

	1957–9	1960–2	1964
Argentina	15·9	16·5	48·5
Brazil	227·8	262·5	255·5
Colombia	61·0	73·7	94·8
Chile	55·4	78·0	120·1
Mexico	131·4	185·5	300·5
Peru	62·6	72·5	91·9
Venezuela	11·6	21·1	32·0

SOURCE: ECLA/FAO/IDB, *El Uso de Fertilizantes en América Latina*, 1966.

varieties of seed and pest control, is responsible for the remarkable rise in agricultural yields achieved in the developed countries over the last two decades. Fertiliser consumption in Latin America rose from about 500,000 tons of nutrients in 1950 to about 1·3 million in 1964. The present average consumption, however, is still only one-fifth of that for the developed countries as a whole. Table 14.3 gives the figures for overall consumption of nitrogen, phosphorus and potassium in selected countries.

The low consumption of fertilisers in Argentina is due to their scanty use in the pampas region, where cereal production is concentrated. A combination of circumstances—the semi-extensive nature of cereal growing, the possibility of rotating crop farming with livestock production and the natural fertility of the soils—makes it possible to attain relatively high levels of profitability without the use of fertilisers and does not favour development of a tradition of fertiliser use. In fact in most countries the tendency is to concentrate the use of fertilisers on a few crops, generally those for which credit is available and an organised marketing system exists. In Brazil, for instance, 48 per cent of all plant nutrients are used for sugar-cane and coffee; in Peru, 33 per cent for cotton; in Argentina, 60 per cent for sugar-cane and fruit crops. Even in Mexico, where relative prices of fertilisers are lower than in any other country of the region, fertilisers are used for only 18 per cent of the area under maize, whereas the figure rises to 84 per cent in the case of cotton. In Brazil, relative fertiliser prices rose after 1961, as a result of reforms in exchange regulations, and this largely accounts for the decline in consumption. The substantial increase in fertiliser consumption which took place in Brazil during the 1950s had

TABLE 14.4. *Tractors Used in Farming in Selected Countries*
(thousands of units)

	1957	1960	1963
Argentina	70·0	110·6	—
Brazil	57·9[1]	65·9	107·1
Colombia	—	23·5	—
Chile	15·0	—	25·0[2]
Peru	—	—	7·8
Mexico	—	54·5	—
Venezuela	—	3·9[3]	10·0[4]

[1] 1955.   [2] 1965.   [3] 1961.   [4] 1964.

SOURCE: Instituto Interamericano de Estadística, *América en Cifras*, 1965,
and ECLA, *Economic Survey of Latin America, 1966*.

a limited effect on boosting the country's average agricultural yields, since fertiliser use was confined to only 2 per cent of the area under cereals.

The comparatively slow progress of farm mechanisation in the region is largely attributable to the relative abundance of manpower that still characterises the region. Nevertheless, precisely because agricultural expansion continues to take the form of bringing new land under cultivation, mechanisation has helped to increase output in certain countries. Moreover, the rainfall pattern in certain areas hampers adequate land use in the absence of given agricultural equipment. Table 14.4 gives figures for the region's tractor inventory.

The number of tractors per 1,000 hectares of arable land ranges between 0·9, in the case of Brazil, and 5·9 for Chile. It should be pointed out that even in countries where extensive farming is practised, such as Canada and Australia, the number is 13.1 and 8·5 respectively. In countries where intensive farming methods are used, such as France and the United Kingdom, the number of tractors per 1,000 hectares is 46 and 52 respectively. It is interesting to note that Italy, employing a higher percentage of its total active population in agriculture than Argentina, has 24·5 tractors per 1,000 hectares as against 2·8 in the latter country. Although the relatively greater importance of livestock farming in Argentina must be taken into account, this figure sufficiently illustrates the extensive use of natural resources still characterising Latin American agriculture even where higher technical levels are observed.

TABLE 14.5. *Growth of Stocks of Cattle, Sheep and Pigs in Selected Countries*
(millions of head)

	cattle		sheep		pigs	
	1955–6	1964–5	1955–6	1964–5	1955–6	1964–5
Argentina	46·9	42·7	44·5	48·3	4·0	3·6
Brazil	65·2	80·7	18·0	21·2	40·0	56·8
Colombia	12·5	15·4	1·1	1·7	1·7	1·8
Chile	2·9	3·0	6·4	7·5	0·9	1·0
Mexico	16·7	22·3	5·1	6·5	6·5	9·4
Peru	3·5	3·5	16·7	14·3	1·3	2·0
Uruguay	7·4	8·4	23·9	22·0	0·3	0·4
Venezuela	6·3	6·6	—	—	2·3	3·5

SOURCE: ECLA, *Economic Survey of Latin America, 1966.*

LIVESTOCK FARMING

Even more than agriculture, livestock production trends reveal the difficulties facing the region in raising the technical level of its rural activities. Table 14.5 gives figures for the increase in the principal species of livestock in selected countries.

In the case of pigs, inventories expanded significantly in most of the countries considered. In Venezuela the increase was 54 per cent, in Peru 47 per cent, in Mexico 46 per cent and in Brazil 42 per cent. In the case of sheep there was stagnation or even decline in the inventories of the region's major wool-producing countries, Argentina and Uruguay. Cattle stocks in Argentina, Chile, Peru and Venezuela remained stationary or even decreased. In Brazil and Colombia the increase was around 24 per cent and in Mexico 34 per cent. Thus the growth of cattle herds in the region as a whole failed to match that of the population. Considering that the income-elasticity of demand for meat is relatively high, it must be concluded that meat consumption was confined to an increasingly restricted group of the population.

The expansion of livestock production in the region continues to be based almost entirely on the opening up of new lands, which provide natural pastures, often simply by burning the forest cover. The pastures cleared in this way can support only a low density of animal population, and, since the lands tend to be increasingly distant from urban centres, raising the costs of fattening and transporting the animals, stock-farming yields decline. Consequently the meat production statistics available indicate that it lags behind the increase in herds. With the exception of Argentina, Uruguay and Southern Brazil, the economic yield of Latin American livestock production is extremely low. The calving rate ranges from 40 per cent to 60 per cent, whereas in the United States the rate is 85 per cent. This is due to the fact that cows calve every two years instead of every twelve months, as they would do if properly fed. Moreover, the slaughtering rate, that is, the ratio of animals slaughtered annually to total stock, is also extremely low and in some countries slightly below 10 per cent. Finally, average carcass weights are relatively low. Consequently, not only is there a slow increase in herds, but the number of animals that can be slaughtered without affecting the growth of the herd is relatively small, and the meat yield per animal slaughtered is relatively low. Thus, if Argentina and Uruguay are excluded, meat production per head of stock in the region averages 22 kilograms as against 52 kg in Australia and 77 kg in the United States. Argentina, where meat yield per animal slaughtered averages 54 kg, occupies an exceptional position in the Latin American livestock production record, due to the high quality of its pastures, even in the case of natural pasturelands. Nevertheless, unlike other countries where new lands continue to be reclaimed for livestock-farming, livestock production in Argentina can only be expanded by taking over crop lands or improving existing pastures.

Even more than in the case of agriculture, whose expansion in many areas still reflects simply the growth of the rural population, the development of Latin American livestock-farming is now essentially dependent on the improvement of its technical levels. The extensive forms of growth which have hitherto characterised it are no longer sufficient for production to keep pace with the region's population growth, and still less to meet the growing demand consequent upon the rise in per capita income. It is more likely that in many countries beef will be replaced by other sources of animal protein, particularly poultry and fish. None the less, except for Argentina and Uruguay, indices of meat consumption and of animal proteins in general are extremely low, which signifies that there must be an increase in the meat supply if meat consumption is not to be restricted to an increasingly small proportion of the population. This increase could easily be achieved by raising the technical level of livestock-farming, particularly if there were improvements in nutrition and greater attention to animal health problems. Given the fact that the region possesses extremely favourable conditions for the development of livestock-farming, and that the supply of meat has fallen off at a time when demand has been expanding, it becomes evident that Latin American economies, particularly in the case of the agrarian sector, display little aptitude for the assimilation of technological progress.

TABLE 14.6. *Agricultural Production* (*Principal Commodities*) *in Selected Countries* (*in thousands of tons*)

	1956–7	1960–1	1964–5
wheat			
Argentina	7,100	4,200	10,100
Mexico	1,243	1,190	2,134
Chile	892	1,123	1,276
Brazil	855	713	643[1]
Colombia	110	145	85
Peru	123	153	161
rice			
Brazil	4,072	5,392	6,344[1]
Colombia	300	450	576
Peru	246	328	341[1]
Mexico	235	327	274
Argentina	193	149	268
Venezuela	47	72	166
maize			
Brazil	6,095	6,886	8,106[1]
Mexico	5,460	5,415	7,760
Argentina	1,958	2,744	3,062
Colombia	802	715	741
Venezuela	287	398	443
Peru	235	246	279
potatoes			
Argentina	1,311	2,072	2,488
Brazil	1,003	1,113	1,264
Peru	1,013	1,146	1,300
beans			
Brazil	1,585	1,745	1,951[1]
Mexico	432	723	892
Chile	86	91	89
soya beans			
Brazil	122	271	475
Colombia	—	19	49

TABLE 14.6 (*cont.*)

	1956–7	1960–1	1964–5
	coffee		
Brazil	979	1,797	1,560[1]
Colombia	365	462	480
Mexico	124	124	145
El Salvador	95	103	114
	cocoa		
Brazil	161	178	154
Ecuador	26	44	47
Mexico	14	24	31
Dominican Rep.	33	35	38
Venezuela	23	19	20
	sugar cane		
Brazil	43,976	56,927	63,723[1]
Mexico	14,597	19,167	21,836[1]
Argentina	9,874	9,650	11,827[1]
Peru	7,033	8,663	7,350[1]
Colombia	14,480[2]	14,569[3]	—
	bananas		
Brazil	4,481	5,127	6,828[1]
Ecuador	1,953	2,075	3,300[1]
Venezuela	894	1,332	1,456[1]
	oranges		
Brazil	1,576	1,918	2,223[1]
Mexico	625	766	855[1]
Argentina	610	717	715[1]
	cotton (lint)		
Brazil	400	536	652[1]
Mexico	426	470	566
Peru	115	130	133
Argentina	105	124	119
	linseed		
Argentina	620	562	815
Uruguay	72	67	64
	sunflower seed		
Argentina	625	585	757
Uruguay	79	57	80

[1] 1963–4.   [2] 1957–8.   [3] 1961–2.

SOURCE: Instituto Interamericano de Estatistica, *America en Cifras*, 1965.

CHAPTER 15

INDUSTRIAL SECTOR

STRUCTURE OF LATIN AMERICAN INDUSTRY

The manufacturing industry, which at present contributes 23 per cent to the region's gross domestic product and employs 14 per cent of its labour force, is the key factor responsible for the structural changes that have taken place in recent years. With regard to the region as a whole, the average annual growth rate of manufacturing for the period 1955–60 was 6·4 per cent and, in the first half of the sixties, 5·8 per cent. This decline largely reflects the loss of momentum of Brazil's industrialisation process, as can be seen from Table 15.1.

The manufacturing sector made good progress in the smaller countries of the region with the exception of Paraguay, the Dominican Republic, Uruguay and Haiti. In the Central American countries, as will be apparent from the detailed analysis of the regional integration experience in a later chapter, there was a dynamic expansion of manufacturing output, particularly in the second five-year period under consideration.

From the point of view of its degree of structural diversification, the manufacturing sector varied a great deal from one Latin American country to another. In countries in which manufacturing has been contributing more than one-fifth to the domestic product over the last decade, more than half the total industrial output is accounted for by the intermediate goods and engineering industries. Because they play a key role in bringing about structural economic change, these industries have been described as 'dynamic' industries.[1] In the group of countries referred to, comprising Argentina, Brazil and Mexico, the food, beverage and tobacco industries contributed 27 per cent to the total value of manufacturing output, and the textile, clothing and footwear industries contributed 15 per cent. In countries at the intermediate stage of industrial development—Chile, Colombia, Peru, Uruguay and Venezuela—the contribution of these two groups of traditional industries was 32 per cent and 20 per cent respectively. In the remaining countries, all at an early stage of industrialization, the food and related industries contributed 57 per cent to the total industrial product, while the textile and allied industries contributed 17 per cent.

[1] Term used by the Technical Secretariat of the United Nations Economic Commission for Latin America (ECLA).

Industrial Sector

TABLE 15.1. *Recent Evolution of Industrial Production in Selected Countries* (*average annual growth rates*)

	1955–60	1960–5
Argentina	3·7	5·7
Brazil	10·3	3·9
Colombia	6·1	5·6
Chile	3·2	7·3
Mexico	8·1	8·1
Peru	6·1	7·7
Venezuela	7·7	9·5

SOURCE: ECLA, *Economic Survey of Latin America, 1967.*

These figures clearly show that industrialisation in the region starts with the simple processing of agricultural products for food, with textile activities marking the transition to modern industry. Once beyond the first stage, the relative importance of the textile sector tends to decline more rapidly than that of the food sector, while the manufacturing sector becomes more complex, with a more than proportional growth of industries whose market is the industrial sector itself. In the group of so-called 'dynamic' industries, the first to develop are the pulp and paper and rubber products industries. Where favourable conditions exist, petroleum refineries may be installed before the chemical sector is developed. However, it is the metallurgical industries, and particularly the metal-transforming and engineering industries, that define the structure of the industrialisation process at its most advanced stage. In countries in the initial stage of industrialisation this group of industries accounts for only 3·6 per cent of total industrial output, whereas in those at the intermediate stage this share rises to 13·6 per cent, and in the three countries with a more advanced industrial structure it rises to 25 per cent.

TEXTILE INDUSTRY

The textile industry merits special attention not only because of its present relative importance but because of its potential role in the development of the region's exports of manufactures. Since Latin America is currently a leading exporter of natural fibres, it is favourably placed for participating in the world market for textile products once the highly industrialised countries realise the advantages to be gained from a greater decentralisation

TABLE 15.2. *Installed Capacity in the Cotton Textile Industry*
(*millions of spindles*)

	1955	1963
Brazil	3·4	3·9
Mexico	1·1	1·4
Argentina	0·7	1·0
Colombia	0·4	0·6
Others	1·0	1·2

SOURCE: ECLA, *La Industria Textil en América Latina*, 1968.

of manufacturing activities on a worldwide scale. Given the limited extent to which the textile industry can be integrated with other industries and the fact that it does not significantly benefit from economies of scale, it offers considerable possibilities for geographical decentralisation. For example, the value of United States imports of textile products increased from 562 million dollars to 1,072 million dollars between 1958 and 1962, and in the latter year 37 per cent of the total imports came from underdeveloped countries. Of the United Kingdom's textile imports, amounting to 220 million dollars in 1960, 60 per cent came from the developing countries. In 1963, Latin America's exports of fabrics amounted to only 82 million dollars, of which 11 million represent internal transactions. In this same year, its imports amounted to 216 million dollars, indicating that the region is still at the 'import-substitution' stage in the sector for which it has all the makings of a world supplier.[1]

The production capacity of Latin America's textile industry increased by 1·5 million spindles between 1955 and 1963, one-third of which were installed in Brazil, one-fifth in Mexico and another fifth in Argentina. The most notable increase, however, was recorded in Colombia.

During the period under review, i.e. between 1955 and 1963, the capacity of the Indian textile industry increased from 11·9 to 14·7 million spindles, that of Pakistan from 1·4 to 2·4 million and that of Egypt from 0·6 to 1·3 million. The growth of Latin America's production capacity, although relatively slow, was not always accompanied by a corresponding increase in output, an indication that demand was very sluggish. Per capita consumption for the region as a whole is relatively low—4·0 kg

[1] For a survey of Latin America's textile industry, its present situation and future prospects in the world market, see ECLA, *La Industria Textil en América Latina*, XII: *Informe Regional*, UN, 1968.

Industrial Sector

TABLE 15.3. *Recent Evolution of Textile Production in Selected Countries* (*Index: 1963 = 100*)

	1956	1960	1965
Argentina	131	134	148
Brazil	70	94	88
Colombia	65	84	103
Chile	73¹	75	108
Mexico	76	91	123
Peru	76	94	122
Venezuela	38	72	117

¹ 1957.

SOURCE: ECLA, *La Industria Textil en América Latina*, 1968.

annually as against 9·7 kg in Western Europe and 16·3 kg in the United States—and its growth rate has been abnormally sluggish at around 0·6 per cent annually. This figure is one of the indicators that the living levels of the bulk of the Latin American population have hardly been affected by the developments of recent years.

In Peru and Venezuela, particularly in the latter country, growth largely reflects the progress of the import-substitution process. In the other countries, however, locally manufactured goods have for some time satisfied more than 95 per cent of the domestic market requirements.

Latin America's textile machinery inventory, despite large-scale recent replacements, still includes a good deal of obsolete machinery and equipment, mainly because of the relative age of the Brazilian and, to a lesser extent, the Mexican industries. With regard to spindles, 44 per cent of the 8·1 million cotton spindles installed are modern, 30 per cent can be modernised and 26 per cent are obsolete; in the artificial and synthetic fibre sector, 88 per cent of the spindles installed are modern, and in the wool sector only 37 per cent are up to date. As regards looms, the automatic looms in operation represent 20 per cent of the installed capacity for wool, 33 per cent for man-made fibres and 44 per cent for cotton. Table 15.4 indicates the disparities between various countries.

Brazil excluded, Latin America's cotton textile industry is reasonably up to date, and in the case of Colombia modernity indices are exceptionally high. The latter country has the highest indices not only for modernity of equipment, but also for productivity of both labour and equipment.

TABLE 15.4. *Modernity Indices for the Cotton Textile Industry*

	spindles			looms		
	modern	modern-isable	obsolete	total	auto-matic	mech-anical	total
Argentina	83	12	5	100	67	33	100
Brazil	21	42	37	100	25	75	100
Colombia	91	8	1	100	99	1	100
Chile	81	19	—	100	83	17	100
Mexico	66	5	29	100	52	48	100
Peru	31	18	51	100	70	30	100
Venezuela	98	—	2	100	91	9	100

SOURCE: ECLA, *La Industria Textil en América Latina*, 1968.

CHEMICAL INDUSTRIES

The chemical industries now constitute a production sector ranking with the textile industry in order of importance for Latin America as a whole and contributing about 15 per cent to the total value of manufacturing output. Moreover, in contrast with the performance of the textile sector, it has registered one of the highest sectoral growth rates although in the larger countries the import-substitution process is in its final stages. Between 1959 and 1964 the average annual growth rate was 11 per cent, the highest registered being for Mexico (14 per cent) and the lowest for Chile (6 per cent). Nevertheless, the total value of Latin America's chemical production was only 50 per cent of that of West Germany and 80 per cent of that of France.[1] The figures given in Table 15.5 show that the region's chemical industry is still not very advanced.

If natural products (anhydrous alcohol and glycerine) are excluded from the first group, comprising the principal chemical products, its share of the total value drops from 11·4 to 5·3 per cent. This figure, taken together with the considerable importance of tensoactive agents and bleaches, which are final products destined for the consumer market, shows that the structure of the region's chemical industry is still not very advanced. In 1964 Brazil accounted for 38·6 per cent of the region's chemical output, Mexico for 22·7 per cent and Argentina for 19·1 per cent. Latin America's chemical production currently supplies around three-quarters of the

[1] A survey of the region's chemical industry is given in ECLA, *La Industria Quimica Latinoamericana en 1962–4*, UN, 1966.

Industrial Sector

TABLE 15.5. *Chemical Industry Structure in Seven Latin American Countries*[1] *and the U.S.A.*

| | Latin America (1964) | | U.S.A. (1957) |
	f.o.b. value in millions of dollars	%	%
principal organic and inorganic chemical products	333·4	11·4	17·5
chemicals for agricultural use	183·7	6·3	3·3
tensoactive agents and bleaches	600·3	20·5	9·8
pharmaceutical products	449·2	15·4	13·5
explosives, phosphorus, fireworks	73·6	2·5	1·4
cosmetics, essences and flavourings	144·7	5·0	5·0
tar, pitch and similar by-products	99·4	3·4	2·9
other products	1,040·7	35·5	46·6
total	2,925·0	100·0	100·0

[1] Argentina, Brazil, Colombia, Chile, Mexico, Peru and Venezuela.

SOURCE: ECLA, *La Industria Química Latinoamericana*, 1966.

domestic market requirements, a share which has not significantly increased over the last few years, particularly in Argentina and Brazil where local production already supplied more than 80 per cent of the market at the end of the previous decade. It must be concluded, then, that the present structure of the region's chemical industry is less a reflexion of inadequate development in this particular manufacturing sector than of the lack of diversification of the industrial system as a whole. In the region's most industrially developed countries, import substitution has apparently reached saturation point, which seems to be around 80 per cent of the domestic supply in the three countries with the largest domestic markets and about 60 per cent in those with medium-size markets. Table 15.6 gives the figures for the major items in Latin America's chemical production.

TABLE 15.6. *Production, Apparent Consumption and Installed Capacity of Principal Sectors of the Chemical Industry (thousands of tons)*

	production (1964)	apparent consumption (1964)	installed capacity (1965)
	sulphuric acid		
Argentina	158·4	158·4	220·0
Brazil	290·0	290·0	456·8
Colombia	38·0	38·0	—
Chile	167·0	167·0	190·0
Mexico	440·0	440·0	665·2
Peru	47·4	47·5	78·0
Venezuela	51·1	51·2	78·6
	caustic soda		
Argentina	63·0	78·9	95·5
Brazil	103.0	219.6	144.5
Colombia	16·1	43·2	—
Mexico	100·0	124·0	106·8
	sodium carbonate		
Argentina	—	104·1	—
Brazil	76·2	82·2	100·0
Colombia	8·8	17·5	—
Mexico	106·0	201·0	—
	ammonium sulphate (20·5–21% N)		
Argentina	7·6	46·3	13·5
Brazil	9·7	153·3	10·0
Mexico	167·0	229·8	235·5
Peru	15·8	89·8	17·0
Venezuela	43·3	45·6	—
	simple superphosphates (18–20% P_2O_5)		
Brazil	251·3	251·3	—
Mexico	400·0	400·0	—
	triple superphosphates (46–48% P_2O_5)		
Mexico	155·0	155·6	170·0
Venezuela	12·6	12·7	36·0
	viscose fibres		
Argentina	15·0	15·0	—
Brazil	32·0	32·0	—
Mexico	17·0	17·0	—

TABLE 15.6 (*cont.*)

	production (1964)	apparent consumption (1964)	installed capacity (1965)
	polyamide fibres		
Argentina	4·1	4·4	—
Brazil	17·0	17·2	—
Mexico	3·0	3·0	—
	carbon black		
Argentina	11·3	16·3	13·0
Brazil	25·0	27·8	36·0
Mexico	13·0	14·8	40·0
	synthetic rubber		
Brazil	32·7	29·4	47·5
Argentina	—	16·8	35·0

SOURCE: ECLA, *La Industria Química Latinoamericana*, 1966.

PULP AND PAPER INDUSTRIES

The paper and cellulose industry has made rapid progress in recent years not only under the stimulus of import substitution but mainly to keep pace with rapidly expanding demand. Between 1960 and 1965 total paper consumption increased from 2·4 to 3·5 million tons, while consumption of paperboard rose from 1·1 to 1·9 million tons. Domestic production supplied three-quarters of the region's market requirements. As regards newsprint, however, a very different situation obtained, with imports from outside the region accounting for four-fifths of total consumption. Chile is in a special position since it produces an exportable surplus of newsprint and the quantity available for export has been expanding. Domestic production of newsprint covers 40 per cent of the total demand in Brazil, 20 per cent in Mexico and 7 per cent in Argentina. The other countries are totally dependent on imports for their newsprint requirements.

Chile, where a notable reforestation project based on conifers has been carried out over the last twenty-five years, has considerable potential for the expansion of its paper and cellulose industry. The substantial investments still being made in the Chilean industry will boost exports intended to supply the regional market, particularly the Argentine market. In the other countries of the region, expansion of the industry is dependent either

TABLE 15.7. *Paper Production in Selected Countries*
(thousands of tons)

	newsprint		writing paper		other paper		paperboard	
	1957	1964	1957	1964	1957	1964	1957	1964
Argentina	20	22¹	65	84	125	189	104	127
Brazil	49	119	107	149	218	251	106	139
Colombia	—	—	—	—	25	60	12	55
Chile	20	77	15	30	23	38	1	20
Mexico	...	22¹	62	110	104	257	170	175
Peru	...	...	...	6	17	32	12	29
Uruguay	...	...	...	10	25	11	10	9
Venezuela	...	...	...	11	7	62	—	62

¹ 1963.
SOURCE: Instituto Interamericano de Estadística, *America en Cifras*, 1965.

on a reforestation policy based on fairly fast-growing trees, whether conifers or another species, or on the utilisation of hardwoods and other raw materials such as bagasse. On the whole, the technical problems posed by the utilisation of local raw materials are being studied and possible solutions are being explored.

STEEL

Latin America's iron and steel industry currently comprises 14 integrated plants and 35 small semi-integrated mills. More than 95 per cent of the total output, which amounted to 9·7 million tons of ingot steel in 1967, was produced by the integrated steelworks. The establishment of this industry, mainly during the last twenty-five years, marks a vital stage in the transition of the Latin American economies towards the industrial age. Since the establishment of steel industries was essentially due to State action, direct or indirect, one wonders what would have happened if the State had taken the initiative a quarter of a century earlier. In fact, Latin America did have a fairly long tradition of steelmaking, particularly in countries with abundant supplies of high-grade iron ores. In Mexico, the first years of the century witnessed the installation of a coke-fired blast furnace at Monterrey, with a daily capacity of 350 tons; in Chile, the charcoal-fired furnace at Corral came into operation before the First World War, and in Brazil the Belgo Mineira Company had been operat-

TABLE 15.8. *Steel Ingot Production in Selected Countries*
(thousands of tons)

	1958	1960	1962	1963	1964	1965	1966	1967
Argentina	244	277	658	913	1,265	1,368	1,267	1,326
Brazil	1,362	1,803	2,396	2,604	2,923	2,983	3,713	3,667
Colombia	149	172	157	222	230	242	216	256
Chile	348	422	495	489	544	477	577	638
Mexico	1,038	1,503	1,851	1,974	2,279	2,455	2,763	3,023
Peru	20	60	73	73	75	94	80	79
Venezuela	40	37	225	364	441	625	537	703

SOURCES: Instituto Interamericano de Estadística, *America en Cifras*, 1965, and ECLA, *Economic Survey of Latin America, 1967*.

ing fairly large charcoal-fired furnaces since the twenties. Nevertheless, it was not until the forties that concrete steps were taken to establish a modern steel industry in the region. Thus, in Mexico, a second blast furnace with a daily capacity of 600 tons was installed in 1942 by the company already operating in Monterrey. In 1944, Mexico's second integrated mill, specialising in flat products, came into operation at Monclova, and in 1946 the Hojalata y Laminas steel company started operations in Mexico. This enterprise was to become well known for its innovations in the technological field with the introduction of a gas-fired iron-ore reduction mill, doing away with the need for a blast furnace and making it possible to reduce the economic size of the plant. In Brazil the Volta Redonda steelworks, an integrated plant comprising a blast furnace with a daily capacity of 1,000 tons and rolling mills for sections and flat products, came into operation in 1946. In Chile, the integrated plant at Huachipato started production in 1950 with a blast furnace whose capacity was expanded to 800 tons a day. In Colombia the Paz del Rio plant began to operate in 1954; in Peru the Chimbote mill started in 1958; in Argentina the San Nicolas plant started in 1960 and in Venezuela the Orinoco plant started in 1962.[1]

Table 15.8 gives figures for the evolution of production over the last decade.

The ores currently exploited in Latin America have a very high iron content. It is only in Argentina and Colombia that ores are exploited with

[1] ECLA, *El Proceso de Industrialización en América Latina*, 1: *La Industria Petroquímica en América Latina*, UN, 1966.

TABLE 15.9. *Rolled Steel Product Supply in Latin America in 1962*
(thousands of tons)

	production	imports	apparent consumption
bars and light shapes	2,181·2	395·4	2,576·6
sheet and plate	1,450·5	881·5	2,332·0
tinplate	234·2	269·4	503·6
rails and heavy shapes	265·3	258·0	523·3
round bars	545·0	209·3	754·3

SOURCE: ECLA, *El Proceso de Industrialización en América Latina*, 1966.

an iron content ranging from 47 to 53 per cent. The output of coal suitable for coking is, however, insufficient in Argentina, Brazil and Chile. Inadequate local supplies of raw materials, and the size of the markets for which the output of individual producers is destined, are the two chief factors conditioning the development of Latin America's steel industry. In some instances coke has been partly replaced by petroleum, gas or pulverised coal, making it possible to effect substantial economies in the consumption of coke per unit of pig iron. Where abundant hydroelectric power is available at a low opportunity cost, as in the case of Venezuela, the steel industry utilises electric energy. With ores of low phosphorus content, production of sponge iron by direct reduction methods makes it possible substantially to reduce the economic size of the operating unit.

The greatest stumbling block to the achievement of competitive prices for the region's steel products is the size of rolling mills for flat products, with respect to which economies of scale assume considerable significance. In fact, the investment required per ton/year for manufacturing flat rolled products drops from 484 dollars to 199 dollars when the scale of production is raised from 100,000 to one million tons.[1] This problem can be solved only within the framework of a regionally planned expansion of the steel industry.

In view of the industry's inevitable concentration in a few countries and the problems relating to the size of the market for certain production lines, imports continue to play a leading role in supplying the region's steel requirements. In Brazil, Mexico and Chile imports account for less than one-quarter of the total supply of steel products; in Argentina the share of

[1] ECLA, *Las Economias de Escala en Plantas Siderurgicas*, UN, 1967.

imports is about 40 per cent, and in the remaining countries imports continue to be the main source of supply. Chile exports sizeable quantities of steel to neighbouring countries and Mexico has become a regular exporter of certain types of rolled products. The figures given in Table 15.9 show the relative importance of imports, particularly as regards flat products.

ENGINEERING INDUSTRIES

The development of the engineering industries is, in some ways, the crowning point of any industrialisation process. While the term is far too broad, embracing establishments as diverse as maintenance and repair shops for industrial or domestic equipment, foundries or heavy forges and factories manufacturing highly complex machinery and equipment, the relative importance of this sector in industrial production is a clear indicator of an economic system's capacity for transforming itself. Given the key role of the engineering industries in transmitting technological progress to the different sectors of productive activity, the attainment of a degree of self-sufficiency in these industries implies the ability to regulate the diffusion of such progress. Their role is similar to that of imports in the underdeveloped countries, whose access to innovations in forms of production is largely dependent on imported manufactures, so that a relative decline in their capacity to import tends to increase structural rigidity. In fact, in the case of the Latin American countries, the bulk of imports now consists of products manufactured by the metal-transforming and engineering industries. In 1960 the value of imports in this category amounted to 4·5 billion dollars, accounting for 60 per cent of the total. More than half the imports in the category indicated were made up of machinery and equipment for agriculture, industry and transport systems.

In most countries of the region the engineering industry still consists largely of factories manufacturing consumer goods, assembly plants utilising imported parts and components, and maintenance and repair shops. Nevertheless, in the industrially more advanced countries the manufacturing of transport machinery and equipment has made good progress in recent years, and now ranks as the leading sector in the group of engineering industries. In Argentina and Brazil the machine tool industry had already made significant strides by the 1950s. In 1960 Brazil's output of machine tools was 13,000 tons, providing the market with 50 different types and about 150 models. In the period 1957–61 domestic output covered 40 per cent of the country's requirements. In 1960 there were

205,000 machine tools operating in the country, 55 per cent of them of less than ten years' standing.[1] In Argentina the output of machine tools in 1961 amounted to 10,500 tons, and in 1963 the number of machine tools operating in the country totalled 172,000, of which 55 per cent were less than ten years old.[2]

A survey of the equipment required for the expansion of five important groups of industries—(a) petroleum, natural gas and petrochemicals, (b) generation and transmission of electric energy, (c) steel, (d) ship-building, (e) pulp and paper—indicated that Argentina's engineering industry is currently in a position to produce almost three-quarters of its total needs. A similar study was carried out for Brazil and indicated that the local engineering industry could satisfy 90 per cent of the equipment needs of the electrical energy generation sector, 77 per cent of the steel industry's, 66 per cent of the cement industry's and a similar percentage of the needs of the petroleum-refining and petrochemical sectors.[3]

However, the most notable progress in any branch of the engineering industry has undoubtedly been the growth of motor vehicle production. This activity, established before the outbreak of the Second World War in the form of local assembly plants, became a matter of growing concern to a number of countries as a result of the ever-increasing weight of motor vehicle imports in their balances of payments. The rapid expansion of demand, both for utility and passenger vehicles, led to the establishment of quantitative import restrictions with the result that domestic prices tended to be three or four times higher than on the international market. This situation made the production of motor vehicles an attractive proposition, even for relatively small-size factories. The favourable conditions of the market and the ample incentives offered by governments led to a prolifera-tion of enterprises in Brazil and Argentina, countries with relatively large markets and particularly severe balance of payments difficulties. The relatively large numbers of the factories—18 in Brazil and an even greater number in Argentina—and the underutilisation of their capacity brought the industry into financial difficulties once the demand, curtailed by the import shortages of the preceding ten years, had been satisfied. The industry is now going through a stage of remodelling its structure, cutting down on the number of enterprises, all of which are, in fact, subsidiaries of international corporations. The relatively high prices of motor vehicles— twice to four times as high as on the international market—continue to

---

[1] ECLA, *Las Máquinas-herramientas en el Brasil*, UN, 1962.
[2] ECLA, *Las Máquinas-herramientas en la Argentina*, UN, 1966.
[3] ECLA, *El Proceso de Industrialización en América Latina*, 1.

Industrial Sector

TABLE 15.10. *Motor Vehicle Production and Assembly*

	1966	1967	degree of integration[1]
Argentina	179,453	175,318	A
Brazil	224,574	227,552	A
Colombia	2,210	3,100	C
Chile	7,096	12,991	C
Mexico	113,170	118,000	B
Peru	13,170	18,000	C
Venezuela	60,500	61,000	C

[1] Proportion of nationally manufactured parts to the unit weight of the vehicles. A = more than 90 per cent; B = between 31 and 60 per cent; C = up to 30 per cent.

SOURCE: ECLA, *Economic Survey of Latin America, 1967.*

hamper expansion of the domestic market. The problem may be solved, albeit only in part, by the reduction in the number of enterprises and the greater co-ordination of production on a regional level.

PETROLEUM PRODUCTION AND REFINING

The Latin American petroleum industry comprises two essentially different sectors: on the one hand, there is the output of Venezuela, accounting for more than two-thirds of the total and destined basically for export; on the other, the output of the other producer countries, destined almost entirely for their own home markets. Venezuelan production is controlled by the large international consortia, while that of the other countries is in most cases controlled in whole or in part by national enterprises financed from public funds. Heavy investments have been made in the petroleum industry over the last decade, both for drilling operations and for installing refineries. The number of wells drilled in Argentina rose from 284 in 1955 to 712 in 1966 and in Brazil from 73 to 331 over the same period. Bolivia also registered a marked increase in drillings, which rose from 21 to 52 between 1955 and 1961.[1] Output of crude in the latter country increased fourfold between 1958 and 1967, while in Argentina it more than trebled and in Brazil it rose 2·8 times.

Of the countries included in Table 15.11, Brazil is the only one still dependent on imports for a substantial proportion of its crude petroleum

[1] ECLA, *Economic Survey of Latin America, 1967*, Part II.

TABLE 15.11. *Crude Petroleum Production in Selected Countries* *(thousands of cubic metres)*

	1958	1960	1965	1967
Argentina	5,668	10,178	15,625	18,242
Bolivia	546	568	534	2,274
Brazil	3,009	4,708	5,460	8,509
Colombia	7,457	8,867	11,628	11,280
Chile	885	1,150	2,020	1,966
Ecuador	494	438	453	572
Mexico	16,000	17,293	21,008	24,000
Peru	2,978	2,819	3,668	3,690
Venezuela	151,160	165,613	201,533	205,600

SOURCES: Instituto Interamericano de Estadística, *América en Cifras*, 1965, and ECLA, *Economic Survey of Latin America, 1967.*

TABLE 15.12. *Crude Petroleum Refined in Latin America* *(thousands of cubic metres)*

	1955	1960	1965	1967
Argentina	9,537	13,629	19,495	20,852
Bolivia	338	359	512	590
Brazil	4,089	10,412	17,841	22,100
Colombia	2,248	4,221	5,325	6,000
Chile	753	1,727	2,746	3,898
Ecuador	319	674	873	980
Mexico	13,028	17,028	21,444	23,260
Peru	2,356	2,637	3,300	3,560
Uruguay	1,302	1,508	1,867	1,960
Venezuela	31,140	51,339	68,210	67,700

SOURCE: ECLA, *Economic Survey of Latin America, 1967.*

requirements. Nevertheless, the share of imports in this country's domestic supply decreased from three-quarters of the total to around one-half between 1965 and 1967. On the other hand, in Chile the share of imports in total domestic supply increased from one-quarter in 1965 to one-half in 1967 as a result of the stagnation of local output in recent years. Refining expanded even faster than output, as can be seen from Table 15.12.

Industrial Sector

With the exception of Venezuela, which consumes less than one-tenth of its refinery output, the output of Latin America's refineries is destined for the individual domestic markets. Mexico imports a certain amount of by-products to supply outlying areas near the United States frontier, and in turn exports a certain quantity of petroleum products. Apart from Venezuela and Ecuador, whose refineries are all owned by the large international companies, the refineries in the remaining Latin American countries were virtually all installed and are currently operated by national companies, most of which are State-owned. All the refineries in Mexico, Brazil, Bolivia, Chile and Uruguay are under national control. In Argentina, the State controls 63 per cent of the oil-refining industry and in Colombia 49 per cent.

ELECTRIC ENERGY

Electric power generation in Latin America grew at an average annual rate of 9·5 per cent between 1950 and 1960 and 9·6 per cent between 1960 and 1965.[1] For the world economy as a whole, the corresponding growth rates for these two periods were 8·4 and 7·8 per cent respectively. The increase reflects the relative growth of the industrial sector in the Latin American economy, as well as population expansion and rapid urbanisation. Nevertheless, considering that, despite the regional economy's low degree of industrialisation, 55 per cent of the electric energy generated is destined for industrial consumption—as against 50 per cent in the United States and 65 per cent in Europe—levels of per capita consumption are still very low.

The electric energy sector in the Latin American countries was traditionally controlled by large international companies whose headquarters were mostly in the United States. For various reasons, both internal and external, investments by these companies grew very slowly during the period between the 1929 crisis and the end of the Second World War. Thus, most of the Latin American countries—nearly all affected by energy supply shortages in the immediate post-war years—were faced with the problem of creating institutions capable of mobilising the substantial resources needed to expand electric energy generation and transmission capacity. The new resources came almost exclusively from public funds through taxes levied specifically for this purpose or from international financing agencies such as the World Bank and, later, the Interamerican Development Bank. Table 15.13 gives figures for the generation of electric energy over the last decade.

[1] ECLA, *Economic Survey of Latin America, 1966*, Part III.

139

TABLE 15.13. *Electric Energy Generation in Selected Countries*
(millions of kwh)

| | | | | | 1967 | |
| | | | | | | kwh per |
	1957	1960	1965	1966	1967	capita
Argentina	9,418[1]	10,459	14,700	15,400	16,508	718
Brazil	16,963	22,865	30,128	32,200	35,300	410
Colombia	2,850	3,750	6,000	6,350	6,700	356
Chile	4,188	4,523	6,131	6,600	7,100	770
Mexico	8,463	10,813	17,769	19,339	20,926	458
Peru	1,792	2,501	3,808	4,080	4,810	388
Venezuela	—	4,652	8,171	8,900	9,200	985

[1] 1958.

SOURCES: Instituto Interamericano de Estadística, *América en Cifras*, 1965, and ECLA, *Economic Survey of Latin America, 1966* and *1967*.

Despite the considerable increase in generation of electric energy over the last few years, the inadequate supply has been a permanent stumbling block to industrial development in many countries, particularly in Argentina. Of the public-service energy supply, only 24 per cent is destined for industrial consumption in Argentina, 29 per cent in Mexico, 36 per cent in Brazil and 40 per cent in Chile. In the region as a whole, 31 per cent of the public-service supply is used by industry, which consumes, as already noted, 55 per cent of the total energy generated, indicating its dependence on inadequate self-generating plants installed for private consumption. On the other hand, a considerable proportion of the regional population, including urban population, has no electricity. In Argentina 14 per cent of the population is in this position, in Chile 24 per cent, in Brazil 26 per cent, in Mexico 59 per cent and in Peru 61 per cent.

Of the total installed capacity in Latin America, which rose to 31 million kw in 1967, about 60 per cent (17·7 million) was thermal. Of the 13 million kw of installed hydroelectric capacity in the region, 5·9 million kw is installed in Brazil, 2·6 in Mexico and 1·3 kw in Colombia. Nevertheless, the most rapid progress over the last decade has been made in the hydroelectric sector, reflected in the expansion of existing central power stations and the growing interconnexion of networks. This development is making it possible to link up various areas in interconnected systems, integrating thermal and hydroelectric units and raising the load factor. From the projects currently under way it can be predicted that power from hydroelectric sources will account for an even larger share of the region's energy supply in the next few years, with an increase in the average size of power stations and interconnexions between areas with different hydrographic systems. It is also probable that supplies at lower tariffs for industrial purposes will become feasible in some of the more industrialised countries.

CHAPTER 16

DECLINE IN THE GROWTH RATE

OVERALL REGIONAL TRENDS

During the last two decades, the economy of the Latin American countries, taken as a whole, has experienced a marked expansion and has undergone structural changes of real significance. Measured in 1960 prices, the region's gross product, which had barely exceeded 40 billion dollars in 1950, rose to more than 120 billion in 1967. Output of ingot steel, which was just over 1 million tons in 1950, was close on 10 million in 1967. Nevertheless, despite these and similar indicators that could be taken into account, it would be wrong to assume that the regional economy had achieved the combination of conditions needed for development to become self-sustaining. On the contrary: the figures show that the pace of growth of the regional economy has tended to slacken off and, what is even more significant, that this weakening was attributable largely to trends in the economies in which the industrialisation process was furthest advanced. Data for the region as a whole show that the growth rate of the per capita gross product declined from 2·2 per cent in 1950–5 to 1·8 per cent in 1955–60 and 1·6 per cent in 1966–8.[1] These figures obviously conceal wide disparities in trend between different countries, but this does not detract from their overall significance. In effect, this falling off in growth occurred during a period when technological progress was making rapid headway and when the industrialised economies as a whole were maintaining a high rate of growth with no symptoms of weakening.

Present trends can be more readily understood if it is borne in mind that the Latin American economies do not constitute a *system* and that the overall figures are strongly influenced by trends in the region's three major national economies—Brazil, Mexico and Argentina—which together account for over two-thirds of the regional product.

However, it must also be borne in mind that the national economies have been developing along certain common lines and for this reason the evolution of the more advanced economies in some ways prefigures the evolution of those in earlier stages of development. Thus, the structural evolution of economies that experienced in the post-war period a phase

[1] Cf. ECLA, *Economic Survey of Latin America, 1967*, Part I.

of growth under the impulse of expanding exports—such as bananas, in the case of Ecuador, cotton in Central America or fish meal in Peru—was a repetition of a pattern that had already become familiar in the region, as was that of the countries that started import substitution during the last decade. While making no attempt to establish a model of development based on a series of precisely defined stages for the region's economies, which would imply that the experience of the less-developed countries can be anticipated, one must recognise that the *present* performance of these economies can be fitted into a given number of *types*. In certain countries an extremely favourable set of circumstances for a given *type*— the agricultural commodity exporter, the mineral product exporter or the 'import substitute'—made it possible to sustain development over a relatively prolonged period. In others, conditions were less favourable and the period of development of a given type was correspondingly shorter. The overall development curve for the region represents the aggregate of national curves whose behaviour reflects the dynamic of a given number of types operating under a manifold variety of conditions. The slackening of growth can manifest itself in economics corresponding to various types, and the movement of the overall curve will be accentuated or attenuated according to whether the processes occur simultaneously or not.

We have already seen how development induced by the growth of exports of primary products had made industrialisation possible. However, given the conditions that have come to prevail in the world market for primary products, reflected in the persistent downward trend of relative commodity prices, it was widely held that the region's development would become increasingly dependent on the industrialisation process. That the pace of growth should have weakened to the extent we have seen seemed to indicate that industrialisation had failed to become sufficiently broad. In fact, the decline in the growth rate of the region's domestic product largely reflects the poor performance of the Argentine economy in the fifties and the unfavourable trends registered in Argentina and Brazil during the present decade. In other words, it reflects the behaviour of the two countries that, having experienced a period of rapid industrialisation, suffered a decline in the growth rate of the manufacturing sector. The problem that arises, then, is to determine whether Latin America's industrialisation suffers from intrinsic limitations, that is, whether it represents a type of development similar to other types of development experienced by the region up to the present time, which would distinguish it from that of the countries currently regarded as developed.

Economic Development of Latin America

The Argentine experience is particularly interesting because of its precedence, but it can in no way be regarded as representative of the region as a whole. Having achieved a high degree of urbanisation while still at the stage of export-led development, and having established a relatively high level of average wages in agriculture to attract European immigrants, Argentina stands in a class of its own in the Latin American context. However, because of the country's relative importance, the Argentine experience constitutes one of the significant aspects of the region's recent evolution. The intensification of the industrialisation process, which lasted from the war period to the mid-fifties, proceeded behind the strong protection of tariff barriers and the provision of subsidies for the importation of industrial inputs. The consequences were twofold: (a) an increase in the marginal efficiency of investment in the final consumer goods industries, and (b) a change in the internal terms of trade which moved against the agricultural sector. The tendency was thus in the direction of horizontal expansion of the industrial sector, which continued to be largely dependent on imported inputs. This meant the creation of a growing short-term incompressibility of imports at a time when there was an upward-shifting trend in the demand for imported products as a result of expansion in the industrial sector. Underlining the aspect that concerns us here, it can be said that the growth of the industrial sector proceeded less in the direction of creating an integrated system than in that of complementing the import sector. This complementarity did, of course, evolve in the direction of a greater participation for domestic production, which meant that the items still imported became increasingly essential. The level of economic activity became more dependent, in the short term, on the fluctuations of the capacity to import than it had been when the bulk of imports consisted of final consumer goods. The fears underlying Argentine economic policy in the second half of the 1930s and early 1940s, when anticyclical preoccupations prevailed, were thus confirmed. On the other hand, the unfavourable evolution of the internal terms of trade had discouraged investment in the rural sector, the country's traditional source of exports. Furthermore, the stagnation of petroleum production in the 1940s and 1950s created strong additional pressures on the declining capacity to import.

In sum, two processes were simultaneously at work in Argentina: the excessive horizontalisation of industrial growth and the discouragement of investment in the export sector. There has been a tendency to emphasise one or other aspect of the problem according to the intellectual approach of the analyst.[1] There can be no question that the second process would, in any event, have tended to reduce the productivity of investment and increase the instability of the economic system. But it is no less true that if industrialisation had broadened its base sooner, its capacity to bring about overall structural economic change would have been far greater and it is even possible that it would have come to have a favourable impact on the export sector itself, by reducing its relative input prices. It must be pointed out that Argentine industrialisation could only have gained in depth after the 1940s if it had followed a policy based on a diagnosis taking into account the long-term trends of international trade. In effect, industrialisation implied the absorption of manpower from the agricultural sector, which meant a relatively high level of wages. If industrial investments had been channelled towards projects with longer maturation periods and greater capital intensity, the profitability of the industrial sector would have been lower and accumulation less rapid. Given the relative shortage of manpower in the second half of the forties, reflected in the pressure for a rise in real wages, it must be admitted that a more balanced expansion of industry would have called for the active financial support of the government, together with simultaneous investments in the agricultural sector aimed at releasing labour. In practice, policies followed the line of least resistance, which consisted of an expansionary wage policy and a concentration of industrial investments in activities with the fastest capital turnover. This resulted in the inadequacy that characterised both the social overhead facilities and the capacity to import in the mid-fifties. Since then, the main objective of Argentine economic policy has been the recovery of the capacity to import, whether by improving the terms of trade of the rural sector, by reorientating credits towards agriculture or by encouraging an inflow of foreign capital, although parallel efforts have been made in the period 1958–62 to broaden the bases of the industrial system.

CASE OF BRAZIL

The Brazilian experience of a flagging industrialisation process, while more recent than that of Argentina, is more interesting because of the greater representativeness of Brazil's economic structures in the region as a whole. In contrast with Argentina, industrialisation in Brazil proceeded

[1] See, as an example of the first tendency, Aldo Ferrer, *La Economía Argentina*, and, as an example of the second, Carlos F. Diaz-Alejandro, 'An Interpretation of Argentine Economic Growth since 1930', *Journal of Development Studies*, Oct. 1966 and Jan. 1967.

under conditions of a totally elastic labour supply (a similar situation to that now obtaining in practically all the other countries of the region). On the other hand, Brazil had become aware of the need to broaden the bases of its industrial system as early as the 1930s and had recognised that the government must assume the responsibility for carrying out this task. It is significant that, in the midst of the difficulties of the Second World War, the Brazilian government succeeded in providing the country with a modern steel industry.[1] A preliminary plan for public investments in infrastructure (the SALTE plan) was launched in the immediate post-war period. The Banco Nacional de Desenvolvimento Economico (National Bank for Economic Development), established in 1954, was responsible for allocating substantial resources to the basic industries and to the construction of an infrastructure. Petrobras, created shortly afterwards, provided resources for the production, refining and shipping of petroleum. In short, the Brazilian industrialisation base was broadened sufficiently for industrial expansion to continue for more than a quarter-century. By the beginning of the 1960s, domestic output accounted for about 90 per cent of the total supply of industrial products available on the Brazilian market. In the case of consumer durables, domestic production covered more than 95 per cent of the total domestic supply, in the case of intermediate industrial goods about 90 per cent and in the case of capital goods about 80 per cent. Industrialisation had thus made considerable progress towards the creation of an industrial system with a degree of diversification comparable to that of the highly industrialised economies. Mention should also be made of the import-substitution process in the petroleum sector, which started in the second half of the 1950s when petroleum imports accounted for nearly one-fifth of the total value of Brazilian imports. Since then, the value of these imports has been stabilised as a result of the rapid expansion of refining in the first instance, followed by a steady increase in the output of crude. By the early years of the sixties, when the structural diversification of industry was nearing completion and the industrial system was largely in a position to create its own means of expansion, the balance of payments threat constituted by the rapid increase in petroleum imports had been contained. Notwithstanding these favourable conditions, the growth rate of the industrial sector began to show a sharply downward trend, falling from an average annual rate of 10·8 per

---

[1] The Brazilian government's Steel Plan was framed just before the outbreak of the war. The steelworks at Volta Redonda were constructed during the war years with funds provided by the Export-Import Bank and equipment bought in the United States; this was possible only because of the political understanding between the Vargas Administration and President Roosevelt. The plant came into operation in 1946.

cent for the period 1956–62 to a rate of 4·8 per cent for the period 1963–8. In the first period it was around 60 per cent higher than the growth rate of the gross domestic product, whereas in the second it was only 20 per cent higher.

This loss of dynamism in Brazilian development was accompanied by mounting inflationary pressures and an aggravation of social tensions with serious repercussions on the political plane. Furthermore, the radical change in policy since 1964—the containment of inflationary pressures having become the main objective of government action in the economic and financial sphere—had secondary repercussions to the point that the level of industrial production declined by 5 per cent in 1965, with an even more marked decline in manufacturing output. It would be by no means easy to demonstrate that social and political factors were of only secondary importance in the decline of the growth rate discernible in Brazil since 1962. On the other hand, it would be even more difficult to demonstrate that these factors were the prime or principal cause of this decline. Closer examination of the data shows that exports tended to grow much faster than imports. Between 1959–60 and 1965–6 the export coefficient rose, while the import coefficient declined. Thus, it seems evident that the factors responsible for the deceleration in Brazil's economy derive far more from a failure on the demand side than from shortcomings on the supply side.

It has already been pointed out that import-substituting industrialisation is essentially characterised by the fact that demand precedes industrial investment, which means that the demand schedule is defined before industrialisation gains momentum. New investments are consequently orientated towards an existing demand structure, established in the period preceding industrial development. In a country where the structural manpower surplus was practically absorbed in the pre-industrial period—as in the case of Argentina—the problem is not of major importance. However, in countries with a large labour surplus, that is, where there are wide differences between the living levels of the bulk of the population and the middle and upper classes, the composition of demand assumes particular significance, since the market for manufactured consumer goods consists of two distinct sectors making little contact with one another. Since the manpower surplus continues to exert downward pressure on wages, there is little or no change in the standards of consumption of the mass of the population, and the market for general consumer goods grows simply by the addition of new elements moving from conditions of underemployment or disguised unemployment into productive employment. Meanwhile, in the second section of the market, comprising a mere fraction—

less than 5 per cent—of the total population, real income rises, and consumption is diversified along the lines of the new patterns emerging in the more developed countries. Since technological progress tends to increase the capital coefficient per employee and per unit of additional output, the structural situation outlined above is even further aggravated. The slower absorption of manpower contributes to the growing structural labour surplus. Thus the social distribution of benefits deriving from technological progress will be hampered by this very progress. Growth of the industrial sector will therefore be supported by two separate markets functioning in practically watertight compartments. The first, composed of the bulk of the population, grows horizontally only and tends to become more limited with the progress of technology. The second expands dynamically but, given its small size, this very dynamism, reflected in the greater diversification of demand, will limit its real size. For example, the growth of the demand for motor vehicles calls for a greater variety of models, which has a negative effect on industrial productivity. Economies of scale, one of the most significant indications of the assimilation of technological progress, cannot be realised to full advantage.

In the Brazilian case, we find that between 1955 and 1965 the productivity of the labour force employed in the manufacturing sector rose at an annual rate of 5·2 per cent, where the annual rate of increase in real wages in this sector was 1·3 per cent.[1] Thus, even in the sector with the highest rise in productivity, real wages increased less than the per capita income of the population as a whole, that is, less than average productivity. It must be concluded, therefore, that development was accompanied by a decline in the share of total income accruing to wage-earners, particularly if we exclude from this share the earnings of the middle-income groups. We have already mentioned that the agricultural sector's share in the domestic product did not decline between 1955 and 1965, remaining steady at around 31 per cent at a time when the per capita gross product was rapidly expanding. These apparently contradictory data can be explained by the fact that the bulk of the population, deprived of access to the benefits of development, has failed to diversify its consumption and has continued to allocate the same proportion of the family budget to agricultural commodities. On the other hand, there is statistical evidence of the existence of large margins of idle capacity in practically all branches of Brazilian manufacturing, particularly in the capital goods sector.

[1] For the basic data see ECLA and Banco Nacional de Desenvolvimento Economico, *A Evolução Recente da Economia Brasileira*, Rio de Janeiro, 1967.

Decline in Growth Rate

Data for 1965 show that when operating only one shift the capital goods industries use just over 50 per cent of existing capacity.[1]

Although it is difficult to go much beyond preliminary explanatory hypotheses, there can be no doubt that the Brazilian industrialisation process is currently faced with serious obstacles of a structural nature, whose root cause is the failure to achieve a more widespread diffusion of the gains from increased productivity. This tendency towards the concentration of income made it possible to accelerate development when this was based on import substitution. Once the import-substitution process had been exhausted, however, the domestic demand schedule for final consumer goods tended to determine an allocation of investments that led to a persistent decline in the marginal productivity.[2]

The Brazilian experience takes on great significance for Latin America when we consider that it took place in a country with the region's largest population, an extremely favourable endowment of basic natural resources and an entrepreneurial class whose dynamism is widely recognised.

Since the industrialisation of countries such as Colombia, Venezuela and Peru is currently proceeding along lines not very different from the Brazilian pattern—all these countries face the problem of a large structural surplus of manpower—it would come as no surprise if similar phenomena, involving a tendency to stagnation, were reproduced in the near future. This is, of course, merely a possibility and its degree of probability is uncertain. One cannot exclude the possibility, for instance, that these countries will bypass the Brazilian experience and approximate the Mexican model, characterised by a drastic reform of the agricultural sector, paralleled by an industrialisation process in which State action was as far-reaching as in Brazil.

[1] Cf. Werner Baer and Andrea Maneschi, *Import-substitution, Stagnation and Structural Change: an Interpretation of the Brazilian Case* (mimeograph), 1968.

[2] Cf. C. Furtado, *Subdesenvolvimento e Estagnação na América Latina*, Rio de Janeiro, 1967 and *Um Projeto para o Brasil*, Rio de Janeiro, 1968.

VI. INTERNATIONAL RELATIONS

CHAPTER 17

TRADITIONAL FORMS OF EXTERNAL DEPENDENCE

CORRECTIVE POLICIES: AIMS AND INSTRUMENTS

The international system of division of labour, which enabled Latin American countries to initiate their development in the nineteenth century, created asymmetrical relations that were reflected in the close dependence of countries exporting raw materials on the industrialised centres. The development of international economic relations involved not only increased trade between the various nations but also the creation of 'poles of command' controlling financial flows, orientating international transfers of capital, financing strategic stocks of exportable products, intervening in the formation of prices, etc. Expansion of the exportable surplus in a Latin American country depended, almost always, on infrastructural investments financed by foreign capital made available when the increment in production entering the world market matched expectations in the world economy's decision centres. What was involved was thus a form of dependence consequent upon the very structure of the world economy. By making economic decisions little more than an automatic operation involving the transfer of price mechanisms from the micro-economy to the level of international relations, liberal ideology diverted attention from this problem and hindered perception of its consequences for the national economies on the domestic plane.

Reference has been made in earlier chapters to some of these consequences. So long as primary exports continued to play a role in these countries similar to that of investments in the industrialised countries, the instability of raw material prices was bound to have far-reaching internal effects. Administration of the monetary system and public finances became extremely difficult and the operations of the gold standard proved a heavy burden on account of the volume of foreign exchange reserves required and the fluctuations in the level of domestic economic activities implied.

The prevailing economic doctrine made it even more difficult to find a way out since, far from helping to solve these problems, it in some ways obscured the perception of their more important aspects. Orthodox concepts were only gradually abandoned, at first thanks to empiricists in search of solutions to isolated problems and, since the forties, under the influence of economists trying to understand the specific nature of international relations involving primary-exporting economies.[1]

As they came to realise the dependent situation inherent in their integration into the international economy, Latin American countries made several attempts to counter the negative effects of this dependence. On the one hand, they sought to reduce what has come to be called the 'external vulnerability' of their economies by taking steps to control foreign economic and financial relations; on the other, they sought to increase the internal integration of these economies by reducing their dependence on the international system of division of labour. The first line of policy was designed mainly to control real and financial flows in order to reduce the domestic propagation of external imbalance. The second sought to prevent outflows of resources generated within the country and to channel investments towards home market expansion. A line of policy nearly always envisaged more than one aim or, with one particular end in view, attained several others. Hence it is easier to identify a policy through the instrument used, which, as a rule, involved exchange, fiscal or trade control measures.

Exchange control, which tended to be widely adopted in Latin American countries from the 1930s onwards, was designed mainly to reduce external vulnerability. Movements of short-term capital tend to create serious disturbances, particularly at times when inflationary pressures are mounting while the exchange rate remains fixed. An expected devaluation provokes massive flights of capital while the devaluation itself entails

[1] The Executive Secretariat of ECLA, under the guidance of Argentine economist Raúl Prebisch, played a decisive role in furthering the effort to break with orthodox concepts and gain greater insight into the region's economic problems. In a study prepared for the ECLA conference held in 1949, and subsequently published in the March 1961 issue of the Economic Bulletin for Latin America as 'The Economic Development of Latin America and its principal problems', Prebisch made an original contribution to the study of the problems of external dependence and the role of import-substituting industrialisation in the context of regional development. This study had an immediate and marked influence on Latin American economic thinking. It should be added that diagnosis of underdevelopment problems in Latin America is bound up with awareness of the phenomenon of external dependence and has been based on original studies carried out by Latin American economists within the framework of the work undertaken by United Nations research teams that included members from various countries in the region.

sudden movements in the opposite direction. Exchange control was not, however, restricted to capital movements. In many countries it acted as a mechanism for rationing a suddenly reduced capacity to import, making it possible to defend the level of domestic economic activity. Exchange control in the form of multiple exchange rates was used by some countries to modify income distribution and intervene in the orientation of investments. Various types of fiscal policy have been used in the region in an effort to reduce their external dependence. In this field, the experience of mineral exporting countries becomes extremely significant. When production of non-ferrous metals and petroleum is controlled by international consortia, local productive factors generally receive only a small share of the flow of income generated by the exportable product. On the other hand, technological progress tends to reduce the proportion of labour while wages account for a mere fraction of total production costs. Furthermore, it is in the interests of international producing companies to purchase virtually all intermediate products abroad, within the framework of a buying policy designed to supply production units located in several different countries. In the case of petroleum companies, it is common practice to try to limit local expenditures, including wage payments, to the amount received in local currency from sales of fuel in the market of the country in question. Up to the 1930s the existence of 'enclave' mineral-exporting sectors, operating in total isolation from the country granting the concession, with a different level of prices and a separate balance of payments, was a situation that prevailed throughout Latin America. Chile played a pioneer role in this respect, with a policy aimed at *internalising* the costs of the big copper-producing companies. Through a combination of exchange and fiscal measures, the Chilean government managed to retain in the country a growing share of the foreign exchange earned on exports by the major copper companies. In 1928-9 only 17 per cent of these earnings returned to the country. By the end of the 1930s this proportion had more than doubled and the upward trend continued in the post-war period, as we shall see further on.

PETROLEUM POLICY IN VENEZUELA

Venezuela's policy in the petroleum sector is an interesting example of the use of a fiscal instrument to cope with a situation of acute external dependence. The development of the Venezuelan oil industry was carried out under the terms of the extremely liberal 1922 law. As the result of subsequent developments in petroleum technology, the industry cut its labour costs and became more and more detached from the economy of the country. The new fiscal policy introduced in 1946 modified this trend and opened up enormous possibilities for the country. Under the new regulations, oil companies operating in Venezuela paid a royalty per unit of output, a standard income tax and a surtax, the latter having been introduced in 1944. The royalty corresponded to 16⅔ per cent on the value of crude, based on Texan quotations. Taxes could be paid either in money or in petroleum, which enabled the State to develop a national oil-refining industry and to participate directly in exports. The Venezuelan government has been extremely cautious in its use of this prerogative but fiscal legislation leaves the possibility open. Income tax was substantially increased in 1946 and in 1948 a further tax was introduced, establishing the principle that profits from the petroleum industry were to be divided on a fifty-fifty basis between the Venezuelan State and the foreign producer companies. This principle was later adopted by all Third World countries in which oil is exploited by foreign companies. Finally, in 1958, changes in income tax legislation increased the State's share of the industry's gross profits to 60 per cent. The scope of this policy was all the greater because the extraordinary rise in productivity tended to reduce the industry's importance as a source of employment. Between 1948 and 1963, output increased from 490 million barrels to 1,186 million, while the number of workers employed declined from 55,170 to 33,742. Output per worker rose from 8,877 barrels to 35,178. Although average wages rose substantially, the total spent on wages increased by only 49 per cent while output went up by 142 per cent. Between 1950 and 1962, the companies increased their outgoings on labour by 70 per cent, and on the purchase of locally produced goods and services by 110 per cent, while in the same period the amount paid out in taxes to the State increased by 220 per cent. In 1962, tax receipts amounted to twice the total paid out by the oil companies in wages and other local expenditures. Thus, despite the rise in productivity—reflected in the greater share of foreign capital in the income generated by petroleum production—the share of total value returned to the country increased from 55 per cent in 1950 to 66 per cent in 1962. This policy provided the Venezuelan government with ample resources for development purposes, and it was able to finance a modern infrastructure, launch an important development programme for agriculture and establish basic industries (see Tables 17.1 and 17.2).

Traditional External Dependence

The coffee policy followed by the Brazilian government since the beginning of the present century is a notable example of action through trade measures designed to lessen dependence on the outside world. The fact that at the turn of the century Brazil's coffee exports provided four-fifths of the total supply available on the world market meant that any fluctuations in the Brazilian crop had a marked impact on prices. Thus the value of Brazilian coffee exports could suddenly be halved because a bumper crop was forecast, or rise sharply because a frost had occurred. Consequently, the strategic position for the coffee economy became the regulation of stocks. Brazil's position was in some ways like that of the United States in the world cotton market about the middle of the last century. But there was one important difference: in the latter case the American monopoly faced the English monopsony, since the textile industry was then concentrated in England. Prices were not subject to violent fluctuations but the financially more powerful monopsonist was always in the dominant position.

Realising their own strength—which had been used against them as a result of their failure to seize its advantages—Brazilian coffee planters outlined a policy for stabilising supply at a meeting held in 1906 in Taubaté, a city in the State of São Paulo. Surpluses were to be withdrawn from the market and financed through loans negotiated abroad. Servicing of the debt contracted would be covered by a tax levied in gold on every bag of coffee exported. At first this policy encountered resistance from Brazil's international creditors, led by the House of Rothschild, but it was carried through with the support of German and North American financial groups and its initial success soon made it a highly attractive financial proposition.[1] However, its very success was to become the source of its later weakness. Brazil was anticipating by half a century the attempts to organise international markets that have been made in the last decade through commodity agreements. Acting in isolation, Brazil had to assume the entire responsibility for financing the costs of the operation, creating a privileged position for other producers. Coffee came to stand out among tropical commodities for the exceptional stability of its prices at a profitable level. It was only natural, therefore, that production and supply in other countries should tend to rise, which meant that in order to maintain the price stabilisation policy Brazil had to accept a steady decline in her

---

[1] Cf. Celso Furtado, *Formação Económica do Brasil*, for a detailed discussion of Brazilian coffee policy.

TABLE 17.1. *Venezuela:Value Returned to Domestic Economy from Petroleum Production and Distribution*

	millions of bolivars	as % of petroleum exports value	% distribution government revenues	% distribution wages and salaries	local purchases of goods and services
1950	1,838	54·8	55·2	26·8	18·1
1951	2,125	56·0	64·3	25·4	10·3
1952	2,269	53·9	63·5	26·3	10·3
1953	2,233	50·8	67·8	26·4	5·8
1954	2,537	52·8	59·3	27·9	12·8
1955	2,704	49·2	63·4	24·7	11·9
1956	3,131	49·3	65·9	24·7	9·4
1957	3,892	49·5	68·9	22·7	8·5
1958	4,174	58·8	67·3	21·7	10·8
1959	4,109	61·8	68·1	21·9	10·1
1960	4,618	69·5	65·0	21·8	13·2
1961	4,702	68·8	68·8	18·1	13·0
1962	4,784	66·1	67·3	17·8	15·0

SOURCE: Ministerio de Minas e Hidrocarburos, *Petróleo y Otros Datos Estadísticos*, Caracas, 1964.

share of the world market. Nor was this the only difficulty. The policy outline in Taubaté envisaged action on the part of the State governments designed to discourage the rapid expansion of coffee planting which was absolutely necessary, since coffee occupied a privileged position among the country's exportable commodities. This essential feature of policy was neglected and the surpluses to be withheld began to pile up alarmingly. Thus in 1929 production totalled 28·9 million bags while exports amounted to only 14·3 million. It has been estimated that in this same year, investments in coffee stocks amounted to 10 per cent of the domestic product. The catastrophic slump in prices following the world crisis—in twelve months prices tumbled from 22·5 cents a pound to 8 cents—did not affect output, which continued to increase until 1933, as the result of new plantings undertaken in the latter half of the twenties when prices were high. As we have seen in a previous chapter, in the absence of external financing, surpluses began to be financed by means of credit expansion which would provoke inflation but would also cushion the domestic impact of the crisis. World market conditions and the growing output of competitor coun-

TABLE 17.2. *Venezuela: Distribution of Profits from the Petroleum Industry*

	government revenues (millions of bolivars)	%	share of profits retained by companies (millions of bolivars)	%
1955	1,841	52	1,710	48
1956	2,281	52	2,115	48
1957	2,990	52	2,774	48
1958	3,066	65	1,616	35
1959	2,860	68	1,335	32
1960	2,711	68	1,282	32
1961	2,899	66	1,477	34
1962	3,308	66	1,693	34
1963	3,419	67	1,677	33

Note: The figures in the table above reflect the prices of exports f.o.b. declared to the Venezuelan government by the foreign companies and known as 'realisation prices'. These prices differ from those obtaining in international market quotations for crudes of similar quality because of various factors relating to marketing operations and concealed transactions between subsidiaries and parent companies. If Venezuelan petroleum prices are calculated on the basis of international quotations, the share of the companies is 53·3 per cent for 1957, 50·8 per cent for 1960 and 52·7 per cent for 1963. For further details see the estimates made by Hugo Dario Montiel Camacho in *La Explotación del petróleo en Venezuela y la capitalización nacional*, Mexico, 1967.

SOURCE: Ministerio de Minas e Hidrocarburos, *Petróleo y Otros Datos Estadísticos*, Caracas, 1964.

tries ruled out the possibility of finding outlets for the enormous coffee stocks which had continued to accumulate throughout the thirties. Apart from the heavy costs involved in retention, the existence of these stocks was affecting world market prices, which led the Brazilian government to opt for the destruction of part of the surplus as the only feasible solution. Consequently, more than 80 million bags—about two-thirds of present world consumption—were destroyed. Coffee prices were to recover their pre-1929 level in real terms only towards the end of the forties. The upward trend in prices after 1949, accentuated by the Korean war, led to a new wave of planting in Brazil, mainly in the virgin lands of North Parana. Unsold surpluses began to accumulate once more in the latter half of the fifties and this situation led the Brazilian government for the first time to carry out a plan for large-scale uprooting of low-yielding trees, aimed at assuring more effective control of supply. On the other hand, a concerted effort was made to persuade other producers to organise supply, leading at the beginning of the sixties to the conclusion of the first World Coffee Agreement, binding producers and consumers to co-operate in regulating the international marketing of coffee.

ARGENTINA'S EXPORT CONTROL POLICY

Argentine foreign trade policy between 1946 and 1955, carried out through the Institute for the Promotion of Foreign Trade (IAPI), provides the example of the most comprehensive attempt yet made in Latin America to bring exports under the control of the State. The system of multiple exchange rates operated in this country since the 1930s enabled the government to freeze a considerable proportion of the export sector's income during the war years, which made it possible to cushion the inflationary pressure created by the balance of trade surplus. On the other hand, the revenues thus obtained permitted the financing of export surpluses resulting from the bumper crops of 1944 and 1946. To prevent supply fluctuations from having an adverse effect on world market prices at a time when there was a marked insufficiency of supply, IAPI was established, with a monopoly over exports. In this way, domestic market prices and export prices could be separately fixed, while at the same time the marketing of the exportable surplus could be undertaken in accordance with an overall strategy designed to maximise the income of the country's export sector. The way in which this policy was applied had a number of consequences whose interpretation has been the subject of heated debate in Argentina. Given the marked improvement in the external terms of trade—which improved by 41 per cent between 1943 and 1946—the IAPI was able to begin its career by absorbing a substantial share of the increment in the income accruing to the export sector without causing any reduction in the latter's profitability. In fact, between the two years indicated the internal terms of trade for the agricultural sector, which constitute an indicator of this sector's profitability vis-à-vis the other sectors of the country's economy, improved by 25 per cent. Between 1946 and 1948 the external terms of trade continued to improve—the index rose by 18·4 per cent—while the internal terms of trade for the agricultural and livestock sector deteriorated, declining practically to their 1943 level. The agricultural and livestock sector thus lost the relative advantage it had gained between 1943 and 1946, a loss that occurred precisely when the expanding economy was making it possible to raise investment. To what extent this decline in relative profitability was responsible for the fall in investment in the agricultural and livestock sector is not easy to determine. But there is no question that agricultural output fell after 1949. The effects of the deterioration in the internal terms of trade and the decline in the volume of production combined to produce a substantial reduction in the real income of the agricultural and livestock sector. After 1950 government policy was revised and the IAPI began to pay producers prices above those it could obtain in the international markets. Since the Institute's losses were covered by the expansion of credit, its policy became a focus of inflationary pressure during a phase of serious tensions provoked by the marked deterioration in the country's external terms of trade, whose index was practically halved between 1945 and 1952. Agricultural and livestock production responded favourably to the change in policy, and the average level of output between 1953 and 1958 was 25 per cent above that for the 1943–8 period. However, exportable surpluses did not regain their former levels in view of the substantial growth of domestic demand. After 1955 the Argentine government gradually re-established a liberal exchange policy, using credit support to continue its efforts to promote the recovery of the agricultural and livestock sector, although the results were not very different from those achieved in 1953 and 1954. There can be no doubt that the IAPI had proved as effectual in deflecting resources from the agricultural and livestock sector as in re-allocating them to its advantage (see Table 17.3).

PETROLEUM POLICY IN MEXICO

The policy followed by Mexico in the petroleum field also illustrates a number of problems that face the countries of the region in their attempt to counter foreign domination of their economies. In the opinion of authorities such as Jesús Silva Herzog,[1] the Mexican government did not reach its decision to expropriate the oil companies as part of any premeditated plan. The 1917 constitution established the principle of public ownership of the subsoil resources, but shortly afterwards the concessions granted earlier were all ratified. In fact, Mexican output expanded rapidly in the years following the First World War, reaching a peak in 1921 when it accounted for one-quarter of the world's production of oil. Production levels stayed high but began to show a downward trend in the mid-twenties. It is possible that one of the reasons for this decline was the predatory form of exploitation that characterised the early stages. However, the main reason why Mexico lost ground probable lay in the expansion of Venezuelan production, which in 1928 was already outstripping Mexican output. The great productivity of the Venezuelan oil industry

[1] Cf. Jesús Silva Herzog, *História de la Expropriación de las Empresas Petroleras*, Mexico, 1964.

TABLE 17.3. *Argentina: External and Internal Terms of Trade, and Indices of Agricultural and Industrial Product*

	external terms of trade	internal terms of trade	index of agricultural product	industrial product
1943	83·5	97·0	100·0	100·0
1944	84·6	87·2	126·9	120·8
1945	87·7	101·6	104·0	113·2
1946	120·3	122·6	180·7	130·7
1947	143·8	106·5	154·0	151·1
1948	141·7	100·9	157·7	158·2
1949	117·8	91·3	126·0	157·4
1950	100·0	100·0	108·8	152·4
1951	109·5	111·3	122·6	150·7
1952	75·2	113·2	99·6	137·4
1953	100·0	128·2	173·9	130·3
1954	90·0	111·3	148·7	147·4
1955	88·0	104·0	152·4	167·1
1956	76·0	116·0	155·3	154·8
1957	72·5	125·1	177·7	157·6
1958	76·6	130·2	202·9	165·6
1959	81·0	147·3	196·2	145·6
1960	84·5	145·3	188·9	155·4

Note: The internal terms of trade reflect changes in agricultural prices to the producer in terms of prices of industrial goods on the home market.

SOURCE: Data given in Javier Villanueva, *The Inflationary Process in Argentina, 1943–1960* (mimeographed), Buenos Aires, 1964.

was reflected in the fall in world prices, which became more marked after 1930 owing to the economic crisis. It is interesting to note that Venezuelan output declined only slightly during the depression, rising in 1935 to levels above that for 1929. In the same period Mexican production declined steeply, falling in 1932–3 to one-half the 1927 output and less than one-fifth of the levels attained in the first half of the twenties. There had been no new drillings in Mexico since 1927 and the foreign oil companies' determination to cut back on production was having serious repercussions on the social plane. It was these social tensions that brought the companies into conflict with the Mexican government, leading them to the extreme of ignoring a Supreme Court decision, which left the executive power with no alternative but to expropriate their properties.

Traditional External Dependence

In 1937, the year before expropriation, oil accounted for one-fifth of the Mexican export total and about half the output was already destined for the home market. Between 1937 and 1938 exports were practically halved, although production declined by less than 20 per cent. The production level for 1937, amounting to 47 million barrels, was surpassed in 1946 when output rose to 50 million barrels. Thereafter, exploratory activities were intensified and Mexico managed to incorporate new producing areas. Output kept pace with the rapid growth of domestic consumption and in 1963 amounted to 126 million barrels. There can be no doubt that expropriation, perhaps precisely because it had not been planned, was a serious challenge to the country, since failure to organise the exploitation of oil as a national industry would have undermined the Mexican State's authority to such an extent that it would have had great difficulty in implementing its agrarian reform programme. Because it called for the formation of a pool of skilled technical and executive personnel and provided the State with substantial resources for investment, the oil industry came to play a key role in the rapid industrialisation occurring after the 1940s. Petroleos Mexicanos (PEMEX), the company set up by the State to take over the expropriated properties of the foreign oil companies, is at present the largest non-foreign enterprise operating in Latin America (see Table 17.4).

COPPER POLICY IN CHILE

Relations between the Chilean State and the big enterprises engaged in exploiting the country's copper resources provide an equally striking instance of a prolonged effort to integrate into the national economy one of its vitally important sectors, traditionally under foreign control. Copper production in Chile grew strongly after the First World War, rising to 321,000 tons in 1929. This growth was essentially due to the operations of United States companies which had relegated the older national enterprises, established since the previous century, to a completely secondary position. In 1925–9, Chile already contributed 18 per cent of the world's total copper output, ranking second to the United States among world producers. On the other hand, copper accounted for 40 per cent of the total value of Chilean exports. The new industry, employing modern technology, located in isolated regions and paying extremely light taxes, returned only a small share of the value of production to the host country. In fact, one ton of copper produced by the small national enterprises represented as much for the country as four tons produced by the foreign companies.

After the world crisis, the Chilean government made concerted efforts

TABLE 17.4. *Petroleum Production in Mexico and Venezuela*

	Mexico	Venezuela	petroleum prices in the United States (dollars per
	(in thousands of cu. metres)		barrel)
1920	24,971	73	3·40
1921	30,747	230	1·70
1922	28,979	355	1·80
1923	23,781	688	1·45
1924	22,206	1,451	1·45
1925	18,365	3,169	1·65
1926	14,375	5,669	1·95
1927	10,194	9,606	1·30
1928	7,973	16,845	1·20
1929	7,105	21,634	1·25
1930	6,285	21,502	1·15
1931	5,253	18,581	0·60
1932	5,216	18,560	0·80
1933	5,406	18,792	0·60
1934	6,069	21,668	0·95
1935	6,398	23,612	0·95
1936	6,523	24,586	1·05
1937	7,457	29,533	1·20
1938	6,122	29,896	1·15
1939	6,820	32,518	0·95
⋮	⋮	⋮	⋮
1946	7,900	61,763	1·25

SOURCE: ECLA, *Economic Survey of Latin America, 1949.*

to 'internalise' the copper industry. Through fiscal and exchange measures the government sought to increase the domestic share of operating costs and to appropriate a growing share of company profits for the State. These measures made it possible to integrate into the national economy the flows created by a sector which had hitherto existed as an 'enclave', while at the same time significantly increasing the country's capacity to import. The first income tax legislation, passed in 1934, provided for a tax of 18 per cent on the industry's profits. In 1939, when CORFO was established, the tax was raised to 33 per cent. The subsequent course of events was profoundly marked by the disturbances in the copper market provoked by the Second World War and the Korean war. The policy of

Traditional External Dependence

the United States government, in fixing a relatively low ceiling price on copper during the Second World War, left the impression in Chile that the country had suffered serious harm. When the Korean war started and the United States again tried to impose a wartime price ceiling on copper— in 1950 three American companies operting in Chile signed an agreement with Washington providing for a fixed price on copper effective for the duration of the Korean conflict—there was an immediate outcry in Chile and the government was forced to react by intervening more directly in this sector of the country's economy. An agreement was signed between the two governments in 1951, which provided *inter alia* for one-fifth of production to be disposed of by the Chilean government as it saw fit, thus opening the door to government intervention in the marketing of copper. On the basis of this agreement, the Chilean Central Bank began to buy its 20 per cent quota of copper at the prevailing New York price and to sell it at the highest prices obtainable on the world market. These operations provided the Chilean Treasury with profits amounting to 190 million dollars between 1952 and 1955.

The year 1955 saw the beginning of a new phase in Chilean copper policy. Rising taxes on the one hand and the prospect of an increase in African output on the other led the companies to cut back on their investments in Chile. Chile's share of world copper production, which had been as high as 21 per cent in 1948, had declined to 14 per cent by 1953 and the level of output had remained virtually at a standstill. A new law was passed in May 1955, whose main objective was to ease the tax burden on firms while at the same time simplifying the complicated fiscal system created in the past. The law provided for a fixed tax of 50 per cent on profits and a variable surtax of 25 per cent, to be reduced proportionally as production exceeded the quotas fixed for each firm. In some ways, this legislation represented a reversal in terms of previous developments. The *share* of the total value of copper proceeds returned to the domestic economy (the proportion of foreign exchange retained by the country) fell from 82 per cent in 1950–4 to 78 per cent in 1955 and to a low of 56 per cent in 1959. Nevertheless, the value returned in *absolute* terms rose from 160 million dollars in 1950–4 to 170 million dollars in 1956–9 as a result of the recovery in exports. Moreover, the new law created a Copper Department, later to be known as the Chilean Copper Corporation, which was to be the point of departure for systematic action designed to provide a thorough knowledge of all matters concerning the copper industry. Production, which in 1954 had amounted to 364 million tons, a level close to that for 1929, reached 662 million tons by 1964 (see Tables 17.5 and 17.6).

TABLE 17.5. *Chile: Value Returned to Domestic Economy from Copper Before and After 1955 Law*

	millions of 1960 dollars	% of total value of production
1947	113·9	51
1948	142·9	61
1949	117·4	63
1950	129·4	70
1951	137·3	66
1952	200·1	93
1953	172·8	94
1954	166·9	91
1955	245·7	78
1956	217·5	53
1957	156·1	59
1958	125·2	55
1959	182·7	56

Note: The high percentages for 1952 and 1953 are attributable to the fact that the Chilean government sold its quota on the international market at prices well above those declared by the producing companies. The figures refer to exports by the large foreign companies.

SOURCE: On the basis of data taken from Clark Winston Reynolds, in *Essays on the Chilean Economy*, 1965.

TABLE 17.6. *Chile: Copper Production and Exports*

	production in thousands of tons	exports in millions of dollars
1954	363·7	221·5
1955	433·5	327·4
1956	489·2	333·7
1957	480·2	246·0
1958	464·9	195·1
1959	544·8	279·3
1960	532·5	322·1
1961	547·7	304·7
1962	585·9	332·3
1963	601·1	335·9
1964	621·8	374·8
1965	585·3	428·5
1966	661·8	575·7

SOURCE: Chilean Copper Corporation.

Traditional External Dependence

In 1966 a new law was passed redefining Chilean copper policy in an attempt to reconcile the two aims pursued previously: the integration of the industry into the national economy—the principal objective up to 1955—and the encouragement of its expansion with a view to increasing the country's share in world copper production—the major objective of the policy initiated in 1955. The new policy, known as 'Chileanisation', led the State to participate in the formation of joint stock companies while at the same time undertaking to carry out a policy of financing its own investments from part of the revenues derived from taxation and royalties. Thus the Braden Copper Company became the *Compañia Minera El Teniente S.A.*, in which the Chilean State holds 51 per cent of the stock and the United States group (Kennecott Copper Corporation) 49 per cent. A new company was formed to develop the Exótica deposit, with the State holding 25 per cent of the stock and the Anaconda Group 75 per cent. A third company, in which the State holds 25 per cent of the stock, was established to develop the Rio Blanco deposit. An option was secured on the exploitation of new deposits at present under the control of Anaconda. Finally, an agreement signed with the Anaconda Group in June 1969 made it possible to transfer 51 per cent of the Group's stock to the Chilean State, which also secured an option to buy up the remaining 49 per cent by 1982. The agreements with the copper companies included an investment programme involving a total of 566 million dollars, which will raise the industry's production capacity to 1,100,000 tons by 1971. The new policy thus provides for a system of joint production which will enable the Chilean State to participate increasingly in the decision centres controlling the supply of copper on the world market.

CHAPTER 18

NEW FORMS OF EXTERNAL DEPENDENCE

FINANCIAL FLOWS

After the Second World War there was a marked change in the evolution of mechanisms for international financial co-operation. During the two decades following the 1929 crisis the amount of foreign investment in Latin America had declined. The capital markets of Europe and the United States had been closed to bonds issued by public or private entities in the region and the bitter experience of the 1930s had made it only too clear that, given the instability of the foreign exchange earnings of countries exporting primary products, the accumulation of a large external debt ruled out any possibility of carrying out rational economic policies in these countries. On the other hand, in the two decades referred to the development of the region's economies had been entirely financed, in the case of the region's most industrially advanced countries, out of domestic savings. Moreover, a large part of the foreign debt accumulated in the preceding period had been repaid, thanks to the favourable balance of trade of the war years. Besides, the traumatic experiences resulting from the conflicts between foreign-owned enterprises and some of the region's national governments—the expropriation of Mexican oil was only the most spectacular instance—had created a climate that made it difficult to take an objective view of the problems of international financial co-operation.

Two trends emerged in the immediate post-war years. The first was the delimitation of areas closed to the operations of foreign-owned enterprises. The Mexican Constitution was amended in 1938 to reserve to the State all forms of exploiting hydrocarbons. A similar principle was embodied in ordinary legislation passed in Brazil. In Chile and Uruguay the principle of State ownership of the oil industry guided policy from the outset.[1] Even in Venezuela, government policy over the last two decades—

[1] In Uruguay, the oil refining industry is a state monopoly, with half the imports purchased by the State company, ANCAP (Administración Nacional de Combustibles, established in 1931) and half by private foreign companies with marketing interests; there is no local production and the imported crude is processed at the ANCAP refinery, meeting practically

with the exception of 1956-7—has been firmly against the granting of new concessions to foreign enterprises, implying that the long-term objective is State control over the oil industry. Other countries, such as Argentina, have accepted the co-operation of foreign groups in the form of service contracts valid for limited periods. In a less explicit or less coherent form, the same line of policy has prevailed with respect to basic services such as generation of energy and urban and inter-urban transport and communications. In some countries, such as Mexico and Chile, the State has already taken over control of these sectors completely. In others, such as Brazil and Argentina, the State controls the rail transport sector and is steadily extending its control over the energy sector in which virtually all new investments have been public.

The second trend was the growing use of international credit agencies as financial intermediaries for the region's national governments. In the course of the last two decades, the World Bank has made loans totalling 2 billion dollars to private and public enterprises in the region backed with government guarantee. These loans have been used almost entirely for infrastructure projects, especially electric power and transport. Since these sectors had traditionally been financed from resources obtained abroad, the operations of the World Bank have made it possible to reopen a channel of financial co-operation of major importance to the region in the past. Loans granted by this credit agency represent a considerable advance on the external bond issues formerly floated through banking consortia closely supervised by the traditional finance houses of London and New York, both as regards the cost of the money and the pre-investment study of projects. World Bank requirements, particularly in the early years of its operations, which stipulated not only that investment projects be technically sound but that they fall within the economy's investment prospects, were one of the starting-points for the practice of establishing overall projections and preparing development programmes in the countries of the region. The Interamerican Development Bank, which began operations in 1961, is even more representative of the new trend. Between 1961 and 1967 the Bank authorised loans to a total value of 2·1 billion dollars, of which 40 per cent have already been disbursed. Its authorised capital totals 2·15 billion dollars, of which 475 million is

all the country's consumption needs. In Chile, the law establishing state monopoly over the petroleum sector was passed in 1927. The Empresa Nacional del Petroleo (ENAP), established in 1950, is responsible for exploration, production and refining. State enterprises with greater or less control over the petroleum sector also exist in the following countries: Argentina (established in 1922), Peru (1934), Bolivia (1936), Colombia (1948), Brazil (1953), Cuba (1959) and Venezuela (1960).

Economic Development of Latin America

TABLE 18.1. *Latin America: Gross Inflow of Foreign Capital*
(millions of 1960 dollars)

	net direct investment	private loans	public loans	official donations	total
Annual averages					
1950–4	309	45	177	22	553
1955–9	799	345	520	88	1,752
1960–3	282	592	1,022	141	2,037
(excludingVenezuela)					
1950–4	236	45	176	22	479
1955–9	466	344	339	88	1,237
1960–3	426	587	911	140	2,064

SOURCE: ECLA, *Integración, Sector Externo y Desarrollo Económico de América Latina*, 1966.

paid up. With the guarantee of its callable capital, totalling 1,675 million dollars, the Bank has been floating bond issues, on relatively favourable terms, on the U.S. capital market and more recently on the capital markets of Europe. The IDB has thus gradually become the financial intermediary for Latin American governments in the world's capital markets, representing an enormous saving for the individual borrowing countries and offering greater security to creditors. On the other hand, the IDB has been collaborating closely with local development banks or similar financial institutions, thus making it possible to extend credit facilities at relatively low cost to medium-size enterprises in the region and even to make lines of credit available to firms exporting locally produced equipment.

The volume of public international financing channelled into Latin America as a whole rose from an annual average of 177 million dollars to 1,022 million dollars between 1950–4 and 1960–3. The share of these public loans in the gross inflow of foreign capital increased from 32 per cent to 50 per cent (see Table 18.1).

Net direct investment declined from an annual average of 309 million dollars to 282 million dollars between 1950–4 and 1960–3, a decline attributable to trends in the Venezuelan oil industry. In fact, direct investments were largely financed out of profits retained by foreign-owned companies. The disinvestment of 144 million dollars registered in Venezuela in the 1960–3 period indicates that the growth of the oil industry

New External Dependence

TABLE 18.2. *Latin America: Net Inflow of Foreign Capital*
(annual averages in dollars)

| | | service payments | | | | net contribution |
	gross inflow	amortisation	interest	profits	total	
1950–4	553	176	76	801	1,053	− 500
1955–9	752	572	147	20	739	+ 13
1960–3	2,037	984	331	1,015	2,330	− 293
		(excluding Venezuela)				
1950–4	479	174	76	358	608	− 129
1955–9	1,237	423	147	347	917	+ 319
1960–3	2,064	806	314	445	1,565	+ 499

SOURCE: ECLA, *Integración, Sector Externo y Desarrollo Económico en
América Latina*, 1966.

failed to absorb the gross depreciation reserves held by the companies operating in this sector. In other words, the rapid technological progress taking place in the petroleum sector makes it possible to increase production even when the industry is going through a period of disinvestment. The increase in private loans, whose share in total direct investment rose from 8 to 29 per cent, is largely attributable to the relative growth of foreign investment in the manufacturing sector, which was not yet in a position to finance its own expansion by ploughing back profits.

The figures in Table 18.2 show that almost throughout the period a minus figure was recorded for the net inflow of foreign capital. However, if Venezuela is excluded, the net capital inflow averaged over 300 million dollars a year in the second half of the fifties and around half a billion dollars for the period 1960–3.

Comparing the figures in the two tables, we find that the volume of loan funds reached an annual average of more than half a billion dollars in the period 1960–3. However, 80 per cent of these funds were used, in the final analysis, to cover interest payments and amortisation of earlier loans. On the other hand, even if Venezuela is excluded, profit remittances abroad exceeded net direct investment in the period under consideration. Thus, the effective contribution of external funds—considered from the financial viewpoint—was limited to official donations and to 20 per cent of the total value of loans. In most cases the loans were made on hard terms to refinance balance of payments deficits. It is against this background that we must consider the significance of the international credit agencies, whose operations have meant that foreign capital costs much less and amortisation periods are substantially longer. Barring a really effective expansion of their activities, it seems more than likely that in the next decade the region will not only be remitting more profits abroad than it receives in direct investment but will also be incurring a growing volume of external debt to service loans contracted in the past.

If we consider the problem of the foreign contribution to Latin America's recent development strictly from the financial angle, we must conclude that it was only of secondary importance. Even in the period 1960–3, when the inflow of foreign capital reached a fairly high level (as can be seen from Table 18.2), the share of external saving in gross capital formation was only 6·8 per cent, declining in the subsequent four-year period (1964–7) to 5·3 per cent.[1] Moreover, this share becomes virtually nil when we take into account transfers under the head of service payments to foreign-owned factors (interest and profits) not included in the capital account and representing a reduction in the availability of current funds. However, the financial aspect is only one side of the problem. The region's recent development, particularly where it has taken the form of industrialisation, called for assimilation of modern technology, which had to be largely imported. Consequently, it is by studying the way in which the manufacturing sector was organised and how the transfer of modern technology was effected, that we can grasp the real significance of international co-operation for the region's recent development.

Since Latin American imports consisted largely of manufactures, any attempt to reduce the import coefficient (the ratio of imports to domestic product) would have to take the form of industrialisation, that is, a more than proportional growth of the manufacturing sector. Policies designed to attain this end took various forms, one being the offering of special inducements to attract foreign capital to the manufacturing sector. Even without such incentives, however, the decline in the capacity to import of countries such as Argentina, Brazil and Mexico meant that industrial development would have to be intensified and that one of the consequences would be a *loss of markets* for the international groups that had formerly supplied them. Such groups could safeguard their markets only by decentralising part of their economic activity, setting up Latin American subsidiaries to operate local assembly plants or factories manufacturing components of products hitherto imported in their finished state. Two

[1] Cf. ECLA, *Economic Survey of Latin America, 1967*, Part I, 1968.

different factors thus converged: the desire of countries in the region to reduce their import coefficient and the concern of international groups to safeguard their traditional position in the markets of these countries.

ACCESS TO MODERN TECHNOLOGY

At this point we must consider the following question: would the Latin American countries have registered the high rates of growth characterising their manufacturing sectors in the post-war period if they had not been able to count on the effective co-operation of international groups, primarily North American, with considerable industrial experience and easy access to the sources of financing? There can be no doubt that for industrialisation to be achieved within a relatively short period and on an extremely broad front, a complex of productive activities, built up over several generations in other countries, had to be transplanted to certain countries in the region. Technical personnel with a wide variety of specialised skills had to be found and, in the absence of local laboratories, technological institutes and advisory services, it was necessary to secure outside support to ensure that the many technical and economic problems created by the operation of transplanting an entire industrial system would be solved within a reasonably short space of time. Some form of international co-operation was inevitable since sources of technology were located abroad and access to these was in many cases strictly controlled. Primarily, this co-operation took the form of setting up Latin American subsidiaries of companies that had formerly supplied the market, which were to take over a growing proportion of production activities designed to bridge the import gap. The new industries were thus largely under foreign control and closely tied to imports. The production units emerging in the process fit into two different complexes: the national complex in which each unit is located, and the economic complex centring on a parent company located abroad. This dual relationship must be kept in mind when considering the behaviour of the unit concerned. The board of directors, for instance, generally includes two types of person: (*a*) those characterised by their legal experience or social prestige and local connexions, recruited in the country of location of the operating unit; (*b*) those with effective control over technical and economic decisions, acting as delegates of the parent company and nearly always citizens of the country in which the parent company is located. Another significant aspect is the control of stock. Although the parent companies are in most cases public joint-stock companies whose shares are bought and sold on

Economic Development of Latin America

TABLE 18.3. *United States Investments in Latin American Manufacturing Industries (millions of dollars)*

	1950	1965	% increase
Argentina	161	617	280
Brazil	285	722	153
Mexico	133	752	466
Chile	29	39	34
Colombia	25	160	540
Peru	16	79	393
Venezuela	24	248	933
Latin America	780	2,741	251

SOURCES: *Survey of Current Business, November 1966* and earlier numbers.

the Stock Exchange, the subsidiaries are nearly all private in the sense that 99 per cent of the voting stock is in the hands of the parent company's agents. Expansion is carried out primarily by mobilising local resources without this having any effect on the capital structure of the subsidiary enterprise. The control of key decisions by head office personnel and the fixed capital structure are both results of the concern to preserve the unity of the multinational economic complex controlled by the parent company whose economic rationale is based on the whole rather than on the parts. If a subsidiary operated through some form of joint capital venture, particularly with a group controlled by residents of the host country, the production unit's relations with other units in the same complex would have to follow the same lines as its relations with autonomous enterprises, otherwise the transfers of resources implicit in many transactions between enterprises belonging to the same complex could represent a loss for the parent company. If the rationale of the whole is also to be that of the parts, the latter must be homogeneous, that is, the parts must be integrated into the whole to the same degree.

The behaviour of United States manufacturing subsidiaries in Latin America reveals certain aspects of the new type of external dependence that tends to prevail in the region. Capital held by parent companies rose from 780 million dollars in 1950 to 2,741 million in 1965. The bulk of this investment went to the three countries mentioned earlier: Mexico, Brazil and Argentina. In countries where industrialisation started more recently—Colombia, Venezuela, Peru—the subsidiaries registered high rates of growth, which makes it likely that outside control will be even greater

New External Dependence

TABLE 18.4. *Indicators of Economic Growth and of Growth in Sales of North American Subsidiaries in the Manufacturing Sector* (% *average annual growth during period 1960–5*)

	Argentina	Brazil	Mexico	Venezuela
GDP	2·8	4·9	5·9	5·4
industrial product	4·1	4·9	8·0	9·4
sales by subsidiaries	24·0	6·4	13·0	14·0

SOURCES: *Survey of Current Business, November 1966* and earlier numbers.

once these countries achieve the degree of industrialisation of the first three.

Sales by American subsidiaries in the manufacturing sector are expanding rapidly both in countries where development is still intense and in those where growth is relatively stagnant. Table 18.4 above is indicative of this trend.

To finance the vigorous expansion of their manufacturing subsidiaries in Latin America, U.S. corporations have followed a policy of reinvesting undistributed profits and have sought to raise local funds. Thus, whereas enterprises in the petroleum sector, financed entirely out of their own earnings, have retained only 15 per cent of their profits, 60 per cent of the profit earnings of manufacturing subsidiaries have remained undistributed. Even so, undistributed profits have covered less than half of the investment made: in the period between 1958 and 1964, 46·8 per cent of the total investment in manufacturing subsidiaries was financed from their own funds, 18·9 per cent from funds obtained abroad and 36·3 per cent from loan funds obtained in local capital markets.

These figures show that participation by foreign groups in Latin America's recent development is far less a phenomenon of financial co-operation than one of control over productive activities by groups that had already been supplying the markets with exports. Since they controlled trademarks that had become familiar on the local markets and could more easily mobilise technical resources and domestic and foreign credit, these groups occupied privileged positions on the markets where there was a wave of import substitution. Moreover, foreign enterprises could nearly always count on the exceptional facilities extended by Latin American governments.[1] Several countries have given favourable foreign exchange

---

[1] Instruction No. 113, issued by the Brazilian Superintendency of Money and Credit in 1953, established a system which in practice involved discriminating against national companies

treatment to enterprises undertaking to manufacture or assemble locally a growing proportion of the finished product, not only with regard to imports of equipment but also for imports of intermediate products or components for local assembly. In other words, the government is providing resources free of charge for the enterprise to establish itself in the country. Once established, undistributed profits, sinking funds and locally raised resources will enable it to press ahead with its expansion plans. During the initial stages the gap created by the shortage of imports in the preceding period provides an opportunity for excessively high profits. Once supply returns to normal, the market tends to be controlled by one or more financially powerful groups, nearly always linked to the international consortia that had traditionally controlled imports. Resources are mobilised abroad by raising loans that are in many cases guaranteed by the local government, which undertakes to provide exchange coverage for remittances of interest and amortisation payments.

EXTENT OF EXTERNAL CONTROL OF
LATIN AMERICAN INDUSTRY

The quantitative data available are too limited to provide a precise idea of the relative importance of subsidiaries of foreign companies in the manufacturing sector of the Latin American economies. A study of the situation in Mexico at the beginning of the present decade[1] showed that of the 100 major companies operating in the country, 56 were either totally controlled from abroad (39) or had a substantial share of foreign capital (17). Of the remainder, 24 were stock-owned enterprises and 20 were private Mexican-owned enterprises. If we take into account the volume of sales invoiced, the participation of the public sector rises to 36 per cent in view of the relative importance of the petroleum sector, which is State-controlled. However, the participation of the national private sector falls to 13·5 per cent, a very marked difference. If the analysis is extended to the 400 largest enterprises, the participation of the foreign group rises to 54 per cent while that of the public sector falls to 25 per cent. Leaving aside the public sector, whose share in manufacturing is small, we find that 77 per cent of the sales invoiced by the 100 largest enterprises is accounted for by groups controlled from abroad. If we consider the 400 largest

in favour of foreign companies operating in the country, by granting the latter favourable exchange treatment for imports of equipment. This measure led a number of national companies to join foreign groups so as to have access to favourable exchange treatment.

[1] Cf. José Luis Ceceña, *Los Monopolios en México*, Mexico, 1962.

enterprises, foreign-controlled groups still account for as much as 70 per cent.

A study of the economic power structure, carried out in Brazil,[1] covers 276 consortia whose individual capital in 1962 amounted to one billion cruzeiros and over at 1962 prices. This study, which covered private enterprises only, divided the consortia into two categories. The first included groups with capital totalling 4 billion cruzeiros or more, and the second comprised all the other groups. Of the 55 consortia falling into the first category, 29 were foreign, 2 were mixed companies and 24 were national. A more detailed analysis of the data shows that of the groups with a total capital of 4-10 billion cruzeiros, 19 were national and 19 foreign (including one mixed company), and that of those with a total capital of over 10 billion cruzeiros, 5 were national and 13 foreign (also including one mixed company). The 29 foreign groups controlled 234 firms, with an average capital of 1,300 million cruzeiros, while the 24 national groups controlled 506 firms with an average capital of 300 million cruzeiros. Of the 55 largest consortia, 39 operated in the industrial sector, 23 being foreign. In the consumer durables and capital goods sectors 26 were operating, of which 16 were foreign and 8 national. A sample survey carried out among the smaller groups (each with a total capital of between 1 and 4 billion cruzeiros) showed that of those operating in the industrial sector 42 per cent were foreign, while more than half the groups operating in the consumer durables and capital goods sectors were controlled by foreign groups. An overall survey of the 276 groups shows that more than half the capital invested in Brazilian industry is held by foreign groups and that foreign control increases as we move from the consumer non-durable goods industries to the consumer durables and capital goods industries, which are precisely those undergoing the most rapid expansion. A survey carried out in São Paulo[2] indirectly confirms this picture, revealing that the average age of equipment in factories owned by national groups is considerably greater than that of the equipment in factories belonging to foreign groups. A more detailed analysis of the 55 largest Brazilian groups shows that the majority of the so-called national groups are linked, in one way or another, to the foreign groups. In fact only 9 of the 55 groups had no shareholding connexion with foreign interests.[3] In

---

[1] For an outline and analysis of the data on this survey, see the articles of Mauricio Vinhas de Queiroz, Luciano Martins, José Antonio Pessoa de Queiros and Vera Werneck, in *Revista do Instituto de Ciências Sociais*, Rio, Jan.–Dec. 1965.
[2] See José Carlos Pereira, *Estrutura e Expansão da Indústria em São Paulo*, São Paulo, 1967.
[3] See the article by Mauricio Vinhas de Queiroz in *Revista do Instituto de Ciências Sociais*, Rio, Jan.–Dec. 1965.

most cases, part of the capital of the Brazilian group's subsidiaries is held by foreign groups, an association often unavoidable if the enterprise is to have access to the 'knowhow' for certain production techniques.

In broad outline, the pattern typical of the region's most industrially advanced countries is the following: on the one hand we find a group consisting of a large number of national enterprises, of which the most important were established in the first quarter of the present century, in many instances before the First World War. Since these enterprises were established during the phase when the textile, food and building materials (including cement) industries were rapidly expanding, they continue to dominate these sectors. On the other hand, we find a smaller group of enterprises of larger than average size, nearly all established in the second quarter of the century, which are subsidiaries of organisations with headquarters in the major industrialised countries, primarily the United States. This group generally controls production activities that developed in the second phase of industrialisation, particularly the metal-using and engineering industries and the chemical and electrical goods industries. The pharmaceutical industry is in a class of its own. Having achieved considerable development in the first phase of the regional industrialisation process, when it was controlled by national groups, it has undergone a complete change in the last two decades. Local laboratories have been displaced by competition from new products developed as a result of advances in chemical technology. In this case the industry, revolutionised by technological progress, has been taken over by consortia linked to the large-scale international chemical firms.

To complete the picture, it should be added that the Latin American enterprise is still largely a family concern. Not only is the capital still controlled by one family or by a small group of interrelated families, but management is also in the hands of members of these families, in some cases layered according to the hierarchy of generations within the family. Even where management is staffed by semi-professionals, no clear distinction is made between the ownership of an enterprise and its management. In these circumstances, control of the region's manufacturing activities is being competed for by two types of enterprise, corresponding to two stages in the evolution of capitalism: the family enterprise, in which capital ownership and administration are fused, managers being selected from a limited circle on the basis of kinship ties, family connexions and even age, and the completely institutionalised enterprise, with an independent board of directors, in a position to control shareholders' meetings and with managers selected on the basis of their professional qualifications.

New External Dependence

TABLE 18.5. *Foreign Investment and External Debt in 1963*
(in millions of 1960 dollars)

	direct foreign investment	external debt	total
Brazil	3,950	2,750	6,700
Venezuela	5,400	300	5,700
Argentina	1,280	2,250	3,530
Mexico	1,620	1,650	3,270
Chile	920	1,020	1,940
Colombia	550	700	1,250
Peru	680	400	1,080
Bolivia	50	250	300
Panama	210	70	280
Ecuador	150	110	260
Dominican Republic	150	100	250
Uruguay	80	150	230
Guatemala	160	50	210
Costa Rica	90	90	180
Honduras	130	40	170
Nicaragua	50	50	100
Paraguay	20	30	50
Latin America	15,230	10,100	25,330

SOURCE: ECLA, *Integración, Sector Externo y Desarrollo Económico de América Latina*, 1966.

The present situation is, of course, a transitory one. Certain lines of development can be foreseen or have already emerged. Some national groups may evolve towards institutionalisation, a move that could be hastened by State action, whether this takes the form of controlling the penetration of foreign groups or of providing financial support for national groups. National groups may join foreign groups, jeopardising their real autonomy. As we have seen, foreign groups seek to ensure control over technical, economic and financial decisions in the areas where they penetrate in order to safeguard the effectiveness of the supranational complex as a whole. Fusion with national groups tends to involve the transformation of locally recruited directors into public relations officers or their co-option on to the boards of the multinational enterprise. A third line of development, feasible only in the case of large undertakings, is the joint production venture, involving participation of the State and international groups.

Chile's new copper policy, outlined in the last chapter, is a case in point. State participation, even when the government holds a minor share of stock, can have a decisive influence on the management of the enterprise. On the other hand, in certain cases the participation of international groups can take the form of service contracts. At the present time these lines of development overlap, the second, i.e. extension of the area controlled by foreign groups, tending on the whole to prevail. Consequently, just as traditional forms of dependence on the outside world were beginning to be overcome, new and more complex forms have emerged, raising problems that will undoubtedly be central to Latin American economic policy in the coming decade.

CHAPTER 19

TOWARDS THE RESTRUCTURING OF THE INTERNATIONAL ECONOMY

IMMUTABILITY OF EXPORTS

In studying the long-term trends of the Latin American economies, the single most striking feature is the immutability of the region's export pattern. Leaving aside a few special cases, we find that despite the considerable changes that have taken place in the production structures of a number of countries, the region's capacity to import is still dependent on exports of a few primary products, which were already being exported before 1929. However, we have seen that the importance of primary products in the pattern of the world economy and more particularly in the pattern of international trade, has been declining and will tend to decline still further. It is hardly surprising, therefore, that the region's share in world trade should be diminishing, as can be seen from Table 19.1 (p. 180).

The improvement in the behaviour of the Latin American index in the second half of the 1950s is entirely due to the expansion of Venezuelan petroleum exports. However, the evolution of the external terms of trade slightly alters the overall picture. When we consider the value, rather than the volume (quantum) of trade, relative price trends were less favourable to the region in the 1950s than in the 1960s. In fact, the region's share of the value of world exports fell from 11·9 per cent in 1950 to 8·6 per cent in 1955 and to 6·8 per cent in 1960. In 1966 it was 5·6 per cent. The region's external terms of trade, which had deteriorated by around 20 per cent in the second half of the last decade, improved by 7 per cent between 1960 and 1966.

The mere fact that it has remained a region of primary production for export means that Latin America has had to suffer the consequences of the long-term change in the structure of world trade. The extraordinary increase in the volume of the developed countries' external trade, which grew by around 60 per cent between 1960 and 1966, is a reflexion of this change, of which the salient feature is the rapid expansion of trade in manufactured products between industrialised countries. In fact, the other countries of the Third World as a group have also experienced a decline

179   7-2

Economic Development of Latin America

TABLE 19.1. *Recent Evolution of the Volume of World Trade*
(index 1955 = 100)

	world total	developed areas	Latin America
1955	100	100	100
1960	135	136	128
1965	189	196	155
1966	200	213	160

SOURCE: United Nations, *Monthly Bulletin of Statistics*, various issues.

in their share of world trade, despite the substantial increase in petroleum exports from the Middle East. However, changes in the structure of world trade do not sufficiently account for the behaviour of the region's exports. Other factors have accentuated the basic trend. Some of these factors, affecting important export products, are examined below.

Venezuelan *petroleum*, which accounted for more than half the world's oil exports in the immediate post-war period, has lost a substantial part of its share in the world market as a result of the rapidly increasing supplies of crude oils from the Middle East, North Africa and the Soviet Union. A variety of reasons, such as the remarkable average yield of Middle Eastern oil wells, their greater proximity to the major markets of Western Europe, the greater financial participation of importing European countries in the exploitation of African and Asian oil, have helped to account for the decline in Venezuela's share of the world petroleum market, which had been reduced to less than one-third by 1960. To these factors must be added the restrictions on oil imports recently imposed by the United States, restrictions primarily affecting Venezuela since this country sells more than 40 per cent of its output to the U.S.A. The combined action of these factors accounts for the fact that Venezuelan exports, whose dollar value had increased at an average rate of 7·5 per cent a year in the 1950s, have remained stationary since 1960.

Coffee is exported by 15 Latin American countries and is the major source of export earnings for a number of these. Whereas, in the case of oil, consumption is rapidly increasing and supply is controlled by a small number of large consortia, coffee is dependent on a slow-growing demand (the annual increase in world consumption is estimated at 2·5 per cent) and a supply strongly affected by climatic factors. In the absence of stock control, coffee prices on the world market tend to fluctuate widely in accordance with current crop estimates, particularly in Brazil, which

180

TABLE 19.2. *Latin American Export Value* (*f.o.b.*)
(*millions of dollars at current prices*)

	1948–50	1958–60	1965	1966	1967[1]
Argentina	1,244	1,027	1,493	1,593	1,485
Bolivia	102	68	110	126	148
Brazil	1,203	1,265	1,596	1,741	1,630
Chile	303	459	688	881	898
Colombia	335	462	539	508	500
Costa Rica	49	83	111	138	149
Ecuador	48	99	161	192	215
El Salvador	56	115	178	189	210
Guatemala	70	111	167	228	200
Haiti	35	33	40	34	35
Honduras	55	66	92	142	143
Mexico	456	749	1,053	1,228	1,185
Nicaragua	20	65	118	138	137
Panama	21	30	70	88	94
Paraguay	31	31	50	49	49
Peru	168	343	667	765	757
Dominican Republic	80	142	178	138	155
Uruguay	208	122	179	186	154
Venezuela	1,068	2,409	2,481	2,404	2,522
Latin America	5,552	7,684	10,109	10,768	10,666

[1] Preliminary figures.

SOURCE: ECLA, *Economic Survey of Latin America, 1967*, and *The Economic Development of Latin America in the Post-War Period, 1964.*

accounts for more than one-third of the world's exportable production. On the other hand, the efforts being made by certain Latin American countries—mainly Brazil and Colombia—to regulate supply, have provided an incentive to production in African countries, a development the more understandable in that these countries, given their relative backwardness, must avail themselves of all possible means of maximising their external payments capacity. Between 1948–52 and 1962–3, African production was multiplied 2·8 times whereas Latin American production increased only 12 per cent. In consequence, Latin America's share of the world coffee market declined from more than four-fifths in the early 1950s to two-thirds in the second half of the present decade. The displacement of the Latin American product has occurred not only in Western

TABLE 19.3. *Latin American Share in the Total Value of Exports of Under-developed Countries* (% *figures*)

	food products, beverages tobacco	raw materials	fuels	chemical products	manu- factures	total
1955–6	49·3	22·8	32·7	36·2	24·3	34·2
1959–60	47·2	20·9	31·2	35·2	20·3	31·8
1963–4	45·6	25·2	26·3	32·9	19·4	30·8

SOURCE: ECLA, *Economic Survey of Latin America, 1965.*

TABLE 19.4. *Contribution of Selected Countries to Total Value of Latin American Exports* (%)

	1960	1967
Venezuela	30·1	23·6
Brazil	16·0	15·3
Argentina	13·7	13·9
Mexico	9·6	11·1
Chile	6·2	8·4
Peru	5·5	7·1
Colombia	5·9	4·7
Central America	5·5	7·9
Other countries	7·5	8·0

SOURCE: ECLA, *Economic Survey of Latin America, 1967.*

Europe—where the ex-French colonies have gained a privileged position from their associate membership of the Common Market—but also in the United States, where the soluble coffee industry has given preference to the lower-grade and lower-priced coffees (Robusta) produced in Africa. This situation has confronted Brazil with a serious dilemma: whether to place its entire output on the market, provoking a drastic fall in prices which would harm not only its own interests but those of other producing countries, or whether to try to regulate supply, taking into account the slow growth of demand. The second solution would involve financing the withholding of stocks and would facilitate the progressive penetration of low-grade coffees for which there are highly favourable expansion opportunities in Africa. However, this solution has been practically ruled out by the rapid growth of the soluble coffee industry which entails the substitution of the Brazilian product by African Robustas. Brazil has attempted to solve this difficult problem by moving towards the establishment of a local industry manufacturing soluble coffee for export on the basis of low-grade green coffees withheld from the export market. It would be possible to compete indirectly with low-grade African coffees on the markets of the importing countries in this way. However, this solution has come up against the reaction of U.S. soluble producers, concerned to safeguard their own market. In view of this reaction and of the consequent restrictions on soluble imports imposed by the U.S., Latin American producers will find it difficult to defend their share in the U.S. market by these means.

Apart from petroleum and coffee, which together account for more than a third of the region's exports, other products contribute a relatively small share to the total value of exports. The ten agricultural and livestock products ranking next in importance together account for a quarter of the total and the six mineral products ranking below these for slightly less than one-tenth. With regard to the major temperate-zone commodities—wheat, meat and wool—the decline in the Latin American share of the world market is largely attributable to the reduction in Argentina's exportable surpluses brought about by the slow growth of output and the vigorous increase in domestic consumption. This downward trend became apparent in the 1950s and in the present decade the region has failed to recover its former position. Between 1950 and 1960 the region's share in world exports fell from 16 per cent to 9 per cent in the case of wheat, from 27 per cent to 17 per cent in the case of meat and from 19 to 14 per cent in the case of wool.

Cotton, exported mainly by Mexico, Brazil, Peru and the Central American countries, has a special position on the world market because of the relative weight carried by exports to the U.S. On the one hand, restrictions on U.S. cotton shipments help to maintain prices at relatively stable levels; on the other, strong competition from synthetic fibres discourages any rise in prices above certain levels. Although the growth of demand is relatively slow, Latin American countries have managed to increase their share in world exports from 13 per cent in 1950 to 15 per cent in 1960 and to over 20 per cent in the most recent period.

Cacao, exported primarily by Brazil, Ecuador and the Dominican Republic, stands out among the world's major agricultural commodities for the relatively intense growth of demand, which has increased at an average annual rate of 4·5 per cent over the last two decades. The region's contribution to world exports has remained more or less stable at around a quarter of the total. Like coffee, cocoa, as a commodity produced primarily for export by underdeveloped and hence financially vulnerable countries, is subject to sharp fluctuations in price in accordance with current crop estimates.

Sugar, which figures among the exports of all the countries in the region except Chile and Uruguay, provides a classic example of the enormous gap between the degree of organisation achieved in the local markets and the lack of organisation that still prevails in the world commodity market. Major importers such as the United States and the Soviet Union, who are also major producers, allow access to their own markets on the basis of quotas allocated to privileged clients, a trade carried on outside the world market. The open market, receiving only residual surpluses unable to penetrate preferential markets, is thus subject to sharp fluctuations, and prices tend to be well below those obtaining in the protected domestic markets. The elimination of Cuba from the preferential U.S. market at the beginning of the present decade revealed the great elasticity of the sugar supply available in the Latin American countries as a whole. Thus, the drastic cut in Cuban sugar exports to the United States, which fell from 2·9 to 1·9 million tons between 1959 and 1960, was offset by an increase in the combined exports of Brazil, Mexico, Peru and the Dominican Republic, which rose from 1·9 to 2·9 million tons in the same period. Of this increase 90 per cent was sold on the United States market. Latin America's share in the world sugar trade rose from 43 per cent in 1950 to 49 per cent in 1960. In the present decade, despite changes in direction due to the closing of the United States market to Cuban sugar, this improvement has been maintained.

Peruvian *fish products* represent the only significant innovation in Latin American exports over the last two decades. Accounting for more than a quarter of Peru's exports, they ranked among the region's ten major export items in the second half of the 1960s. The basis of the industry is provided by the large shoals of *anchoveta* found close to the Peruvian coast almost the whole year round, thanks to the cold waters of the Humboldt Current. Peru had traditionally exploited her *anchoveta* resources through the extraction of *guano*, deposited by the bird populations attracted by the extraordinary abundance of these fish. The fear that the bird migrations might cease was used for many years as an argument against exploiting the shoals directly. When the exceptional richness of these became known, however, a fisheries industry was established, its rapid development providing yet another instance of the speed with which a productive sector tends to grow in Latin America whenever demand conditions are favourable. The output of Peruvian fish meal rose from 31,000 tons in 1960 to 1,120,000 tons in 1962. By the middle of the present decade, with an output of 9 million tons, Peru had become the world's leading producer in terms of volume of fisheries' output. This spectacular expansion is accounted for by the simple techniques involved in *anchoveta* fishing: shoals, found close inshore, are encircled by nets, which are drawn tight at the bottom when the circle is complete so that the catch can be pumped aboard the fishing boat. 150 tons or more can be caught at one cast, generally enough to fill the hold. When the fish run freely a medium-sized boat can make two or more trips a day. Onshore, the *anchoveta* is pumped out of the boat and delivered to the plant, where the oil is extracted for use in margarine and other cooking fats and the residue is processed as fish meal, a product with a high protein content used in the preparation of feeding compounds for chickens and pigs. The relatively low cost of protein derived from Peruvian *anchoveta* assures the industry a firm place in the world market. Its expansion has been limited, however, by the availability of fish. The inshore shoals have begun to disappear and yields in the industry have started to decline, calling for greater capital investments and leading to a concentration of enterprises, which has facilitated the penetration of foreign consortia. As in the case of so many other sectors connected with the region's exports, the boom phase of rapid expansion and easy profits has been followed by a phase of crisis and consolidation during which financially stronger foreign groups tend to take over control of the industry while at the same time raising its technical level. The phase of dramatic expansion came to an end in 1964, when Peru already provided 40 per cent of the world's fish meal supplies.[1]

Mexican *tourism* also deserves mention as one of the few items making up the Latin American capacity to import that has shown a consistently upward-trend in the post-war period. Under this head we include not only the expenditure of tourists proper, i.e. visitors remaining in the country for more than 48 hours, but also the so-called 'frontier trade'. Actually, the latter can scarcely be considered an export since it is not subject to the restrictions imposed on exports to the United States. Receipts accruing to Mexico under the head of tourism, in this broad sense, rank after petroleum and coffee as a major factor in generating the region's capacity to import. Moreover, the relative importance of tourist income

[1] See Gerald Ellicot, 'The Fishing Industry of Peru', in Claudio Veliz (ed.), *Latin America and the Caribbean: A Handbook*.

has been increasing steadily: in 1948–50 it accounted for 3 per cent of the value of Latin American exports; by 1966–7 this proportion had risen to 9 per cent. During this period, the dollar value of Mexican exports was multiplied by 2·4 and that of receipts from tourism by 4. In 1967, tourist income totalled 959 million dollars, representing 83 per cent of the value of exports, as against 46 per cent in 1950–3 and 68 per cent in 1960–3. Earnings from tourism have not only grown much faster than Mexican exports but have also proved to be more stable. As a function of the income available for consumption in the United States, short-term fluctuations are far less pronounced than fluctuations in U.S. imports, particularly of primary commodities whose price instability is all too well known. Finally, it should be pointed out that Mexico's share in the tourist expenditure of United States citizens has shown an upward trend in the last two decades, which will probably be accentuated in the next few years as a result of the measures recently taken by the United States government to curb travel to Europe.

EXTERNAL FINANCIAL COMMITMENTS

Leaving aside such exceptional cases as that of Peruvian fish meal, Latin American exports over the last two decades have been growing at the slow rate characterising the expansion of world demand for most primary commodities. In the most recent period the increase in external financial commitments has put an additional strain on the capacity to import. Thus between 1960 and 1966 the value of exports increased by 35 per cent, while payments of interest and dividends on foreign loans and investment grew by 67 per cent and amortisation of loans by 41 per cent. Financial services which, for the region as a whole, absorbed slightly under one-fifth of the value of exports at the end of the previous decade, represented a third of this value in 1966. In recent years the situation has tended to deteriorate as a result of the increase in interest rates in international capital markets. Thus the private sector's rates of interest have risen from around 6·5 per cent in 1960 to around 8 per cent in 1967. The IDB has charged interest rates as high as 7¾ per cent on its loans to the private sector. With the rise in the cost of money, the simple renegotiation of loans contracted earlier entails an increase in future financial liabilities. Even the most cautious projections with respect to probable trends in the expansion of exports and new capital inflows indicate that by the end of the coming decade, at least half the value of the region's exports will be absorbed by external financial commitments.

The picture outlined above—which indicates that the region tends to suffer from a growing inadequacy in its capacity to import, with serious repercussions on its development—has highlighted the need for an overall survey of the region's external trade problems.[1] Discussions centring on these problems have taken place in international organisations, particularly ECLA, making it possible to define certain long-term lines of policy which have been followed by governments in the region in an effort, shared with other developing countries, to rebuild the international economy. The two United Nations conferences on Trade and Development—the first held in Geneva in 1964 and the second in New Delhi in 1968—were largely a consequence of Latin America's realisation of the magnitude of the problem. The limited progress made at these two conferences is not altogether unconnected with the fact that, in the other areas of the Third World, structural inadequacy of the capacity to import has not yet become as serious as it is in most of the Latin American countries today.

TOWARDS AN OVERALL STRATEGY

Significant and irreversible change in international economic relations—capable of bringing about a more equitable distribution of the benefits of technological progress between developed and underdeveloped countries and of creating conditions for accelerating the economic growth of the latter—can be achieved only through a determined effort carried out over several decades on a number of fronts. The measures most frequently proposed in Latin America relate to the following fronts:[2] (*a*) international commodity trade, (*b*) international trade in manufactures, (*c*) financial flows, (*d*) international transport, and (*e*) economic relations between underdeveloped countries. The latter aspect will be considered in the next chapter in the context of the pattern of regional integration.

Basic commodities are of overriding concern because they are practically the only source, and for some time to come will continue to be the major source, of export earnings for the countries of the region. Given the lack of organisation of the commodity markets, the average annual rate of fluctuations in commodity prices is around 20 per cent which, with the

[1] For an overall survey of the problem see ECLA, *América Latina y la Política Comercial Internacional*, UN, 1967.
[2] For a formal exposition of the Latin American proposals concerning the reorganisation of the international economy see chiefly the two ECLA documents, *Latin America and the United Nations Conference on Trade and Development*, UN, 1964, and *Latin America and the Second Session of UNCTAD*, UN, 1968; see also, Raúl Prebisch, *Nueva Política Comercial para el Desarrollo*, Mexico, 1964.

tightness of money on the world markets, makes economic planning impractical. Moreover, in the absence of international regulation of supply, commodity prices are subject to a long-term decline entailing a transfer of income from the exporting countries to the importing countries, as past experience has shown. To deal with these problems, it has been suggested that the product-by-product approach should be adopted, taking into account the particular situation of each country. Some basic guidelines have been proposed:

(1) Setting ceilings on self-sufficiency in the developed countries. Since their domestic output enjoys stable and relatively high levels of prices, it is recommended that protective measures should be designed to guarantee a share of the markets of the developed countries for imports from countries of the Third World. For instance, in European Common Market countries there is already a high degree of self-sufficiency in certain products, e.g. 85 per cent in beef requirements, 66 per cent in the case of cereals (excluding wheat), 97 per cent in that of sugar. If coefficients of self-sufficiency were determined, medium-term forecasts could be made for import requirements which would increase as demand expanded. On the basis of an approximate medium-term forecast of demand, supply could be planned within the framework of an agreement between exporting countries.

(2) Free access to the markets of the developed countries for commodities not produced in the latter. With the elimination of customs duties, discriminatory internal rates and taxes and quantitative administrative restrictions, consumption would rise and substitutes would be discouraged. On the whole, since supply is inelastic in underdeveloped countries, tariffs tend to have a depressive effect on world prices, particularly when substitutes are available. The end result is a transfer of income from the underdeveloped producer country to the government of the developed importing country.

(3) International financing of stocks withheld with a view to stabilising commodity supply. Regulation of supply is an essential feature of commodity-market organisation and is particularly important in the case of commodities vulnerable to climatic factors. The financing of stocks is a heavy financial burden, in many cases beyond the resources of the producer country. Moreover, price stabilisation also benefits consumer countries.

Commodity exports, even if substantially increased, cannot solve the problem of the external-sector bottleneck in the Latin American economies. Access to markets for *manufactured and semi-manufactured goods* is the second and undoubtedly most important objective of the effort being made by the Latin American countries in the hope of changing the existing structure of international relations. If the underdeveloped countries have lagged behind in the rapid expansion of world trade that has taken place over the last fifteen years, this is precisely because they have not gained access to the markets for manufactured products. Thus, whereas world trade in manufactured products increased by 78 billion dollars between 1953–4 and 1965–6, the countries of the Third World as a group accounted for only 4 per cent of this increase. With a view to changing this trend, a strategy has been devised, based on a *system of preferences* in favour of manufactures and semi-manufactures exported by underdeveloped countries. These preferences are to be (*a*) general, (*b*) non-reciprocal, and (*c*) non-discriminatory. Basically, the aim is to secure free access—elimination of tariff and non-tariff restrictions on imports—to the markets of the developed countries for manufactured and semi-manufactured goods exported by the underdeveloped countries. This would not, however, imply reciprocity. The concession mechanism could take various forms: a list of products to be included in the preferential system could be drawn up; or a list of exceptions could be prepared, or quotas could be allocated for certain products, fixing a ceiling for imports included in the preferential system. The justification for the preferential system is that the increase in exports of manufactures from underdeveloped countries to developed countries automatically entails the expansion of imports of other manufactures in the opposite direction. In fact, whereas any increase in the income of an underdeveloped country not in balance of payments difficulties entails a corresponding increase in the income of the developed countries, the converse does not hold. Moreover, since the new trade pattern would imply a transfer of resources in the developed countries from the traditional industries to those with the most advanced technology, the vanguard sectors would receive the greatest stimulus. This transfer of resources would require, of course, certain structural adjustments, but the transition could be planned and changes could be staggered over a period of time.

The problem of *international financing* is the third front for joint action. We have already mentioned the financing of commodity stocks. Together with this, *compensatory* or *supplementary financing* would be needed to help underdeveloped countries in balance of payments difficulties caused by sharp falls in export prices or a deterioration in the terms of trade. The aim of this type of financing is to prevent the internal propagation of external imbalances, since without this standby development planning becomes impossible. Finally there is the question of long-term financing for specific development projects. The present inadequacy of this type of financing leads underdeveloped countries to make use of high-cost bank credits. Consequently, although Latin America's liabilities with respect to private banks accounted for only 38 per cent of its external debt in 1966, the servicing of the private debt accounted for 78 per cent of the total service payments in that year, which indicates the burdensome conditions under which private loans are contracted.

Lastly, the *shipping front* must be considered. The present organisation of world shipping discriminates against non-traditional products exported by underdeveloped countries, representing an obstacle to the opening up of new lines of trade which is often extremely difficult to overcome.

CHAPTER 20

INTEGRATION PROCESS IN CENTRAL AMERICA

INSTITUTIONAL FRAMEWORK

As we have seen in earlier chapters, the export of primary products was the starting-point for an initial industrialisation process in many Latin American countries. However, externally induced structural change was dependent on the parallel action of domestic factors such as the relative importance of wage payment flows, the degree of domestic control over the export activity, fiscal policy, the existence of a significant volume of recent immigration of European origin, etc. Among such simultaneously acting factors probably none was quite so important as the *size* of the country, if we take this to mean, firstly, the relative population size and, secondly, the natural-resource base. Thus, in the case of the five Central American countries each with a population averaging just over one and a half million inhabitants in 1950, it can be said that the main cause of their relative backwardness was closely related to their small size.

The Central American isthmus, excluding the present territory of Panama—the latter was an integral part of the Viceroyalty of New Granada and remained a province of Colombia until 1903, when it seceded to become, with the help of the United States, the Republic of Panama—was governed in colonial times from the Captaincy of Guatemala and, when it broke away from Spain in 1821, was organised as a Federal Republic.[1] The federation succumbed to centrifugal forces unleashed during the Wars of Independence and broke up into five nation-states seventeen years later. The export economy, based mainly on bananas,

[1] A year after the break with Spain, i.e. in 1822, the Central American region became part of Mexico. Its independence from the new metropolis was proclaimed a year later when it became first the United Central American Provinces and shortly afterwards the Central American Federation. The Federation fell prey to internal conflicts and was dissolved in 1838. An attempt to establish a Confederation a decade later also failed. In 1885 the Guatemalan dictator, J. R. Barrios, made an attempt, also ending in failure, to unify Central America by force, creating a Republic of Central America.

coffee and cocoa, linked each of the five countries to the outside world, at first to England and soon afterwards to the United States, rather than to its neighbours. But awareness of past unity was kept alive in the region and it was natural that it should have been frequently thought that the solution of many of the problems of the present required the reconstitution, in some form, of the whole formed in the past. More recently, discussion of development problems allowed this idea to be shifted from the political sphere, where its realisation seemed so remote that it had become little more than a myth, to the economic level. However, it would be difficult to account for the rapid advance of the integration movement—ignoring the disputes in the political sphere that have led, on occasion, to the severance of diplomatic relations—without keeping in mind these historical roots.

The starting-point for the present integration movement was a resolution adopted by the five Central American governments at the fourth session of ECLA held in Mexico City in 1951.[1] In this resolution the five governments, represented or advised by economists who had worked together in international agencies, expressed their interest in 'developing agricultural and industrial production and the transportation systems of their respective countries in a form which will promote the integration of their economies and the creation of larger markets through trade, the co-ordination of their development plans and the establishment of enterprises in which all or some of the countries have an interest'. This led to the creation in that same year of the Committee for Economic Co-operation in the Isthmus and the Organisation of Central American States (ODECA). From then on, the Central American integration movement was to advance along two mutually reinforcing fronts: the creation of institutions that could provide the process with continuity, and the progressive liberalisation of trade among the five countries.

After 1951 a series of bilateral free trade agreements, applicable to limited lists of goods, were entered into by the following countries: El Salvador–Nicaragua (1951); El Salvador–Guatemala (1951); Costa Rica–El Salvador (1953); Guatemala–Costa Rica (1955); Guatemala–Honduras (1956); El Salvador–Honduras (1957). The multilateral treaty on Central American Free Trade and Economic Integration was signed in 1958, consolidating the lists of duty-free goods established under the earlier agreements and paving the way for complete free trade. The

[1] See the ECLA study, 'Contribución a la Política de Integración Económica de América Latina', in ECLA, *Hacia la Integración Acelerada de América Latina*, Mexico, 1966; see also ECLA, *Evolución de la Integración Económica en Centroamérica*, UN, 1966.

Integration in Central America

Agreement on the System for Central American Integration Industries was signed at the same time as the general treaty. This Agreement was the first major step towards the creation of a new productive structure and superseded the more limited objective of integrating existing industries. It provoked strong reactions, particularly from the U.S. government, which held that its purpose was to create State-supported enterprises with exclusive rights to the market. In fact, the system aims to provide a guaranteed regional market for industries—designated 'integration industries'—that are of interest to a number of the Central American countries and require access to the whole or to a large part of the Central American market for their expansion. The Central American Convention on the Equalisation of Import Tariffs was signed the following year, with a view to co-ordinating policies in this key sector in order to pave the way for a uniform external tariff. Finally, in 1960, the decisive step was taken of transforming the emerging free trade area into a genuine Economic Community. The preferential tariff system was replaced by a general provision establishing immediate free trade for 'all natural products originating in the territories of the contracting parties and goods manufactured therein'. On the other hand, the scope of the articles governing the circulation of goods was extended to include the movement of factors of production, guaranteeing 'the free circulation of persons, goods and capital between their territories...with no restrictions other than those established by the national laws' of the five countries. The new Treaty of Economic Association (later the General Treaty of Central American Integration) was initially signed by Guatemala, El Salvador and Honduras, shortly afterwards by Nicaragua and in 1962 by Costa Rica. Thus, in the course of a decade, the structuring of an economic framework comprising the five national economies had been accomplished, establishing mobility of goods and factors within the union and a common external tariff vis-à-vis the outside world.

The movement was not limited, however, to the liberalisation of economic and financial flows between the five countries. It was accompanied by the creation of several different types of institution, all related to the idea of forming a unified economic space. Thus in 1954 the Central American Institute for Public Administration (ESAPAC) was established, with headquarters in Sao José, Costa Rica, and in the following year the Central American Institute for Industrial Research and Technology (ICAITI), located in Guatemala City. In 1960 the general treaty gave rise to the Central American Bank for Economic Integration (CABEI), the Central American Economic Council (comprised of the Central American ministers of economy), the Executive Council and the Permanent Secretariat for Central American Economic Integration (SIECA). Other regional institutions created within the integration framework were the Monetary Council, composed of central bank directors and, more recently, the Central American School for Textile Training. Lastly, we must mention the concerted effort to improve regional interconnexion: the construction of a road network has been given top priority and, more recently, a start has been made on the interconnexion of electric power systems.

ACHIEVEMENTS AND PROSPECTS

The practical achievements of the Central American integration effort, in so far as can be judged from the trade flows, have been considerable. Between 1950 and 1961, the annual growth rate of the value of intra-Central American trade was 21 per cent, while in the period following the general treaty (1961–7) it rose as high as 35 per cent. In 1950, trade between the Central American countries accounted for only 4 per cent of their exports; by 1967 it accounted for more than a quarter of the total, the value rising from 8·6 million dollars to 220 million. This remarkable expansion did not affect traditional lines of export to countries outside the area, since these exports consist of a few commodities with a limited local market and are practically the same for all five countries. In fact, in recent years, manufactured goods have accounted for nearly 70 per cent of the total value of intra-Area trade.

Analysis of the macroeconomic data shows that the region experienced a marked acceleration of development during the period under review. The growth rate of the domestic product, which averaged 4 per cent annually in the preceding decade, rose to 6 per cent in the 1960–7 period. At the same time there was a significant diversification of productive structures, with the industrial sector's share in the domestic product rising from around 12 per cent in the mid-fifties to 16 per cent in 1965.

By providing the small Latin American countries with a combined market of approximately the same size as that of Peru, and with a relatively high import coefficient—around 17 per cent in 1960—the integration movement created conditions for starting industrialisation along the same lines as the process experienced in earlier periods by all other countries of the region of similar economic dimensions. In the 1960–7 period, Central American manufacturing output grew at an average rate of 9 per cent a year. However, the region's rapid overall growth cannot be attributed solely to the integration process, since exports to the outside world also

TABLE 20.1. *Central America: Evolution of Exports and Intra-Area Trade* *(millions of dollars)*

	1960	1963	1965	1966	1967
traditional exports					
cotton	36·7	104·6	144·4	131·5	117·4
bananas	66·3	70·1	84·7	109·3	116·0
coffee	212·0	229·8	282·9	284·5	244·3
total exports to outside world	397·3	524·0	636·2	667·2	625·3
intra-area exports	32·7	66·2	136·0	176·3	220·0
total	430·0	590·2	772·2	843·5	845·3
% of intra-area exports in total	7·6	11·2	17·6	20·9	26·0

SOURCE: ECLA, *Economic Survey of Latin America, 1965* and *1967.*

TABLE 20.2. *Central American Countries: Evolution of GDP in the 1960s*

	GDP in 1960 (millions of dollars)	Annual rates of growth (%)		
		1960–5	1965–6	1966–7
Guatemala	1,094	6·4	4·5	3·4
El Salvador	698	6·6	5·7	3·4
Costa Rica	568	6·1	6·5	8·3
Honduras	406	5·7	4·7	3·5
Nicaragua	359	8·3	3·8	3·8
Central America	3,125	6·6	5·0	4·3

SOURCE: For data on GDP, ECLA, *Economic Bulletin for Latin America, Oct. 1967;* for rates of growth, ECLA, *Economic Survey of Latin America, 1967.*

experienced a relatively vigorous expansion during this period, permitting a slight rise in the import coefficient even when intra-regional trade is not taken into account (see Table 20.1). If integration was able to proceed fairly smoothly, this was apparently because the region's import capacity vis-à-vis the outside world continued to increase rapidly. The decline in traditional exports in the latter part of the period had an immediate effect on the growth rate of the region's gross domestic product, which fell from an average of 6·6 per cent in the first half of the decade to 5 per cent in 1966 and 4·3 per cent in 1967 (see Table 20.2). The experience of the last two years has shown that the integration process has failed to reduce the Central American economies' dependence on their traditional exports. A fall in cotton exports or a drop in coffee prices—as in 1967, for instance— has immediate repercussions on the public sector, with a consequent reduction in government-financed investments. Investments connected with integration would not suffice to offset the depressive effect of the factors indicated. Consequently, unless the governments can count on a broader means of compensatory action than those available at present, there is a likelihood that the integration process will tend to lose its dynamism as a reflexion of the slower growth of exports to the outside world.

Central American industrialisation over the past decade is largely attributable to the growth of the traditional export sector and the enlargement of the market consequent upon integration. This enlargement has been based simultaneously on the customs union, the positive measures taken to create a common infrastructure and the incentives offered to investment projects of regional interest. The process, then, is not one of straightforward import substitution, which implies growth of the manufacturing sector accompanied by a decline in the import coefficient for industrial products. In some ways, Central American industrialisation is similar to the industrialisation that took place in Argentina and Brazil before 1929. It seems more complex on account of the larger number of enterprises involved and the greater support of the government, as well as the more marked presence of foreign capital and techniques. The degree of industrialisation being attained in the current decade has created the opportunity for the region to embark on a second stage in the near future, which may take the form of the classic Latin American import-substitution model or may be based on overall regional development planning. In either case, the region must move towards even greater integration of the decision centres on the monetary, foreign exchange and fiscal planes. In short, the real difficulties of integration will become apparent only when development can no longer base itself on the expansion of traditional exports.

CHAPTER 21

LAFTA AND THE ANDEAN GROUP

MONTEVIDEO TREATY AND ITS OPERATION

The four southernmost Latin American countries—Argentina, Brazil, Chile and Uruguay—had traditionally carried on a relatively important reciprocal trade in primary products. The bulk of this trade was between Argentina and Brazil, consisting on the part of Argentina mainly of wheat, and on the part of Brazil of tropical products—coffee and cocoa—and timber, an exchange which generally resulted in an adverse balance for Brazil. During the Second World War, difficulties in securing external supplies boosted intra-regional trade. Argentina increased her imports from Brazil and stepped up her trade with other Latin American countries. After 1945, balance of payments difficulties led to an intensification of bilateralism, within the framework of which trade among the southern countries mentioned could continue to develop. In 1950, exchanges between these four countries accounted for 9·2 per cent of their total foreign trade and in 1953 for 12·2 per cent. From the mid-1950s, however, the movement towards trade liberalisation and multilateralism in Argentina and Chile and, later, in Brazil, led to a sharp decline in their reciprocal trade, a problem which caused increasing concern in the region. To some extent, bilateralism had performed the role of a protectionism extended over a wider area and, given the characteristics of the national economies concerned, it could reasonably be held that its disappearance would entail a fall in the level of activity. In fact, since these countries could not afford to incur balance of payments deficits in their reciprocal trade if they were to avoid having to settle their accounts in convertible currency, and since short-term financing involved obtaining lines of credit in the major financial centres, serious payments problems arose within the area. This led the countries concerned to seek bilateral equilibrium at lower levels of trade than had prevailed when the trading pattern did not involve multilateral repercussions.

This unsatisfactory state of affairs induced the four countries most concerned—Argentina, Brazil, Chile and Uruguay—to enter into negotiations with a view to devising adequate payments arrangements and recovering their former levels of trade, if possible by creating a free trade area compatible with other international obligations. This movement, albeit modest in its objectives, was speedily reinforced by the line of ideas that had been crystallising within ECLA almost since the setting up of this body in 1948. In fact, in its report for 1949, written by Raúl Prebisch, ECLA had drawn attention to the intrinsic limitations of an industralisation restricted to isolated national Latin American markets. At that time, the problem had already arisen for the Latin American countries that had advanced beyond the first stages of industrialisation. With each successive shift from light to heavy industry, from non-durable consumer goods industries to durable consumer goods industries and the beginnings of a machinery and equipment industry, the problem of the size of the market became increasingly important. From the mid-1950s, several studies on regional industrialisation and the location of basic industries, as well as explanatory analyses of the low rates of economic growth registered in Argentina and Chile, had highlighted the stumbling block that the small size of the national markets tended to place in the way of the industrialisation process. These views, repeated over and over again at meetings convened by ECLA and other international agencies concerned with the region, had no immediate practical outcome but they helped to create the psychological climate that led to the creation of a free trade area in 1960.[1]

The Treaty of Montevideo, establishing the Latin American Free Trade Association (LAFTA), was signed in February 1960 by the four countries already referred to and by Mexico, Peru and Paraguay. Colombia and Ecuador joined the Association in the following year and Venezuela and Bolivia have subsequently become members. Thus, by 1968, LAFTA encompassed all the South American countries and Mexico. The Montevideo Treaty is conceived in the spirit of GATT in two respects: in its objective, which is to liberalise trade within the area rather than to form a customs union, and in its operational procedures, which involve bilateral negotiations on a product-by-product basis and exclude the automatic and linear trade liberalisation schemes characterising the development of the European Free Trade Association and the European Economic Community. This is an important point, since it indicates that the Treaty is a response to the limited problems that have arisen over the past decade in relation to trade among the southern countries rather than a major step

[1] See the ECLA study, *Contribución a la Política de Integración Económica de América Latina*. Also, Instituto Interamericano de Estudios Jurídicos Internacionales, *Instrumentos Relativos a la Integración Económica en América Latina*, Washington, 1964. For an overall survey see also M. S. Wionczek and others, *Latin American Economic Integration*, Frederick A. Praeger, New York, 1966; Victor L. Urquidi, *Teoría, Realidad y Posibilidad de la ALALC en la Integración Económica Latinoamericana*, Mexico, 1966; José Maria Aragão, 'La Teoría Económica y el Proceso de Integración de América Latina', *Integración*, no. 2, Buenos Aires, 1968.

towards the restructuring of economic relations between the countries of the region on a completely new basis. The Treaty provides for two methods of achieving the liberalisation of trade within the area. The first consists of annual bilateral negotiations with respect to specific products, leading to the granting of concessions which should benefit all members of the Association. Such concessions must be equivalent each year to not less than 8 per cent of the weighted average duties applied by the country concerned to imports from third countries. A total of 3,246 concessions were agreed upon during the first round of negotiations and 4,397 during the second, but since the third annual round the number of additional concessions has been sharply reduced. Between the third and sixth rounds of negotiation, the latter held in 1967, a total of 1,831 tariff concessions were made. The concessions negotiated in these annual rounds form *National Schedules*, listing all the tariff reductions granted by each individual country to the remaining members of the Association. However, these National Schedules do not constitute a permanently binding obligation, a fact which accounts for the large number of concessions negotiated in the first few rounds. Each country is free to withdraw any concession listed in the National Schedule or to limit itself to extending concessions granted earlier. The second method of achieving liberalisation consists of transferring items from the National Schedules to a *Common Schedule*, negotiated every three years. The Common Schedule is irrevocable and products included in it are to be freely traded within the area by 1973.

Since concessions on items listed in the National Schedules may later be withdrawn, they cannot be of major significance from the viewpoint of creating new economic activities. Because of this, particular importance was attached from the beginning to the Common Schedule, to be negotiated every three years and to constitute an additional 25 per cent of the value of the trade carried out among member countries at the end of each three-year period. The first list of products for the Common Schedule, negotiated in 1964, included 180 products corresponding to 25 per cent of the aggregate value of the trade among members of the Association in the period 1960–2. However, a detailed examination of this common list shows that it consists mainly of primary commodities traditionally traded in the region. The practical scope of this first stage of the Common Schedule is therefore negligible. The second list of products for the Common Schedule, which was to have been drawn up in 1967, has proved far more difficult to negotiate, since it was no longer relatively easy to reach agreement on a common list without including a significant number of industrial products or items such as petroleum, which posed particular trade problems. The lengthy negotiations concerning the second common list, which had still not been brought to a successful conclusion at the end of 1968, made it clear that the signatories to the Montevideo Treaty did not really have in mind any drastic changes in their traditional trading patterns. This seems to be particularly true in the case of Argentina and Brazil, whose mutual trade continues to constitute the bulk of intra-regional trade.

In addition to the product-by-product negotiations, the Montevideo Treaty provides for sectoral or 'complementarity' agreements, designed to promote co-ordination at the production level. The idea was to facilitate industrial integration by enabling producers to divide complementary activities among themselves and so gain access to a larger market. In the absence of priority planning by the individual countries, sectoral agreements were left to the initiative of private groups, particularly international groups already operating in the region. Even so, very little progress has been made in this direction. During the first six years of the Treaty's existence, only four complementarity agreements have been signed: on data-processing machines (Argentina, Chile and Uruguay), electronic valves (Argentina, Brazil, Mexico, Chile and Uruguay), domestic appliances (Brazil and Uruguay), and certain products of the electronics and electrical communications industries (Brazil and Uruguay). Products included in these agreements represent less than 0·5 per cent of the trade between LAFTA countries. In December 1967 the first complementarity agreement of some importance was signed by all LAFTA countries. It included 125 chemical products, intra-area trade in which amounted to 28 million dollars in that year.

Finally, the Treaty makes allowance for the special position of the relatively less advanced member countries—Bolivia, Ecuador and Paraguay. These countries have to grant only partial reciprocity for the concessions they obtain and may receive concessions that are not extended to the more developed LAFTA countries. More recently, LAFTA has come to recognise a difference, for the purpose of discrimination in the concessions made, between the three largest countries—Argentina, Brazil and Mexico—and the intermediate-sized countries, possessing markets of insufficient size. Uruguay, although one of the countries with the highest per capita income in the region, was included in the group of the less-developed countries on account of its special characteristics.

The practical achievements of LAFTA have been extremely modest. The countries that had traditionally carried on a significant mutual trade recovered and even exceeded their former levels of trade. Other countries, such as Mexico and Colombia, whose intra-area trade had always been

TABLE 21.1. *Evolution of Trade among LAFTA Countries*
(value of exports (f.o.b.) in millions of dollars)

	1953–5	1959–61	1965	1966	1967
Argentina	205	133	231	243	171
Brazil	133	86	197	182	161
Colombia	3	5	16	29	15
Chile	59	35	53	54	60
Ecuador	9	7	13	13	19
Mexico	5	6	36	57	47
Paraguay	13	9	17	20	16
Peru	50	37	54	52	35
Uruguay	29	4	16	27	17
total	508	321	635	675	641

NOTE: LAFTA was established by the Montevideo Treaty in 1960. Venezuela joined the Association in 1966 and Bolivia in 1967.

insignificant, achieved some export gains. Trade among the group of nine countries that originally formed the Association, i.e. excluding Venezuela and Bolivia, amounted to 635 million U.S. dollars in 1965, as against 321 million in 1959–61 and 508 million in 1953–5. After 1965, however, trends in intra-area trade began to waver both for the traditional trading partners and for the countries that had recently entered the regional trade flows. This evolution showed that the machinery created by the Montevideo Treaty had failed to make a significant impact on the regional economies. Since then, there began a new stage of discussions, culminating in a meeting at presidential level held in Punta del Este, Uruguay, in 1967. At this meeting it was established that the aim of the Latin American governments was to move progressively towards the integration of their economies in a common market. The year 1970 was set as the target year for beginning the integration process, to be substantially achieved by the end of the fifteen-year period following this date.

NEW SUB-REGIONAL ORIENTATION

A second consequence of the meagre results produced by LAFTA was the attempt to find new avenues for development through the sub-regional approach. This movement was inspired largely by Chile, the country in the region whose limited domestic market most obviously constitutes a brake on the progress of the industrialisation process. Realising the problems posed by an integration process involving economies of such widely differing sizes as Brazil, Argentina and Mexico on the one hand and the remaining LAFTA countries on the other, the medium-sized countries sought closer co-operation in an attempt to promote integration at the sub-regional level. Since these countries—Chile, Peru, Colombia and Venezuela—are all linked by the Andean Cordillera, the new association became known as the Andean Group.[1] The designation became fully justified by the inclusion of Ecuador and Bolivia. The declared aim of the group is simply to prepare for the integration of Latin America as a whole. But there can be no doubt that if it makes rapid headway the Andean Group will tend to achieve internal cohesion and will come to form, on the economic plane, a subgroup of comparable importance to that of the region's three largest countries. The strategy underlying the structuring of the Andean Group is essentially different from that governing the creation of LAFTA. Automatic and irrevocable liberalisation of trade is envisaged, particularly for products not produced in any of the Andean countries at present, simultaneously with harmonisation of tariffs applicable to imports from third countries. In other words, the creation of a customs union is planned. Even before agreements were formalised, the Corporación Andina de Fomento (Andean Development Corporation), with headquarters in Caracas, was set up with responsibility for 'expediting the regional integration process...through the creation of production and service enterprises and the expansion, modernisation or adaptation of existing enterprises'. The new institution, the first entirely Latin American multinational financial agency, has an authorised capital of 100 million dollars.

Like the Central American Common Market, the Andean Group is starting from a situation in which trade among member countries is virtually non-existent. Nevertheless, a relatively developed transport infrastructure already exists, since all the Andean countries are interconnected through the shipping lines serving the region's traditional foreign trade. Steps are being taken to co-ordinate regional shipping, and a joint air freight line has already started operations. On the other hand, in contrast with the Central American countries in the pre-integration period, the countries of the Andean Group—or, at any rate, the four largest countries in the Group, representing 84 per cent of the population—are at a relatively advanced stage of an industrialisation process based on import substitution. However, since the national industrial systems have not yet

[1] Cf. Carlos F. Díaz Alejandro, 'El Grupo Andino en el Proceso de Integración Latinoamericano', *Estudios Internacionales*, Santiago de Chile, July–Sept. 1968.

reached the high degree of integration characterising the industries of the 'Big Three' LAFTA countries, there is likely to be less resistance to industrial complementarity between countries and—given the growing importance of economies of scale—import substitution may become the main operative factor in opening up the national economies to intra-area trade.

PROSPECTS FOR INTEGRATIONIST MOVEMENT

The creation of a regional common market is a declared aim of the economic policy pursued by all Latin American governments at the present time. This *idée-force*, which will undoubtedly play a key role in the region's development over the next few decades, has rapidly gained sway in the last few years largely as a reflexion of the realisation that small and isolated countries cannot cope with the growing problems raised by the need to overcome their underdevelopment. However, recent experience has already demonstrated the enormous complexity of the task ahead and the sterility of conventional blueprints for approaching the problem. Straightforward trade liberalisation schemes in the tradition of free trade areas and even of customs unions may be meaningful in particular situations, as in the case of the Central American countries, characterised by a similar degree of development and on the point of embarking on the first stage of industrialisation. But for countries already at a relatively advanced stage of industrialisation geared towards the achievement of self-sufficiency —the case of Argentina and Brazil—or countries whose degrees of development are vastly different, such schemes are of little value in themselves. In fact, by creating privileged conditions for international consortia in a position to plan their development on a region-wide scale, these systems may lead to forms of 'integration' that ignore or tend to undermine the national decision centres without providing genuine multinational planning for regional development. It is now regarded as more or less obvious that the real problem is not simply a matter of liberalising trade but of promoting the progressive creation of a *regional economic system*—a far from easy task in view of the previous orientation of development, the wide discrepancies in present development levels, the risk of aggravating the geographical concentration both of economic activities and development gains, the considerable autonomy with which powerful international consortia controlling not only traditional export activities but also a large proportion of the modern manufacturing sector have hitherto operated in the region, the differences in national policies governing the exploration of natural resources, particularly oil, the ineffectiveness of the nation-states in controlling and orientating economic processes and many other no less important factors.

In short, the problem is much less the creation of a unified economic framework by means of a progressive mobility of goods and factors of production—which would be feasible only if the national economies had attained a far greater degree of homogeneity in their internal structures and were at approximately the same level of development—than the reorientation of development on the national plane towards a growing integration of the national economies into a coherent whole. Customs unions and free trade areas are a belated outcome of *laissez-faire* ideology, whereas the type of integration that could benefit the Latin American countries presupposes a considerable advance in planning at national level. The most important decision centres, those that are of a political nature and able to interpret the aspirations of collective groups, will continue to exist on the national plane for a long time to come. It is to be hoped, however, that economic 'integration' so-called, at present no more than a development policy instrument of the national governments, will set in motion an evolutionary process involving the political structures, a development corresponding to the urgent changes called for in international relations. The need for a more realistic definition of their relations with the great power blocs of the present-day world, particularly with the United States, has led Latin Americans to attach greater value to what they have in common and to move towards the framing of a regional project that will condition socio-political evolution on the national plane in an increasingly perceptible form. To overcome the natural misgivings of countries with a long history of external dependence, this evolution will require a clear definition of development objectives at national level. On the basis of these national objectives, it will be possible to define those sectors of activity in which there would be undeniable integration benefits from economies of scale, advantages of location or conglomeration phenomena of various orders, that could be shared among all the parties concerned. It is therefore likely that until economic planning becomes an effective policy instrument at national level, the so-called 'integration' movement will continue to make slow progress and disappointments in this field will be frequent.[1]

[1] A vigorous defence of the integration thesis can be found in the proposals to Latin American presidents put forward, in response to a letter from President Frei of Chile, by four directors of international agencies operating in the region: José Antonio Mayobre (ECLA), Felipe Herrera (IDB), Carlos Sanz de Santamaría (Alliance for Progress) and Raúl Prebisch (Latin American Institute for Economic and Social Planning). This document is included in ECLA, *Hacia la Integración Acelerada de América Latina*. For a different approach to the problem see C. Furtado, *Um Projeto para o Brasil*.

VIII. STRUCTURAL RECONSTRUCTION POLICIES

CHAPTER 22

ECONOMIC PLANNING EXPERIMENTS

METHODOLOGICAL BASIS

External vulnerability, a reflexion of fluctuations in the prices of primary commodities on the world market, led several Latin American governments to assume growing responsibilities on the economic plane even before the 1929 crisis. We have seen how the need to regulate coffee supplies obliged the Brazilian government to undertake heavy financial commitments, with far-reaching repercussions on the monetary and fiscal planes, and how these commitments took the form of a compensatory policy in the 1930s, with profound consequences for the subsequent evolution of the national economy. We have also drawn attention to the complex exchange controls practised by Argentina during the decade of the Great Depression in order to cushion the domestic impact of external instability. We have likewise pointed out the positive form taken by the Chilean reaction during the same period: a greater appropriation of resources generated by the export sector (controlled by foreign groups) and their allocation to strategic sectors, through a state agency specifically established for this purpose with a view to diversifying productive structures.

By and large, the period extending from the end of the 1929 crisis to the end of World War Two is characterised by a development geared to the national domestic markets which Prebisch would call 'development inwards' as opposed to the 'development outwards' of the preceding period, based on growing participation in the international system of division of labour. After a time, this new development pattern raised the immediate problem of remodelling and broadening infrastructures. Not only was it necessary, in most cases, to rebuild existing transport systems on a completely different basis, but there was also an urgent need to increase the available supply of electric energy. These needs arose at a time when traditional forms of international financial co-operation had practically disappeared. In some countries, such as Argentina and Brazil, governments had to buy foreign-owned railroads and other infrastructural installations which had in many cases been rendered obsolete by the failure to replace outworn equipment after 1929 and by the very reorientation of development.

The need to rebuild and broaden economic infrastructures and the determination to exercise some control over the external sector prompted the first economic programming experiments in the immediate post-war period. These were essentially public works programmes and financing schemes in the transport and electric energy sectors. Domestic financing was obtained, as a rule, by means of taxes on liquid fuel consumption and surcharges on electric energy tariffs. Since the investments to be undertaken required a substantial margin of foreign exchange cover, particularly in the case of the energy sector, the problem of their medium-term impact on the balance of payments had to be met. Assessment of this impact called for a projection of the capacity to import and of the margin available to meet service payments on the new financial commitments involved. At the same time the new credit agencies, primarily the World Bank, began to insist on such projective analyses, which generally highlighted the severe limitations on the development prospects of the countries in the region imposed by the capacity to import. Theoretical consideration of the latter problem made it possible to gain a clearer insight into the nature of the development process taking place in the region, and particularly of the role played by import substitution.

From 1949 onwards, ECLA's overall surveys of regional development laid the groundwork for a better understanding of the nature of external dependence, which was reflected in the long-term deterioration in the terms of trade and of the specific characteristics of industrialisation based on import substitution. As a result of these analyses it was no longer possible to accept a working hypothesis based on the possibility of reverting to a situation in which exports of primary products would act as the main driving force in regional development. On the other hand, it became obvious that any attempt to increase the volume of investments would have adverse effects on the balance of payments since capital formation had a high import content and the consumer goods for which demand was most elastic to rises in income were generally imported. If development called for a curtailment of the import coefficient, it had to be taken into account that this could not be spontaneously achieved in an orderly way. Hence, the regulation of import substitution clearly required a prospective analysis of the overall development process.

Economic Planning Experiments

ECLA's ideas on economic programming consequently sprang from a concern to regulate the import-substitution process, which had been the basis of industrialisation and development in the region's largest countries since the external sector crisis.[1] This constituted an entirely new approach in the evolution of ideas on economic planning, since it differed not only from socialist planning—an outcome of the determination to change the overall economic structure and the need to co-ordinate investment decisions in a system involving greatly diminished consumer freedom—but also from planning in Western Europe, for which the starting point was the concern to co-ordinate sectoral programmes or to achieve conditions of full employment for labour.

The methodology worked out by ECLA and later widely adopted in the region is based on a diagnosis of the national economy in question and on a set of macroeconomic projections established essentially on the basis of hypotheses concerning the evolution of the capital output ratio. Recognising that, given its relative *scarcity*, capital is the strategic factor in the development of the region's economies, an attempt is made to measure its productivity in the national economy as a whole and in the different sectors of productive activity.[2] On the basis of the capital-output data and the analysis of inter-industrial relationships, a system of projections can be worked out that makes it possible to forecast the structural inadequacy of the capacity to import, the rate of private domestic savings or of fiscal revenue in terms of various hypotheses as to the probable growth of the domestic product, the increase in the demand for exports and probable

[1] The first ECLA study to consider the planning problem explicitly was the essay entitled *Theoretical and Practical Problems of Economic Growth*, presented to the ECLA conference held in May 1951. The last chapter is entitled 'Preliminary discussion on the elements of an economic development programme'. However, this study does not touch on the methodological aspects of programming technique. These were expounded in detail in a study presented to the 1953 Conference entitled *An Introduction to the Technique of Programming*. The full version was circulated only in mimeographed form but a condensed version was published in 1955 as the first volume of a series entitled, *Analyses and Projections of Economic Development*. With the establishment of the ECLA-sponsored Latin American Institute for Economic and Social Planning (ILPES) in 1962, a more systematic study of planning and the publication of a number of works reflecting the theoretical orientation discussed above became possible. See ILPES, *Discusiones sobre Planificación*, Mexico, 1966, Gonzalo Martner, *Planificación y Presupuesto por Programas*, Mexico, 1967, Hector Soza Valderrama, *Planificación del Desarrollo Industrial*, Mexico, 1966. The last two works are based on study courses given at the Institute. For an overall assessment of ECLA ideas see the recent study prepared by the Technical Secretariat, *La CEPAL y el Análisis del Desarrollo Latinoamericano*, UN, 1968.

[2] This basic hypothesis does not exclude the recognition that skilled manpower, including trained managerial personnel, is an equally scarce factor. It is held, however, that the improvement of the human factor can be achieved only through investment and is thus also dependent on the availability of capital.

trends in relative export prices as well as in terms of the estimated income elasticities of demand for the major items of consumption. In other words, the technique involves a prospective analysis that makes it possible to define the conditions of internal and external balance, given certain development targets.

DEGREE OF EFFICACY OF THE PROJECTIONS

The analyses carried out on the basis of ECLA's programming techniques made it clear, since the first half of the 1950s, that it was necessary to intensify the industrialisation process in countries such as Brazil and Argentina if their development was to proceed at a reasonable rate. The *Target Programme* carried out in Brazil in the second half of the 1950s was directly inspired by this type of diagnosis.[1] The implementation of this programme enabled Brazil to substantially broaden its industrial system at a time when the export sector was registering adverse trends. The experience also served to expose the serious problems that arise when medium-term programmes are carried out without any effective co-ordination of short-term policies. Aggravation of inflationary pressures and a sizeable external debt were the counterparts of the considerable success achieved in meeting the physical targets set for the industrial sector.

In 1961, through the Charter of Punta del Este,[2] Latin American governments recognised that planning was the fundamental instrument for carrying out the development policy to be pursued in the region. Most countries in the region were experiencing serious balance of payments difficulties at the time, and the mobilisation of external resources was becoming increasingly difficult. Planning was regarded as a means of regulating government action and of giving concrete expression to the need for certain reforms, particularly of the tax system, considered essential to development in view of the growing responsibilities assumed by governments. The plans prepared since then consist of a general diagnosis, a relatively detailed prospective study of the external sector, a set of

---

1 In working out the *Target Programme*, extensive use was made of preliminary studies carried out by an ECLA mission working with the Brazilian National Development Bank, published in 1955 under the title, *Análise e Projeções da Economia Brasileira* and later issued as volume II of the ECLA series, *Analyses and Projections of Economic Development*.

2 At the Punta del Este conference, which launched the Alliance for Progress—a policy conceived by President Kennedy with a view to creating a climate of better understanding and more effective co-operation between the United States and the Latin American countries—the countries of the region formally declared that within a period of eighteen months they would undertake planned economic policies covering some basic reforms, including tax and agrarian reforms.

Economic Planning Experiments

TABLE 22.1. *Target (Development Plan) Rates and Actual Rates of Growth in Selected Countries* (*percentages of annual growth rates*)

	GDP	agri-culture	industry	imports	invest-ment	exports
Colombia						
plan (1959–64)	5·7	4·1	8·6	7·2	12·9	4·2
actual rates (1959–64)	4·7	2·2	6·1	10·3	5·4	2·3
Chile						
plan (1960–5)	4·8	3·7	5·0	6·6	12·0	5·5
actual rates (1960–5)	4·1	2·0	6·2	7·0	10·1	4·6
Mexico						
plan (1962–5)	5·4	4·5	6·9	8·8	8·6	4·8
actual rates (1962–5)	7·3	4·4	10·1	9·3	12·4	5·4
Venezuela						
plan (1963–6)	7·6	7·9	12·0	2·2	—	4·6
actual rates (1963–6)	6·0	6·9	9·0	1·7	8·8	1·7

SOURCE: ECLA, *Economic Bulletin for Latin America, October 1967.*

projections in the form of overall and sectoral targets, a vague statement of the particular social policy goals and an assessment, generally none too precise, of the structural changes required if the targets are to be achieved without causing undue economic imbalances and social tensions. However, the plans establish detailed requirements at the operational level only with regard to public investment schemes and the need to mobilise external resources. In these two sectors there has been a remarkable advance in the formulation of government policies. In the case of public investment, for instance, not only has it been possible to ensure greater compatibility with regard to longer-term objectives, but considerable progress has been made in the techniques of preparing individual projects and controlling financial flows at the implementation stage. From the data given in Table 22.1, the targets established in a number of plans can be compared with the actual economic trends in the countries concerned.

With the exception of Mexico, in the countries included in Table 22.1 exports failed to grow at the target rate established by the planners. Similarly—and Mexico is again the exception—agricultural output grew less than forecast; generally speaking, these two sectors act as independent variables and planners confine themselves to *forecasting* their probable behaviour. In the case of exports, this is because of the uncertainty governing world trade in primary products, particularly when a country is dependent on exports of a few primary commodities, and in the case of the agricultural sector it is because of the rigidity characterising agricultural production in the region which makes it insensitive to the policy instruments used by Latin American governments. In Colombia and Chile, total investment was lower than envisaged, whereas imports expanded more than planners had considered desirable.

Even a cursory examination of the data shows that planning possibilities are greatest when export earnings are most stable and hence easier to forecast. This is the present situation of Mexico, largely as the result of the growth of tourism and the diversity of Mexican exports. In the case of Venezuela, the relative stability of petroleum prices meant that the flow of income and the capacity to import generated by the petroleum sector were relatively easy to forecast. The failure to meet planning targets seems to indicate a lack of sufficient data on the policy of the oil companies. In most countries of the region, however, only a substantial progress in organisation of world markets would make it possible to establish reasonable projections for the export sector. In the absence of such projections or of adequate international arrangements for compensatory financing, planning possibilities, in the framework of the techniques currently employed, will be seriously limited. These limitations will be added to those imposed by the rigidity of the agricultural sector.

The planning experience of the last three five-year periods has tested the capacity of the region's governments as agents for regulating economic processes and promoting development. Noteworthy progress has been made in the rationalisation of public investment, both through the systematic introduction of medium- and long-term projects and through the use of budget programmes. There has also been definite progress in orientation of private industrial investment. The establishment of development banks or similar institutions and the enactment of complex legislation creating development incentives have provided governments with the means of influencing private investment decisions or bridging the investment gap, at least in the case of sectors considered strategic for the attainment of the targets established in the plans. None the less, progress in the direction of really effective planning has been much slower, despite such initial successes as the Brazilian Target Programme and the more rational allocation of public investment in various countries. This slow progress is attributable to three main factors: (*a*) short-term fluctuations—the external sector and the difficulties encountered in increasing the capacity to import, (*b*) the extreme rigidity of the agricultural sector, and (*c*) the inelasticity of the public sector's mobilisation of resources. We have already referred to the first of these factors, and the second will be considered in greater detail in the next chapter.

INELASTICITY OF FISCAL SECTOR

As Latin American governments assumed greater responsibility on the economic plane, particularly at the financial level, the inadequacy of existing fiscal systems as instruments for mobilising potential resources became increasingly apparent. The adoption of development plans almost necessarily implies a greater effort in the formation of capital, i.e. a rise in the rate of investment. Since such an increase generally requires a more than proportional growth of investments designed to change the productive structure—which have long maturation periods—greater mobilisation of resources by the State is called for. If the State is not in a position to raise the additional funds needed through the tax system or the domestic capital market it will have to resort to external borrowing, with the consequences previously analysed, or to dubiously effective inflationary expedients. Thus the fiscal system's capacity to provide the State with the resources needed to carry out its new functions became the decisive test of its effectiveness as an agent for promoting planned development. An analysis of the data available for 1960–6 shows that the expenditure of the region's national governments was generally inelastic to the growth of the domestic product. In many cases the reduction of the import-export coefficient and the liberalisation of intra-regional trade caused a fall in fiscal revenues that was not subsequently offset. In Guatemala, which can be regarded as representative of the Central American Common Market countries, the contribution of various taxes and duties on foreign trade to the country's total fiscal receipts declined from 46 per cent to 32 per cent between 1960 and 1966, reflected in the fact that the rate of growth of tax revenue failed to keep pace with that of the domestic product. The same situation occurred in Venezuela, as a result of the relatively slow growth of the petroleum sector in the period under consideration. Mexico again provides the exception in that public-sector expenditure—excluding State-controlled enterprises—grew at a faster rate than the domestic product. On the other hand, the share of public expenditures that Latin American governments financed out of tax revenue also increased, indicating their failure to raise additional resources in domestic capital markets. In Brazil and Chile public-sector expenditure barely kept

TABLE 22.2. *Elasticity of Public (Central Government) Expenditure, and the Tax Structure in Selected Countries*

	Argentina		Brazil		Chile		Guatemala		Mexico		Venezuela	
A. increase in public expenditure increase in GDP (1960–6)	1·015		1·008		1·042		1·540		1·273		1·417	
B. tax revenue as % of public expenditure												
1960–2	84·4		68·1		76·9		67·7		70·0		84·0	
1964–6	73·3		83·5		82·8		74·4		76·5		97·6	
C. tax structure (all countries)	1960	1966	1960	1966	1960	1966	1960	1966	1960	1966	1960	1966
% direct taxes	25	26	34	29	23	27	11	14	38	47	10	14
% indirect taxes	38	49	54	62	43	40	43	54	35	37	8	9
% external taxes	37	25	12	9	34	33	46	32	27	16	82	77

SOURCE: ECLA, *Economic Survey of Latin America, 1967*.

pace with the growth of the domestic product but an increasing share was financed out of tax revenue. In Argentina, public expenditure grew at a rate commensurate with the growth of the product, although a smaller share was financed from taxes, indicating the inelasticity of the fiscal system.

An analysis of the region's tax structure shows that revenue from foreign trade is declining. However, it is still of vital importance and will remain so for a long time to come in countries where exports of mineral products are controlled by foreign enterprises. In Brazil and Argentina the proportion of tax revenue accounted for by indirect taxation is twice that represented by direct taxes, and in both cases the tax system has become increasingly regressive in the course of the present decade. In Mexico, indirect taxes already represented a far smaller proportion of public revenue than direct taxes in 1960, and the fiscal system has become increasingly progressive.

CHAPTER 23

AGRARIAN REFORMS

ROOTS OF THE AGRARIAN MOVEMENTS

In spite of their modest aims, the economic planning experiments carried out in the Latin American countries served to pinpoint the major obstacles hampering the region's development. By establishing targets and identifying the agents on whose decisions their attainment depended, the development planners initiated discussion of the motives guiding these agents and the means that would have to be mobilised in order to intervene in the behaviour of the policy-makers. It soon became apparent that projecting the expansion of an economic system simply by means of extrapolating rates of growth was limited in scope, and that planning based on the traditional behaviour patterns of the agents involved could not guarantee the attainment of even modest targets. What was needed was a study in depth of the structural elements delimiting the range of options open to the decision-making agents so that the factors hindering the development process could be properly identified. Thus the framework of analysis was imperceptibly broadened as the relevant agents were gradually more clearly identified and observed in their own context. Greater knowledge of the real structures was gradually built up and in many cases this involved going beyond the conventional framework of economic analysis.

The structuralist approach to the development process tended to stress the importance of agrarian problems which, until quite recently, had earned scant attention from economists whose interest had been focused on the study of industrialisation. On the basis of the classical European experience, it had been implicitly held that the expansion of the industrial sector would act as the dynamic pole for bringing about changes in the traditional structures. But as obstacles to industrialisation mounted and the industrialisation process proved itself less effective than expected as a factor for inducing structural change, a completely new approach began to emerge. Field studies of the present-day agrarian structures, such as those mentioned in chapter 7, were carried out in several countries and at the same time there was a more systematic analysis of the historical evolution of the land system and of recent changes in agrarian structure. Land reform, the cornerstone of any attempt to bring about economic and social structural change in the region, began to be seriously studied. As a result of these investigations, there was a clearer understanding of the relationship between production systems and socio-political organisation.

The basic unit of the present-day organisation of agricultural production in Latin America is the large landed estate: the *hacienda*, in the strict sense,[1] originally devoted to stock farming or agricultural production for local consumption, or the *plantation*, originally devoted to production for export. As we have already seen, the large estate reflected a decentralisation of the power system. The estate owner was in a position to organise his labour force in a production system capable of yielding a surplus for local use or for export. The *hacienda* was not, however, established in a vacuum. In the most important regions of Spanish America—Mexico and the Andean Highlands—there was a dense indigenous population, living in static communities and with a social organisation closely bound up with the communal use of land. In their attempt to preserve their identity, these *communities* clung to traditional forms of land use. During the colonial period the Spaniards, being limited in numbers, preferred to dominate the communities and extract from them a surplus in the form of crops or labour rather than to break them up. This, at any rate, was the orientation assumed by Spanish legislation and the action of the Religious Orders. In regions where there was a less dense population or where social structures were less bound up with the pattern of land utilisation, the communities tended to disappear and their surviving members were either absorbed by the *haciendas*, or began to live in isolation on the outskirts of the estates or of the administrative centres established by civil or religious metropolitan authorities.

In regions where agriculture was geared to the export market from the very beginning, the *hacienda* took the form of a commercial enterprise, frequently employing slave labour imported from Africa, as in the case of Brazil and most of the Caribbean region. Given its greater capital requirements and its dependence on unstable foreign markets, the agricultural enterprise underwent prolonged periods of crisis and in some cases disintegrated into a number of small productive units devoted primarily to subsistence activities. In any event, wherever agricultural enterprises or plantations were set up, isolated farmers or smallholders moved in, either

---

[1] The term *hacienda* (or *fazenda* in Brazil) was originally applied to properties devoted to stock farming. In Brazil, *fazenda* tended to become widely used in a more general sense. In the Spanish-speaking countries, several terms are used to designate the large estate. The term 'plantation', in the sense of a large agricultural estate, is not used in Latin America. The terms *hacienda*, *latifundio* or *large estate* will here be used to refer generally to any large agricultural property with the dual connotation of a production unit and a type of social organisation.

because the highly specialised commercial enterprise created a local market for farm products or was not in a position to absorb the natural increase in the free labour force it employed, or because in times of financial difficulty it laid off some of the labour it had attracted. Thus the smallholder—the starting-point for the future mass of *minifundistas*—had two different origins in the region: on the one hand there was the element composed of former members of indigenous communities that had broken up, who began to cultivate tiny individual plots of land for their own subsistence needs while at the same time spending the better part of the day working on the large estate; on the other, there was the element indirectly created by large-scale commercial agriculture both in its phase of expansion and in the periods of disintegration. In regions where land was abundant, these small farmers often performed a pioneering role, clearing new lands for farming and introducing commercial crops. However, given their rudimentary farming techniques, where land was scarce or controlled by the large estates, the population increase forced them to subdivide the land, leading to the achievement of a Malthusian balance between population and soil resources.

In sum, it can be said that although the *hacienda* was the basic element of the region's agricultural organisation, it nowhere existed entirely on its own. Roughly speaking, the different areas of the region can be divided into three broad groups: areas in which the large estate existed side by side mainly with the community, areas in which it co-existed mainly with the small production unit and areas in which it had virtually disappeared. The latter case is exceptional and occurred only in Haiti where the struggle for political independence took the form of a revolt against slavery. Here the elimination of slavery put an end to the system of agricultural organisation based on the large plantation, and the smallholding became practically the only form of organising production. The areas where the dominant pattern became *hacienda*–community were those in which there had been a relatively dense indigenous population and the Spaniards and *assimilados* had remained a small minority. Lastly, the large estate–small production unit pattern generally prevailed in areas where land was relatively abundant and where agriculture had been largely commercial in nature from the very beginning.

It was in the regions where the *hacienda*–community pattern prevailed that mounting agrarian unrest gave rise to the land reform movements that became a major landmark in Latin American social evolution in the present century. The coexistence of *hacienda* and community took a number of forms. At one extreme we find the isolated estate, providing employment opportunities for some of the community's members but interfering hardly at all with community balance. At the other extreme we find estates that *occupy* several communities and come to exercise strict control over all their activities. It is in the evolution of these relationships between estate and community that we can trace the roots of the major social tensions that were to trigger off the agrarian revolutions of Mexico and Bolivia.

AGRARIAN REFORM IN MEXICO

In Mexico, relations between estate and community were influenced by the Reform movement of the mid-nineteenth century and by the intensification of development that took place in the last quarter of that same century. With the spread of the *hacienda* system in the country's central region, community lands had been appropriated and the communities confined to the poorer-quality lands. Dispossession and confinement drove the community to further close its ranks and sharpened its hostility to the constituted power exercised through the *hacienda*. Convinced that progress presupposed the full enforcement of a private-property system and that the Mexican Indian would only be *free* when the archaic institutions that kept him in a fossilised state had been destroyed, the 'Científicos' of the Porfirio Díaz period encouraged the shift of large areas of public domain that had been used by the communities into private hands. Many of the land concessions granted at the time were taken up by foreigners, who frequently started irrigation projects and introduced new farming techniques, heightening the contrast between their prosperity and the extreme poverty of the communities confined to the poorest lands. This situation sparked off a number of uprisings which led many landowners, backed by the central power, to institute local reigns of terror. Two underlying factors set the stage for the Mexican agrarian revolution: the existence of the community, with its bonds of solidarity strengthened by the circumstances outlined above, and the vigorous expansion of commercial agriculture, which had led to the expulsion of communities from most of the better lands available. If powerful community bonds had not existed, part of the displaced population would probably have emigrated to other regions, particularly to the south where new lands were still being brought under cultivation by means of rudimentary techniques.[1]

The Mexican Revolution, which started in 1911, paved the way for the

[1] On this point see Henri Enjalbert, 'Réforme Agraire et Production Agricole au Mexique (1910–1965)' in *Les Problèmes Agraires des Amériques Latines*.

communities to recover a large proportion of the lands that had been taken from them. Thus the initial uprising developed into a spontaneous and irreversible social movement, that radically altered the course of a political revolt whose urban leaders had essentially envisaged the establishment of a democracy inspired by liberal ideas. By incorporating the principles that had fired the agrarian leaders, the 1917 Constitution laid the foundations for the country's social evolution up to the present day. When the revolutionary process started there were some eight or nine thousand large estates in Mexico, controlling virtually all the good land in the country. Alongside these estates, four or five thousand communities were eking out a living on poor quality and frequently tiny plots of land. The *hacienda* system was spreading both in the southern part of the country and in the north, while in the central region it had already taken over all the best land. In 1910, the Mexican agrarian structure provided an extreme instance of concentrated land ownership: 1 per cent of the population owned 97 per cent of the land while 96 per cent of the population owned a mere 1 per cent.[1]

The three decades preceding the Revolution were a period of expansion for the *hacienda*, which seemed to be an institution capable of bringing new areas under cultivation, of introducing new crops, of assimilating technology and of investing in capital improvements. However, it was not in a position to provide enough employment to enable the rural masses to live in conditions at least resembling those they had known before they were dispossessed of their land. Thus the root of the problem was of a social nature. The Mexican land reform was essentially designed to solve this social problem. Hence the introduction of the *ejido* system, stipulating that a peasant must be a member of a community to have access to the land. The government gives the community a collective property, the *ejido*, which is divided among the members of the community for their personal use. By law, individual parcels of *ejido* land cannot be sold or rented. In this way the land is tied to the community, which means that the peasants are socially organised in terms of the use of the land. Consequently, the disappearance of the *hacienda* as the basis of the power system did not signify the disorganisation of the peasant masses. The *ejido* was organised as a social and political entity which enabled the new power system established in the country to maintain contact with the bulk of the peasant masses.[2]

---

[1] Cf. Rodolfo Stavenhagen, 'Aspectos Sociales de la Estrutura Agrária en México' in *Les Problèmes Agraires des Amériques Latines.*

[2] An overall survey of the Mexican agrarian reform process and a description of its institutions is found in Moises T. de la Pena, *Mito y Realidad de la Reforma Agrária en México*, Mexico, 1964.

Agrarian Reforms

Mexican agrarian reform was a complex social process that unfolded over several decades. The repossession of land by the communities entailed, in the central area in particular, the break-up of the large estates. Since these were in most cases integrated units whose resources of crop lands, pastures, woodland and water were complementary, enabling them to attain a certain level of productivity and profitability, the redistribution of their lands among the communities using rudimentary techniques to cultivate small individual plots inevitably entailed a drop in productivity and an even sharper reduction in the surpluses formerly available to the urban populations. It was natural, therefore, that this should provoke several types of reaction. Consequently, in the period extending from 1920 to 1935, agrarian reform made slow progress and in large areas the programme made virtually no impression. On the other hand, it was soon realised that the agrarian reform would only achieve its objectives if it succeeded, at the same time, in bringing new land under the plough and increasing the irrigated areas. In 1926 a government commission—which later became a ministry—was appointed to study and carry out major irrigation projects. At the same time an attempt was made to siphon off some of the pressure exerted by land-hungry peasants, by promoting the settlement of certain regions in the north which, although semi-arid, could support seasonal crops. The large cattle estates could cede some of their land without affecting their profitability, in exchange for a guarantee of survival. Furthermore, the new agrarian legislation allowed *haciendados* to keep the nucleus of their estates with some 200 to 300 hectares of land, or 100 hectares in the case of irrigated farmland. This small private property, or so-called 'small estate', with access to abundant credit facilities rapidly became the cornerstone of the country's agriculture.

The Lázaro Cárdenas government initiated a new and decisive stage in the agrarian reform process. Between 1934 and 1940, 17·6 million hectares of land were transformed into *ejidos* and distributed among the peasants, whereas between 1911 and 1934 only 10 million hectares had been redistributed. The intensification of the process revealed a number of weak points in the new agricultural system that had been created in the country. The *ejidos* were generally too small, which meant that *ejidatarios* soon became *microfundists*. Since land reform was carried out in response to the demands of populations living within a 7-kilometre radius of the estate that was to be expropriated, claimants were frequently far too numerous to be accommodated on the available land. The situation was aggravated by the repatriation of large numbers of *braceros*, who had been forced to return to Mexico by the economic crisis in the United States. Under the three governments following the Cárdenas administration, i.e. up to 1958, agrarian reform came to a virtual standstill. During this period, substantial investments were made to extend the crop lands in the large irrigated areas of the north. Half the new land brought under cultivation was distributed in the form of the *ejidos*, and the other half was sold as private property in parcels averaging 30–60 hectares and in some cases as much as 100 hectares. The *ejidatarios* received plots averaging 4–6 hectares. These arrangements were severely criticised by the advocates of land reform and there was a change of direction under the presidency of López Mateos (1958–64) with a policy aiming to reserve all land brought under irrigation for crop farming through the investment of public funds for the creation of new *ejidos*.

An overall assessment of the Mexican agrarian reform yields the following conclusions. Its social objective, which was to do away with the autocratic control exercised over the communities by the large estates and to give access to the land to the greatest possible number of people, has been essentially achieved. The *ejido* system has proved an effective means of employing, and hence keeping on the land, a structural population surplus that would otherwise have failed to find jobs either in agriculture or in the urban areas. The fact that this population surplus remained on the land meant a drop in the productivity of labour as compared with the levels formerly attained on the estates, but it also meant that a large proportion of the product remained in the hands of the working population. In certain regions there was a decline not only in the productivity of labour but also in the productivity of natural resources, with a fall in overall output. On the other hand, the estate had been the capitalisation mechanism and its disappearance could have entailed a reduction in the formation of capital in the agricultural sector. This was avoided because in most cases the *haciendas* were whittled down to medium-sized estates (up to 300 hectares), which benefited from substantial public and private credit. The conversion to medium estates permitted the emergence of a type of agricultural enterprise geared to the full utilisation of its land resources, a considerable advance on the pattern of land use of the traditional estate, on which under-utilisation of the land factor was generally prevalent. The *ejido* system has been the subject of much controversy, in part because it has been considered almost exclusively from the social angle by some and from the economic angle by others. Even if we disregard possible distortions—plots of land too small to employ two people, disguised rent, etc.—it must be recognised that the *ejido* has a number of limitations.[1] It is certainly not a system of private property. But then, neither is it a system of collective ownership. The process of capital formation on the *ejido* is thus seriously curtailed. Furthermore, since it cannot be expanded, it is unable to absorb the increase in population. In fact, the additional population tends to remain on the *ejidos* so as not to lose its statutory rights and as a consequence families of more than twenty individuals are often crowded on to a small plot of land. The latter problem is a reflexion of the situation in the economic system as a whole, which has shown itself unable to create enough employment to absorb the increase in population. In this case, the *ejido* acts as a mechanism for cushioning the social impact of the economic problem, the solution of which does not depend on the *ejiditario*.[2] On the other hand, if the *ejido* is to be in a position to increase capital formation, it must raise the standards of farming techniques, which in most cases presupposes a restructuring involving a reduction in the number of associates or an increase in the area of available land. The basic problem is thus the land–man relationship. Experience in the new irrigated areas, with *ejidos* divided into plots averaging as much as 20 hectares, shows that the other problems can be solved.

The controversy aroused by the implementation of the Mexican agrarian reform programme since the 1920s, and the understandable fears, exaggerated and exploited by its critics, that it would paralyse capital formation in agriculture and force the urban population to depend on imports of food—which in fact did happen during the 1930s—made the agrarian problem the central issue for the Mexican government. Irrigation works and other infrastructural projects for agriculture were given top priority. A network of banks was created to meet the agricultural credit requirements of both the *ejido* and private sectors. The Mexican government thus assumed full responsibility for capital investment in the agricultural sector. It is true however that capital was more readily available for the private sector, a circumstance indicating its remarkable capacity to adapt itself to the new conditions created by agrarian reform. Thus—and from a strictly economic point of view—it can be said that the Mexican agrarian reform achieved no small success, since it is difficult to conceive the rapid expansion of production in the private sector without the substantial investment provided by the government. In fact, both public investment and the creation of a strong private sector made up of

[1] On this point see the summing up in Ramón Fernandez y Fernandez, 'La Reforma Agrária Mexicana: una Gran Experiencia' in *Les Problèmes Agraires des Amériques Latines*.
[2] For an assessment of the role of the *ejido* in the social evolution of Mexico during the last half-century see François Chevalier, 'The *Ejido* and Political Stability in Mexico' in Claudio Veliz (ed.), *The Politics of Conformity in Latin America*, London, 1967.

medium-sized units are a counterpart to the introduction of the *ejido* system and a direct outcome of agrarian reform.

It is also worth mentioning the effects of land reform on the functioning of the Mexican State. The traditional estate, as an instrument for controlling the rural population, was the cornerstone of the power system on which the State was based. The possibility of carrying out a far-reaching industrialisation policy was for a long time challenged by the rural interests, who feared a rise in the prices of manufactured imports. With the elimination of this pressure group, the Mexican State was free to pursue an industrialisation policy, which has now been carried out without hindrance since the 1920s. And when Cárdenas reformed the party controlling the country's political life to create a solid peasant-based organisation, the rural sector became a factor for stabilising the political system, since it could be mobilised by the State political machine.

According to the figures given in the latest census, there were around 20,000 *ejidos* in Mexico in 1960 with approximately 1·5 million active associates, representing a quarter of the country's agricultural labour force. Slightly over one-fifth of this labour force (22 per cent) consisted of property owners of whom two-thirds were smallholders owning plots of up to 5 hectares. The remaining 33 per cent were landless agricultural labourers. Between 1950 and 1960, the relative proportion of both *ejidatarios* and smallholders declined while that of owners of medium-sized and large properties and of wage-earners in particular, increased, rising from 46 per cent to 53 per cent.[1] This position may, however, be changed, in view of the large-scale redistribution of lands to *ejidatarios* undertaken during the López Mateos administration. Although there is still a sizeable manpower surplus in Mexican agriculture, its capacity to raise technical standards and to increase and diversify output constitutes a unique case in Latin America, a phenomenon difficult to explain without the agrarian reform.

AGRARIAN REFORM IN BOLIVIA

Bolivia made the second major attempt experienced in Latin America in the present century to bring about a change in social structures. It differed from the Mexican attempt in several respects although the starting-point for both was the same: conflict between community and estate. However, in contrast to the situation that existed in the days of Porfirio Díaz in Mexico, agriculture in Bolivia was not expanding on the eve of the revolution that set the stage for agrarian reform in 1952. As we have seen,

[1] Cf. Rodolfo Stavenhagen, 'Aspectos Sociales de la Estructura Agrária en México'.

in pre-revolutionary Mexico the *hacienda* was on the increase and had proved an adequate instrument for promoting capital formation and extending the country's agricultural frontier. The situation in Bolivia was entirely different, reflecting the greater lack of development in the country's economy as a whole. The *indigenous community*, which had maintained its close attachment to the traditional *ayllu*, was in 1952, as indeed right up to the present day, still of considerable importance in the Bolivian social structure.[1] According to the 1950 census figures there were around 3,779 indigenous communities in the country, with a total population of about one million. Even if these figures are challenged, there can be little doubt that this traditional form of social organisation is the predominant pattern in Bolivia. These communities have evolved, and individual cultivation of the land has largely replaced the once prevalent system of farming communal plots. The large estate had penetrated less than in other Latin American countries and had also acquired certain features that distinguished it from those characterising the Mexican situation on the eve of the revolution. It has been estimated that in 1950 there were around 5,000 *haciendas* in the country, on which some 200,000 indigenous families lived and worked. In that same year, there were not more than 50,000 small-holders, which indicates the secondary role of this type of farm organisation in the Bolivian context.

Generally speaking, the Bolivian *hacienda* was less an enterprise designed to take over community lands for its own use than a semi-feudal type of system designed to appropriate part of the community's production directly. It incorporated one or several 'captive' Indian communities, which maintained their traditional social institutions. The community was thus preserved as a framework for social organisation with its own traditional authorities, but its relations with the land were altered. Part of the land was divided into plots and assigned to individual families, while the part that had been communally owned, or its equivalent, was worked directly for the *hacienda*. The worker divided his time between his own plot of land and the estate lands, the latter taking up between three and five days of work a week, as in the *corvée* system of medieval Europe. The indigenous community, strictly controlled by the large estate, was entirely cut off from the outside world; internal monetary flows were reduced to a minimum and artisan activities to meet community requirements were encouraged. All economic and political contacts with the outside world were made through the *hacienda*. However, the most significant feature

[1] See the study by Arturo Urquidi Morales, 'Las Comunidades Indígenas y su Perspectiva Histórica'.

was the change in the relationship with the land. As we have seen, this relationship was inseparable from the community form of organisation. Since *free communities* existed side by side with 'captive' communities, the situation of the latter was considered a form of social degradation regardless of the material living conditions prevailing in each. Open conflict between *hacienda* and community, which flared up when some of the community's members were expelled from their land by estate owners with 'progressive' inclinations, was the exception, although such cases came to be increasingly important in the agrarian reform process, since the expelled *comuneros* went to the cities, where their awakened political consciousness was sharpened by the knowledge of the exploitation they had suffered at the hands of the estate owners. Thus it was not the exploited community, deprived of their best lands, that rose in revolt but individuals who had been drawn into the process of urban life. When the time came for a redistribution of land, these former *comuneros* frequently clashed with those who had remained on the *hacienda*.

The aim of the Bolivian agrarian reform was to do away with the exploitation of the community by the *hacienda*. This was attempted by breaking up the *hacienda* in areas where it had essentially been an instrument for exploiting the indigenous population, in other words, where it could be classified as a *latifundio*. In areas where the *hacienda* was classified as a medium property or *agricultural enterprise*, expropriation was restricted to lands exceeding the limits established by the law. These limits were variable and were determined in accordance with the nature of the agricultural activity. The immediate result of reform was the creation of smallholdings, nearly always *minifundios*, from the plots of land on the *hacienda* which had been cultivated by individual indigenous families for their own subsistence needs. The lands formerly cultivated for the estate were retained as communal property. The aim was not only to *free* the community but to maintain it as a framework for social organisation. Its members became smallholders but were still bound together by the tie of collective ownership of part of the redistributed lands.[1]

Agrarian reform was carried out largely under the direction of *rural syndicates*, which had been organised, with urban political support, on the large estates. The MNR (Movimiento Nacionalista Revolucionário), responsible for carrying out the 1952 revolution, was a strictly urban-based political movement with a strong following among the miners. However,

[1] For an overall analysis of the Bolivian agrarian reform see Henri Gumbau, 'Les Changements de Structure à la Suite de la Réforme Bolivienne' in *Les Problèmes Agraires des Amériques Latines*.

by destroying the traditional power structure, it removed the support for the system of oppression exercised by the large estates. Moreover, by bringing the spontaneous freedom movement of the communities into the revolutionary process, the MNR gave a far greater depth to the process than it would otherwise have achieved in a country where 80 per cent of the population lived on the land. A decade after the agrarian reform started, the government had granted about 200,000 titles in the Altiplano region, which meant that nearly all the families living on the former estates had become independent farmers.

Just as in Mexico the idea of organising labour along collective lines on the *ejidos* had proved difficult to put into practice, so in Bolivia the aim of retaining part of the estate lands for collective farming has gradually been dropped. In the first place, to prevent individual plots from being too small, the communal lands have in many cases been reduced to very little. It should not be forgotten that on the former *haciendas*, these lands did not always justify commercial organisation since the property was organised as a mechanism for exploiting the indigenous community rather than as a commercial agricultural enterprise. Barring fairly substantial investment, the only way to improve the community's living conditions was to allow it to keep its produce. In Mexico, as we have seen, the break-up of the large estate often meant a less efficient utilisation of natural resources. This was not the case in Bolivia, where the communities were already living on the estates and continued to practise the same rudimentary farming techniques. The drop in the agricultural surplus available for the urban populations was inevitable in view of the improved standards of consumption of the rural masses living on the estates. Agrarian reform thus had a dual consequence: it altered the income distribution pattern in favour of the rural masses and it enabled the communities, formerly 'imprisoned' by the large estates, to recover their independence on the social plane. They were drawn into the political life of the country through the peasant syndicates. The number of rural schools (which had been prohibited on the large estates) built and run by the communities themselves are an indication that their contact with the outside world is beginning to bear fruit. The elimination of the authoritarian control exercised over the communities by the *haciendas*, the new status of *comuneros* as smallholders and their contacts with the outside world, created conditions for increased mobility of the Altiplano population. This is a really significant development since Bolivia has abundant land and an extremely scattered population pattern. Both the indigenous community itself and the semi-feudal system established by the *haciendas* had traditionally helped to preserve the ancient pattern of settlement, concentrated in the Altiplano. Agrarian reform, by highlighting the problem of agricultural shortages in the urban areas, created a growing awareness of the need to open up new lands, which presupposes a greater population mobility than had traditionally existed in the country. To encourage this mobility, substantial infrastructure investments have been made in recent years. A new road has been built linking Cochabamba with Santa Cruz and several facilities have been provided to encourage the colonisation of virgin land. A new agrarian structure is emerging in the tropical *llanos* (grasslands) of the Yungas area. The new pattern is not yet clear but large consortia organised along co-operative lines and modern capitalist enterprises have been established. The output of cotton, sugar, rice and coffee has expanded steadily in the course of the present decade, enabling the country to diversify its agricultural production.

AGRARIAN REFORM IN AREAS CHARACTERISED BY
THE LATIFUNDIO–MINIFUNDIO PATTERN

In both Mexico and Bolivia agrarian reform was the consequence of the estate–community dualism, which had evolved in different ways in the two countries but had inevitably created mounting social tensions. The agrarian problem had quite different characteristics in countries or regions where the community had been dispersed and the large estate existed side by side with small isolated farmers. This was the situation prevailing in Brazil, Colombia, Chile, Venezuela, Central America (excluding Guatemala) and in nearly all the recently settled areas. Competition between small farmer and large estate meant that the poorest land—whether from the point of view of its soil resources or of its location—was left to the smallholders. As the best land was usually in the hands of the large landowners, the small farmer was faced with the choice of moving to the pioneer zones, in which case he would have to undertake the task of clearing new lands for farming, or dividing what little land he owned among his heirs, who thus found themselves joining the ranks of *minifundio* farmers. On the other hand, since the large estate was the only source of employment, the owner could dictate his terms to the population dependent on it. Thus, when slave workers on the sugar cane plantations of north-eastern Brazil were freed, they accepted a *corvée* system resembling the system which the Spaniards had imposed on the native communities since the seventeenth century. It should be added that in tropical areas it is difficult to continue farming the same family plot, with the rudimentary techniques generally practised, for any length of time. Except in those privileged areas where soils are not subject to constant erosion, the land generally has to be abandoned after two or three years of cultivation, which makes it difficult for the small farmer to consolidate his position. The smallholder thus carries out the task of clearing forest land and opening up new areas to be taken over by the estate, or otherwise lives on a *minifundio* and depends on the estate for employment to complement his subsistence-level income.

In areas where the large estate–*minifundio* pattern predominates, the rural population is totally controlled by the estate, since the so-called municipal authorities[1] are in fact agents of the landowning class. The *minifundio* farmers, who work on the estate as sharecroppers, do not form a real community and they identify themselves through the ties binding them to the landowner. Those living outside the estate are indirectly dependent on it for obtaining credit and for marketing their surpluses. These disorganised and unprotected populations are a breeding-ground for violent movements, labelled by the landowning classes as no more than variant forms of banditry. However, the rural population is in no position to offer any organised resistance against the domination of the estate and still less to present a viable alternative. The absence of any organisation among these rural masses has prevented them from taking part in the movements that have occasionally arisen to challenge the traditional power system in their respective countries. Hence Bolivia, despite its relative backwardness, had more means at its disposal for transforming the agrarian structure than Colombia or Brazil.

The lack of any social organisation that can seriously challenge the power of the landowning classes means that the agrarian structure will begin to arouse genuine concern only when the chronic shortage of agricultural supplies becomes an obstacle to the development of urban activities. It is this type of concern that has largely inspired the agrarian reform movements that have arisen in Latin America during the present decade. Half the countries in the region have already enacted complex land-reform legislation. Of these, Venezuela and Chile deserve closer attention since they have achieved some results in their bid to remodel agrarian structures.

The Venezuelan agrarian reform consists of a government-financed colonisation programme.[2] Agriculture contributes only slightly over 6 per cent

[1] The municipality or 'municipio' is the basic local unit of government, a county-like administrative division comprising several districts.
[2] Cf. William Larralde, 'Primeiros Ensaios de Reforma Agraria em Venezuela' in *Les Problèmes Agraires des Amériques Latines*.

of the country's domestic product and the number of persons it employs has remained stationary over the last decade. However, the smallness of this contribution is an indication of backwardness rather than development, which is evident from the fact that the output per person employed in agriculture is less than one-fifth of the national average. A large proportion of the country's rural population consists of *conuqueros*, or itinerant small farmers with extremely low living standards, whose main function is to clear land of its forest cover in the areas later taken over for extensive stock farming by the large estates. The principal objective of the land-reform programme was to attach these *conuqueros* to the land by providing them with a means of becoming smallholders equipped with enough technical and financial resources to attain an adequate level of productivity. Since the land for these new settlements was acquired under extremely burdensome conditions an attempt was made to overcome this obstacle by settling a large number of families on public land situated in unfavourable areas. This meant that the effectiveness of the public investment being made was considerably reduced and that the settlers were being condemned to a situation entailing distinct handicaps. Between 1960 and 1965, land was given to slightly over 70,000 families and, despite the fact that a large part of the land distributed was publicly owned, the programme cost the government more than 100 million dollars. The target originally envisaged in the programme was the settlement of 350,000 families in ten years.

The Chilean agrarian reform is possibly the only case in Latin America in which social and economic objectives have been explicitly defined from the outset. In Chile, agriculture contributes around 11 per cent of the domestic product and employs about a quarter of the economically active population. The productivity gap, in terms of the national average, is much narrower than in Venezuela. Nevertheless, Chilean agriculture is characterised by a notorious incapacity to raise its technical standards and improve the living conditions of the population it employs. Over the last two decades, Chile has been facing a serious dilemma: whether to wait until the rural population has completely drifted away from the land, which in the long term would force landowners to raise their technical levels, or whether to bring about planned reform of the agrarian structure. The first option would mean a bottleneck in agricultural production that would hamper development and reduce the possibilities of creating new urban employment, thus increasing the likelihood that the population migrating to the cities would suffer a process of social degradation. The second solution would entail a fall in agricultural production over a

Agrarian Reforms

prolonged period unless it were preceded by thorough technical preparation and could be given substantial financial backing. It was thus imperative that the expropriation of land for redistribution should not require too great an initial financial effort. The Chilean agrarian reform was at first delayed by the strong opposition in Congress to the promulgation of the Land Reform Act. On the other hand, the costs of carrying out the programme proved to be much higher than originally envisaged. The target, which was to settle 100,000 families within a period of six years, i.e. by 1972, will be difficult to attain considering that by the end of 1967 only 8,350 families had benefited from the reform. However, the fact that 1,250,000 hectares had already been expropriated by then, indicates that the agents responsible for carrying out the reform have not abandoned its objectives. If Chile attains its land reform targets it will have succeeded in giving smallholder status in a relatively short space of time to a quarter of the country's landless rural families, which in relative terms corresponds to the number of *ejidatarios* in Mexico. These smallholders will have a substantially higher living level than the present landless workers and will form a new sector within the agrarian structure in a position to assimilate new techniques and to respond to a production incentive policy. Lastly, this population, which had been virtually imprisoned on the large estates, is being organised in rural syndicates and is beginning to be effectively drawn into the political life of the country.

Venezuela and Chile are countries in which agricultural and livestock production contribute a relatively small share to the domestic product and in which the rural masses account for no more than a quarter of the total population. On the other hand, in these two countries fiscal revenues largely depend on exports originating in a sector which is practically cut off from the rest of the economic system of the nation. It should be added that the State, in both cases, can command considerable resources in comparison with other countries in the region. In Chile, for instance, central government expenditure represented 23 per cent of the domestic product in 1964-6 and in Venezuela 20 per cent, whereas in the other countries of the region this proportion was nowhere higher than 15 per cent in the same period. In these two countries the State is therefore in a privileged position and, given the relatively small size of the agricultural sectors, they may well succeed in transforming their agrarian structures by fairly conventional means. In the case of Brazil, Colombia or Peru, however, the problem takes on another dimension. In both Colombia and Peru, for instance, if a quarter of the present number of landless workers were to be given smallholder status, this would involve settling not 100,000 but half a million families. However, neither of the two governments concerned has the financial or even the technical resources available to the Chilean government. Consequently, if the Chilean programme is fully implemented, its success will not mean that a generally applicable formula has been found. It is far more likely that in the case of Latin America agrarian structures the path to reform will tend to fall midway between the Chilean and Mexican–Bolivian solutions. This means that radical changes will depend on the progress of movements designed to organise the rural population and to prepare them for the struggle against latifundian structures. It also means that governments must be prepared to direct the transition process.[1]

[1] For an overall review of the Latin American agrarian problem see Jacques Chonchol, 'Land Tenure and Development in Latin America' in Claudio Veliz (ed.), *Obstacles to Change in Latin America*, London, 1965. See also Moisés Poblete Troncoso, *La Reforma Agraria en América Latina*, Santiago de Chile, 1961.

CHAPTER 24

ECONOMIC ASPECTS OF THE CUBAN REVOLUTION

SINGULARITY OF THE TRADITIONAL CUBAN ECONOMY

Cuba displays a number of peculiarities worth analysing separately in an overall study of the Latin American framework. Along with Puerto Rico, the island remained under Spanish rule until the beginning of this century, which means that the colonial period in this area lasted a century longer than in the rest of Latin America. When the Cuban people's struggle to win their independence created impediments to U.S. trade, the United States government used the conflict as a pretext for taking over the remnants of Spain's former Empire in the Americas and Asia. Consequently, the Cuban National State started its independent life under the occupation of United States forces, an occupation that has not yet entirely come to an end—the United States government still has a base on Cuban territory—and that up to 1934 could have been extended to the whole island at any time, 'in the interests of the Cuban people' as adjudged by the President of the United States, in accordance with the provisions of the famous 'Platt Amendment'. The delay of almost a century in starting the process of building a nation-state, and the particular circumstances attending its emergence under the tutelage of a powerful neighbour, make the Cuban process unique in the Latin American context. However, Cuba's singularity lies even deeper and its roots are to be found in the economic evolution of the island within the framework of the Antillean region.

The Spaniards first used the Caribbean islands as defence bases for their lines of communication with the mainland colonies. The indigenous populations, living at an extremely rudimentary cultural level, were practically wiped out and extensive stock farming was established on the larger islands to supply the metropolitan fleets. From the seventeenth century, the smaller islands were occupied by the French and the English, who wanted to secure a foothold for an assault on the mainland. With a view to eventual penetration of the Spanish Empire, they encouraged white colonisation of the islands they had occupied, founding settlements of small planters who combined the growing of subsistence crops with the production of tobacco and indigo for the European market. These

Economic Development of Latin America

settlements, which had been of political value to the metropolitan countries because they could provide colonial militias[1] to be mobilised against the rich Spanish Empire, underwent profound changes during the latter part of the seventeenth century when the cultivation of sugar-cane was introduced into the islands by the Dutch settlers who had been driven out of the Brazilian Northeast. In fact, Dutch interests were responsible for developing sugar production in the Antilles. They financed sugar mills and the importation of slaves, provided technical assistance and guaranteed markets. Sugar ushered in a period of great prosperity for the island settlements, which had formerly lived in conditions of extreme poverty. But prosperity had its price: the social pattern of the islands was profoundly changed. White settlers emigrated, or became small planters marginalised on the poorest lands, while large sugar plantations were established, worked by Negro slaves imported from Africa and owned by a small number of wealthy proprietors or corporations of shareholders who lived in the metropolis. The island of Barbados offers a striking example of this process: between 1643 and 1667 the number of landowners in the island fell from 11,200 to 745 and the slave population increased from 5,680 to 82,023.[2]

While the French and English Antilles were becoming vast sugar plantations with a dense population of African origin, Cuba remained a scantily occupied territory of large cattle estates and small tobacco plantations. This situation is explained by the fact that Spain was herself a sugar producer and that the international sugar trade was almost entirely controlled by the Dutch. Consequently, although sugar was the most important commodity in international trade for more than two centuries, in the Spanish colonies it was produced for local consumption only. In the first half of the nineteenth century important changes occurred in the Antillean economy. The Haitian War of Liberation (1791–1804) brought about the collapse of the export economy of a colony that was at that time the world's leading coffee producer and one of the world's major sugar producers. The abolition of slavery in the English colonies in 1832, and in the French possessions in 1848, did not radically alter the living conditions of the Negro population but it did produce changes in the agrarian structure. Wherever land was available, even if of poor quality, former slaves tried to establish themselves as small independent producers, becoming subsistence farmers on *minifundios* in much the same way as in Haiti. However,

[1] Léon Vignols, 'Les Antilles Françaises sous l'Ancien Régime', *Revue d'Histoire Economique et Sociale*, 1928.
[2] V. T. Harlow, *A History of Barbados*, Oxford, 1926.

232

Economic Aspects of Cuban Revolution

since land was generally in short supply or held by the big plantation owners, the pattern that tended to prevail was a system whereby former slaves were obliged to combine subsistence farming on their own undersized plots of land with some form of wage labour on the plantation whenever this happened to suit the owners. It should be added that with the rise of beet sugar production, which had started during the Napoleonic Wars, the Antillean product began to lose its leading position on the world sugar market, largely as the result of the protection enjoyed by beet sugar on the European markets. To these factors for change in the pattern of the Antillean economy must be added the remarkable expansion of the United States market, whose geographical proximity made it the principal outlet for the region's exportable surpluses.

The expansion of Cuban sugar production in the nineteenth century took place with an eye to the U.S. market, which was not bound by commercial treaty to other parts of the West Indies.[1] In this way, close bonds of trade were established between the United States and Cuba during the colonial period. The fight against Spanish rule, intensified after 1868, created a climate of insecurity for the big plantation owners linked with the metropolis and facilitated the penetration of U.S. interests. After 1901, with the elimination of Spanish power, and the American military occupation which lasted, with a number of interruptions, up to 1908, penetration of U.S. business groups was consolidated and extended and, at the same time, the island's economy was completely transformed. Thus, in the short space of two decades—between 1901 and 1920—the output of sugar rose from 1·5 million to 5 million tons, while radical changes were introduced into Cuban economic structures. Cane plantations spread rapidly and the amount of land controlled by the sugar corporations, largely foreign-owned, increased even more dramatically. Small planters were relegated to the tobacco-growing areas or to poorer lands on the lower slopes of mountains. The bulk of the rural population became agricultural labourers on the plantations, while the shortage of labour in the harvest season gave rise to a current of immigration mostly from the neighbouring islands.[2]

A comparison of the different forms of sugar economy in the Antilles will help us to identify certain distinctive features of the pre-revolutionary Cuban economy. To simplify, it can be said that three types of sugar economy developed in the region. In the first we find slave labour, in the

[1] For data on Cuban sugar exports during the nineteenth century see Ramiro Guerra y Sánchez, *Azúcar y Población en las Antillas*, Havana, 1944.
[2] *Ibid.*

second a combination of rural wage earners and subsistence *minifundio* farmers, and in the third the prevalence of a rural proletariat. The slave system, characterised by a marked rigidity in production costs—all costs were fixed since there was no difference between investments in equipment and in the labour force—was part of an economy completely geared to foreign trade. The system introduced into the English and French Antilles after the abolition of slavery brought an important element of flexibility, since the labour force could pay for itself in part by growing subsistence crops. This greater flexibility of costs enabled sugar-cane growing to survive on several islands despite the impoverishment of soils and the difficulties created by the advent of beet sugar and the consequent increase in price instability. The third system was the one that came to prevail in Cuba during the present century. The abundance of land and the island's semi-integration with the U.S. economy made it possible to create a sugar economy in which, given the wage levels prevailing in the region, productivity was high enough to permit formation of a rural proletariat that remained idle for more than half the year. This situation reflected the high rate of profits in the industry on the one hand and the relatively low cost of labour on the other. It also reflected the very special position of the industry since the high profitability of the sugar corporations was the result not only of the abundance of land and the proximity of the U.S. market but also of a particular type of integration with the United States economy. On the other hand, the relatively low cost of labour, which made it possible to employ large numbers of workers who were unemployed for long periods every year, can be accounted for only by the lack of alternative sources of employment. The development of the sugar industry in Puerto Rico, where integration with the U.S. economy took a different form, underlines the importance of this latter point. Since workers had the possibility of emigrating to the United States and since industrialisation created new employment opportunities in the island itself, there were serious obstacles to the development of the Puerto Rican sugar industry, whose output fell short of the basic quota it had been allocated by the U.S. government. Consequently, despite a substantial rise in the productivity of labour—the number of workers on the cane plantations fell from 124,000 to 49,000 between 1934 and 1959—Puerto Rican sugar production has remained stationary over the last three decades.[1]

In the case of the Cuban economy, the cycle of expansion based on the export of sugar came to an end in the first half of the 1920s. This expansion had taken the form of a rise in the export coefficient and an increase in the

[1] Rafael Picó, *Puerto Rico: Planificación y Acción*, San Juan de Puerto Rico, 1962.

product accompanied by growing integration with the United States economy. At one point the sugar industry contributed as much as 30 per cent to the domestic product and accounted for 80 per cent of the export total. The situation of the Cuban economy during this period was in some respects similar to that of the Venezuelan economy in the 1950s, with the difference that, whereas prices on the international oil market are remarkably stable, sugar prices were—and indeed still are—extremely unstable. In the period immediately following the First World War, the price of sugar rose steeply, reaching a record level of 22 cents a pound, only to fall in the early 1920s to 4 cents a pound. The ensuing crisis revealed the vulnerability of the economic system that had been created in the country. Economic activity became increasingly dependent on U.S. financial groups. The country's banking network was taken over largely by foreign banks and the very existence of an independent monetary system was seriously challenged. Cuba sheltered behind a preferential tariff system, exporting her sugar to the United States under conditions similar to those obtaining in the Lesser Antilles, whose exports were given preferential treatment by the respective metropolitan countries. The Reciprocal Trade Agreement of 1903, which had reduced U.S. tariffs on Cuban sugar imports, also gave products from the United States preferential entry to the Cuban market. The system worked along the lines of a free trade zone, enabling each country to specialise in those products it was best able to supply. In practice, however, Cuba was able to supply one product only, while the United States could produce a range of hundreds, if not thousands, of products. Moreover, the prices of such products were set in the U.S. market, which meant that on average they would not fluctutate too far above or below the level of prices in the country, whereas sugar prices were determined in the international market (the situation obtaining before the quota was fixed) in terms of the surpluses released onto this market by a large number of countries producing mainly for their own home markets. To accommodate fluctuations in external demand, sugar producers kept large tracts of land in reserve, which meant that land tended to be permanently under-utilised and its yield neglected.

The problems created by tariff disarmament vis-à-vis the United States could in part have been overcome had Cuba possessed an independent monetary system. In default of this, any policy designed to defend the domestic level of income was doomed to failure. Cuban banks, predominantly foreign-owned, operated with a high liquidity ratio and held a large part of their assets in foreign currency. Consequently, a fall in the value of exports could create unemployment without causing serious balance of payments problems. This situation contrasted sharply with that in other countries of the region where a contraction in the value of exports had drastic effects on the balance of payments, forcing devaluation of the exchange rate and indirectly creating a protection mechanism resembling a rise in tariffs. The Cuban economy operated as if its circulating medium consisted entirely of foreign exchange, while the banking system enjoyed a liquidity ratio of 50 per cent. In short, the country lacked the minimum decision-making autonomy necessary to initiate the processes that form a national economic system.

Reaction against the situation outlined above came in the latter half of the 1920s, leading in 1927 to a change in tariff legislation that became the starting-point for the first attempt to diversify the Cuban economy. The period saw the beginning of an industrialisation process resembling the process started in other Latin American countries in the late nineteenth century under the impulse of expanding exports. In Cuba, however, the process had barely begun before the 1929 crisis, which assumed the proportions of catastrophe for that country because of the complete lack of defence mechanisms. Following the announcement of protectionist measures by the U.S., the bottom fell out of the sugar market. With prices plummeting to incredible levels—the lowest level for 1932 corresponded to 2·5 per cent of the highest level reached in the preceding decade—the country's economic life was almost paralysed and the resultant unemployment rate can seldom have been paralleled in any other country.

Industrialisation being virtually non-existent, Cuba was in no position to handle this crisis in the same way as other countries in the region with similar levels of per capita income and domestic markets of comparable size. In other words, the minimum conditions for starting an import-substitution process had not been created. It cannot be asserted *a priori* that if Cuban industrialisation had begun a decade earlier the country's evolution in the depression period would have proceeded along the same lines as that of the region's more developed countries. None of these countries was so closely bound to a dominant economy as to lack an autonomous monetary system, which was the case in Cuba. Import-substituting industrialisation in this period was promoted through inflation and exchange controls, a situation hard to envisage in the case of a country whose banking system was controlled from abroad. None the less, the crisis proved to be an acid test and the considerable influence exercised by foreign interests in the country is evident in the fact that a way out was sought in the direction of closer integration with the U.S. economy.

Economic Aspects of Cuban Revolution

In 1934 the U.S. government abrogated the Platt Amendment as part of President Franklin D. Roosevelt's Good Neighbour Policy. The United States kept the Guantánamo military base but there was no longer any legal justification for the U.S. government to exercise the right to intervene that it had claimed since the defeat of Spanish power. In that same year, the first steps were taken to link the Cuban economy more intimately to that of the United States, on a basis which experience had already shown to be non-viable. To counter the wave of protectionism that had swept the United States during the crisis, leading to the displacement of the Cuban product in favour of sugar produced domestically and in Puerto Rico and Hawaii, Cuban interests demanded a *quota* on the U.S. market. As a result of this pressure, Cuba was assigned a basic quota of 28 per cent of the U.S. market under the Costingan–Jones Law of 1932. The quota signified a guaranteed market share substantially smaller than the proportion accounted for by Cuban sugar in the past. On the other hand, it created a new form of dependence: quota exports of Cuban sugar were sold at American market prices, which were well above prices obtaining in the world market and also more stable. In other words, Cuba could take advantage of a U.S. government policy that had been designed to organise the domestic commodity market and to defend the income levels of the country's farmers. In the same year that American legislation extended to Cuba some of the benefits arising from the New Deal Policy of defending the real income of U.S. farmers, the Cuban government signed a complementary trade agreement with the United States in which tariff disarmament was taken a stage further: the margin of preference in favour of U.S. exporters was increased and new items were added to the list of products to be given preferential treatment.

Thus, just when the Cuban State was taking a decisive step towards consolidating its position following the repeal of the Platt Amendment, the Cuban economy became more dependent and less viable. Industrialisation was sacrificed—in this period several recently built factories were demolished and the equipment was sold to other countries in the region that were fostering the development of local industry—in favour of strengthening the sugar economy within a framework that implied its stagnation. The only rational basis for the guidelines implicit in the policy adopted in 1934 would have been a growing integration with the U.S. economy along the lines of the pattern that was to prevail in Puerto Rico after the 1940s. As it was, the stagnation of the sugar sector meant that land, labour and capital resources were considerably under-utilised. Since no Cuban product could hope to compete with U.S. imports, these

237

resources could not be utilised. The Puerto Rican solution was to subsidise investment in the island with funds provided by the U.S. government, while at the same time encouraging the absorption of surplus manpower by the United States. In fact, within the space of a quarter of a century, the Puerto Rican population living in the metropolis equalled that remaining on the island.

In Cuba, where political developments had been moving towards the consolidation of a nation-state, the guidelines adopted in the early 1930s led to an impasse in the economic sphere. The export sector, on which all other economic activities were dependent, made no progress between the 1920s and the 1950s, while the country's population doubled. The economy tended to adapt itself to conditions of permanent underemployment of the country's labour force, a situation which led to the reinforcement of trade unions committed to defending stability in employment. Capital resources formed in the country tended to find their way abroad and the economy's investment rate was extremely low. Part of the resources available were invested in land, which was used to establish extremely unproductive cattle *latifundia*.

In the years following the Second World War, systematic studies of the Cuban economy undertaken by the country's economists and by international agencies drew attention to its intrinsic irrationality. As a result of these studies an attempt was made to provide the Cuban State with wider means of action, particularly at the monetary level. The Cuban National Bank was founded in this period and a number of other institutions were established with a view to promoting the country's development. After 1952 the government began to intervene directly in the marketing of sugar, through the National Bank. Unsold stocks were withdrawn from the market along the lines of the coffee policy adopted in Brazil at the beginning of the present century. The aim of this policy was to prevent crop fluctuations attributable to climatic factors from having an adverse effect on world market prices, while at the same time cushioning the impact of income fluctuations in the export sector on the economy as a whole. In addition to the attempts made to regulate the export sector, the Cuban government sponsored investment in the agricultural, livestock and manufacturing sectors with a view to promoting import substitution. It has been estimated that between 1954 and 1958 fixed capital investment in the manufacturing industry, financed largely by the State, amounted to 250 million dollars. Of this total, 68 million dollars were invested in oil refineries and 17 million dollars in the chemical industry. The pulp and paper industry, using cane bagasse as its raw material, began to develop

Economic Aspects of Cuban Revolution

in this period.[1] However, despite the new bearings in government policy, the annual growth rate of gross domestic product per capita between 1948 and 1958 was only 1 per cent, as compared with a rate of nearly 2 per cent for the region as a whole. It should be added that the counterpart to the State's efforts to finance the private sector's investments in the 1950s was a marked increase in the external debt and a no less considerable decline in the country's gold and foreign exchange reserves. Cuba was on the verge of a crisis which would have forced the government either to back down on its investment programme in order to build up its reserves of foreign exchange—at the cost of aggravating unemployment—or to take a decisive step forward in the direction of doing away with the preferential system and the reciprocity agreements that were subjecting the Cuban economy to semi-integration with the economy of the United States.

REDISTRIBUTIVE STAGE OF THE REVOLUTION

The 1959 revolution precipitated the course of events and impelled the country towards the second alternative at a spectacular pace. The reaction of the United States and the subsequent economic blockade of the island imposed by the Washington government, together with the support given to the new Cuban government by the Soviet Union and other socialist countries, caused events to move with incredible speed, changing the very essence of the range of options arising out of the country's previous evolution. The revolution must be regarded as part of the formative process of the Cuban nation-state, a process that had begun with the country's struggle for liberation from Spanish power. But the later course of the revolution cannot fully be understood without taking into account the fact that the last act of this liberation process was played out against the United States at the critical time when the balance of nuclear power called for a strict demarcation of the spheres of influence of the two super-powers. Thus, the international circumstances surrounding the Cuban Revolution came to play a decisive role in the course it was to follow.

From an economic point of view, the evolution of post-revolutionary Cuba can be divided into two periods. The first is marked by a policy designed to change the power structure and the distribution of income; the

---

[1] For a retrospective analysis of Cuba's industrial development and the present structure of Cuban industry see 'El Desarrollo Industrial de Cuba', a document presented by the Cuban government to the *Latin American Symposium on Industrialization* organised by ECLA in March 1966, and included in the ECLA publication of that name.

second by a concerted effort to bring about the country's economic reconstruction.

The revolution's first major act in the economic sphere was the promulgation of an Agrarian Reform Law which differed from other Latin American land reform legislation in that it did not aim to divide up the land. The maximum landholding permitted was 30 *caballerias*[1] (402·6 hectares) and any land in excess of this area was expropriated. Where the land was already divided and had formerly been worked by tenant farmers or sharecroppers, it was distributed to them in parcels of 5 *caballerias*, i.e. 67 hectares, each. Where estates had been run as a single economic unit, the unit was preserved and co-operatives or State farms (*granjas*) were set up. Medium-sized properties of between 5 and 30 *caballerias*, permitted under this first reform, were done away with by the Second Agrarian Reform Law promulgated in October 1963. Essentially, the reform involved the abolition of rural rents formerly paid by some 100,000 small farmers, and the introduction of State control over all medium and large estates, formerly run as agricultural enterprises, through a powerful State institution created specifically for the purpose: the National Land Reform Institute (Instituto Nacional de la Reforma Agraria—INRA). Independent smallholders, both old and new, owning around 7·2 million hectares of land, were organised in a National Association of Small Farmers (Asociación Nacional de Agricultores Pequeños—ANAP). Medium and large farms, controlled by the State through INRA, account for around 11·4 million hectares divided into some 1,500 agricultural units.[2]

In addition to the agrarian reform, several other measures helped to change the pattern of income distribution.[3] In March 1959, urban rents were lowered by between 30 and 50 per cent and at the same time higher wages were paid to urban and rural workers. Government expenditure on social services (health, education and housing in particular) was raised from $390 million to $1,321 million. Conservative estimates have allowed that the sum effect of the various measures adopted between 1959 and 1961 was to transfer at least 15 per cent of the Cuban national income from property-owning groups to the working masses. The Cuban Revolution was thus, in its initial stage, closer to the distributive spirit of classic socialist ideology than to the developmental socialism that had prevailed in the

---

[1] One *caballeria* is equal to 33·16 acres.
[2] For a complete survey of the Cuban land reform see Michel Gutelman, *L'Agriculture Socialisée à Cuba*, Paris, 1967, René Dumont, *Cuba, Socialisme et Développement*, Paris, 1964, and Julio le Riverend, 'Conclusiones sobre la Reforma Agrária en Cuba' in *Les Problèmes Agraires des Amériques Latines*.
[3] ECLA, *Economic Survey of Latin America, 1963*.

Eastern European countries. In the latter case, income was transferred to the State with a view to raising the rate of capital formation.

The initial orientation of the Cuban Revolution may be accounted for by the fact that its leaders had been influenced by studies of the country's economy before the revolution, which invariably emphasised the existence of considerable unused productive capacity attributable to the lack of effective demand and the extremely inequitable distribution of income. It was felt that a policy directed towards remedying this situation would bring about a rapid growth of the product, although it would at the same time create balance of payments problems over the medium term. To forestall these problems the external sector of the economy would be brought under effective control. This policy was to lead the Cuban State to place the country's economic relations with the United States on a completely new footing. In fact, the margin of idle capacity in the industrial sector was substantial: ECLA has estimated that the proportion of utilised capacity in the major branches of industry, including textiles, was not more than 60 per cent in 1959. This explains why the domestic product was able to grow sufficiently in the first two years of the revolution to absorb a large part of the expansion of monetary demand brought about by the rise in wages.[1] The short-term elasticity of supply was not, however, confined to the manufacturing sector. The sugar harvest in 1961 was the second largest in Cuban history and between 1958 and 1962 rice production rose from 163,000 tons to 300,000 tons, maize production from 134,000 tons to 257,000 tons and production of beans from 33,000 tons to 78,000 tons.[2]

The lack of structural diversification in the Cuban economy meant that any attempt to speed up the rate of growth would bring immediate pressure on the balance of payments. It was thus only to be expected that the external sector would rapidly develop a severe foreign exchange bottleneck that was to determine the future course of the Cuban Revolution. Exchange control, the rationing of scarce foreign exchange, the need to find new markets for the country's sugar surpluses and new credit lines to finance imports of equipment, whose overall volume had to be rapidly increased, became pressing problems. This came at a time when the expropriation of land, largely owned by North American citizens, had led to the formation of a powerful pressure group in the United States violently opposed to any form of public or private co-operation between

---

[1] For an introduction to this first stage of the revolution, from the economic point of view, see Dudley Seers (and others), *Cuba: The Economic and Social Revolution*, London, 1964.

[2] Michel Gutelman, *L'Agriculture Socialisée à Cuba*.

the United States and the revolutionary government in Cuba. The Cuban government began to diversify its sources of supply and it was the purchase of crude oil from the Soviet Union, to be refined at the island's U.S.-owned refineries, that provoked the incident that was to snowball into the nationalisation of all property owned by North American citizens in the island whose assets were worth over 1,000 million dollars.

Whatever may have been the original intention of Cuba's leaders, there can be no doubt that after the severing of economic relations with the United States they were left with very little room to manœuvre. With U.S. supplies close at hand, the Cuban economy had traditionally operated with limited stocks, a far from negligible advantage. Once these stocks had been used up, the shortage of spare parts became a serious problem. Integration with the centrally planned economies called for a number of adjustments on the part of these and for radical changes in Cuban economic structures. Such changes could not be made overnight, and domestic supply problems of no mean order were to arise during the transition period. The gravity of these problems was apparently not grasped at first and it was thought that a concerted effort to promote import substitution both in the agricultural and in the industrial sectors would ease the pressure on the balance of payments within a reasonably short space of time. As a result of this policy, a large number of new projects were launched in the agricultural sector—the country had been largely dependent on imports of food in the pre-revolutionary era—and imports of industrial equipment were considerably stepped up. The consequences were extremely unfortunate: there was a drop in the productivity of the agricultural sector and the shift of factors away from sugar production began to affect the country's only means of earning enough foreign exchange to boost the dwindling capacity to import. As for the industrial sector, it soon became apparent that industry would continue to be heavily dependent on imported intermediate products for some time to come.

Besides the above-mentioned problems, we must bear in mind the speed with which the country's entire economic structure was changed. A vicious circle was created in which the government tended to bring all economic decisions under strict central control without having the technical and administrative resources needed for their implementation to be effective. Medium and large agricultural enterprises were taken over by the State at a time when large numbers of qualified technicians formerly employed in the agricultural sector were leaving the country. Similarly, the entire industrial sector was brought under direct State control when the majority of experienced managers and industrial engineers were emigrating.

Economic Aspects of Cuban Revolution

The structural organisation of the industrial sector is based on several ministries—the Ministry of Industry, the Ministries of the Food, Sugar and Building Industries—and central government agencies such as the National Fisheries Commission and the Cuban Tobacco Institute. These various ministries and autonomous agencies control consolidated *enterprises* which in their turn are responsible for the direction of *establishments* or production units. By and large, the enterprises administer between 10 and 25 factories each. In 1965, 172 factories accounted for 70 per cent of the value of production and for 49 per cent of the labour force employed in the manufacturing sector.[1] Given the lack of diversification of the industrial sector—the structure of the Cuban industrial system in 1964 resembled that of the Central American countries—and the poor development of local resources of raw materials, both agricultural and mineral, the import content of the industrial product is very high. As a consequence, to achieve a rise of one dollar in the output of the food industry, excluding sugar, 30 cents must be spent on direct and indirect imported inputs. In the textile industry the amount required would be 22 cents, in the chemical industry 34 cents, in the metal-using and engineering industries 43 cents, etc.[2]

RECONSTRUCTION PHASE IN THE EXTERNAL SECTOR

The new line of post-revolutionary economic policy has been taking shape since 1963–4. In 1963 the balance of payments deficit amounted to 323 million dollars, corresponding to 37 per cent of the total value of imports and approximately 10 per cent of the domestic product. Sugar production, which had risen to 6,767 million tons in 1961, i.e. 1 million tons above the average for the preceding decade, fell to 4,815 million tons in 1962 and to 3,821 million tons in 1963. The decline was in part attributable to extremely adverse weather conditions but there can be no doubt that the main reason was the reduction in the area planted to sugar cane—in some cases involving the ploughing up of highly productive cane lands—and the acute shortage of labour at the peak of the sugar harvest. The Cuban experience of this period made it very clear that to transform the economic structure of an underdeveloped country it is not enough to have a power structure with the ability to extract resources from the collectivity in order to increase capital formation. It is equally necessary to have a certain margin of capacity to import, in the absence of which the assimilation of technological progress will be insufficient. Even if Cuba had shifted privately owned productive resources confiscated in the early stages of the

---

[1] Government of Cuba, 'El Desarrollo Industrial de Cuba'.   [2] *Ibid.*

revolution towards capital formation—in the same way that the Eastern European countries channelled to this end resources taken from the agricultural sector—the possibility of transforming the economic structure would still have been dependent on the capacity to import, simply because the capacity to *transform* resources in an underdeveloped and under-industrialised economy is extremely limited. The Cuban Revolution had begun by redistributing income with a view to raising the consumption level of the masses, which meant not only that the rate of investment would fail to rise but that the capacity to import released by the reduction in consumption of the wealthy classes was absorbed by the increase in imports of non-durable consumer goods or intermediate products and raw materials needed to produce such goods locally. In fact, the value of imports rose from 638 million dollars in 1960 to 867 million dollars in 1963 and 1,015 million dollars in 1964, the increment being financed entirely by external aid, almost exclusively provided by the Soviet Union. In 1964 the import coefficient was over 30 per cent, a level which, since 1930, had been matched in the region only by Venezuela.

The new policy directives formulated after 1963/4 were essentially aimed at the recovery of the capacity to import through the more systematic exploitation of the country's comparative advantages in sugar production and other agricultural and livestock products. Thus, Cuba returned to the basic pattern of her economic evolution but in a new context. The Soviet Union undertook to increase its imports of Cuban sugar from 2·1 million tons in 1964 to 5 million tons by 1970. Sugar prices are unlikely to create serious difficulties since, even if the Soviet Union pays prices well above those prevailing in the world market, it will still be saving a considerable amount of money in view of the much higher costs of locally produced sugar.[1] In other words, the price paid can be twice the world market price and still be only a third of local production costs. This example emphasises the considerable advantages to be gained from the organisation of international markets. By using Cuban imports to meet the rise in domestic sugar consumption, the Soviet Union can reduce the domestic prices of sugar while at the same time providing Cuba with a stable market for its exports over the medium term. The Cuban government has fixed a target of 10 million tons of sugar in 1970, which means raising output by 50 per cent in terms of the level attained in 1961. To reach this target, not only must the area under cultivation be extended but the average yield per hectare must be raised from 45 tons to 50 tons. This is a comparatively modest aim since the average yield in Mexico and the

[1] Cf. René Dumont, *Cuba, Socialisme et Développement.*

Economic Aspects of Cuban Revolution

United States is 57 tons, in Puerto Rico 68 tons, in Peru 155 tons and in Hawaii 204 tons. However, given the extent of the island's cane lands, Cuba faces a shortage of water which must be shared with other crops. Meanwhile, the possibility of expanding sugar production will encounter economic limits likely to be reached within the next few years. It is true that such limits may be altered by improvements in the overall level of the country's agricultural techniques. Nevertheless, it must be borne in mind that the relative advantages of cane production largely reflect the low level of capital formation in the economy as a whole and the relatively abundant supply of comparatively cheap labour. Any change in these basic conditions will obviously affect the present comparative advantage of sugar.

In recent years the Cuban government has been assessing possibilities for developing new export lines. Stock farming is in a strong position in this respect and it is hoped to raise productivity sufficiently to enable the country to export between 40 and 50 tons of meat a year by the beginning of the coming decade. Nickel could also become an export item of increasing importance. Although its exploitation involves special technical problems, Cuba has exceptionally rich deposits and in 1965, with sales totalling 15 million dollars, nickel ranked third among the country's exports. Coffee and citrus fruits are being planted or replanted with an eye to export possibilities. In the case of coffee, the aim is to practically triple present production so as to attain the official target of an exportable surplus of over 800,000 bags.[1]

As a consequence of the new policy directives, the area dedicated to a number of crops—maize, cotton and oilseeds—has been reduced. The area planted to rice, which competes with sugar cane for irrigation water, has also been transferred to other uses. As it was impossible to continue increasing imports, general rationing has had to be introduced. On the other hand, to provide the investments required by the plan to expand the capacity to import, almost all the industrial programmes conceived in the first stage of the revolution have had to be altered, which implied scrapping a large number of projects for which equipment had already been imported. The industrialisation effort was slowed down and reoriented towards reinforcing the agricultural economy and taking advantage of the external economies it created. Top priority was given to industrial sectors related to agriculture such as chemical fertilisers—nitrogens and phosphates—and agricultural machinery. Food-processing industries, particularly dairy products and citrus juice industries, both partly geared

[1] An official account of the export expansion programme is to be found in Government of Cuba, 'El Desarrollo Industrial de Cuba'.

towards the export market, have also been stimulated, as has the fishing industry. Another development priority is the building materials industry and cement production, which was just under 800,000 tons before the revolution, and is expected to rise to 2 million tons by the beginning of the coming decade.

The keystone of Cuba's new economic policy is, as we have seen, the recovery and expansion of sugar production with a view to providing the country with a basic capacity to import which will leave room to manœuvre in transforming its economic structures. The policy is based on the fact that in an organised international market, such as that constituted by the Socialist countries as a whole, Cuba has an obvious comparative advantage in the sugar sector. However, the targets envisaged for 1970 are far more ambitious than is warranted by her entry into the international trade of the Socialist countries. In fact, in fixing a target of 10 million tons, the Cuban leaders were planning to sell 7 million tons to the centrally planned economies and to dispose of 2½ million tons on the world market. But available estimates indicate that the so-called *free market* cannot absorb such a volume of sugar and the result will be that current prices, already well below production costs in Cuba, will remain depressed for an indefinite period, signifying a deterioration in Cuba's terms of trade. Nor is this all: if free market prices are low there will obviously be pressure on export prices to the Socialist countries, which have to be periodically renegotiated. Moreover, the 2½ million tons destined for the free market may well be increased to 3 or 3½ million tons, since unforeseen developments in the Socialist bloc cannot be excluded. Of the 7 million tons referred to, 5 million are destined for the Soviet Union under the terms of a trade agreement which provides for the purchase of an increasing volume of Cuban sugar at the fixed price of 6 cents a pound. One million tons are to be sold to other European Socialist countries and one million will be taken by China, under the terms of a trade agreement drawn up along the lines of Cuba's agreement with the Soviet Union. Since 1967, trade difficulties have arisen with China, highlighting the new type of problem that Cuba may well be facing in the future.

Before the revolution the Cuban sugar industry had a production capacity of around 7 million tons a year, but a quarter of this capacity generally remained idle. After the setbacks of 1963 and 1964, the revolutionary government proved that former levels could be rapidly recovered and harvests of over 6 million tons were achieved in 1965 and 1967. Sugar experts have estimated that it would not require very heavy investment (around 150 million dollars in industrial inputs) to raise production capacity in this sector of the Cuban economy to 8·5 million tons, the maximum which Cuba could reasonably hope to sell in 1970 without bringing too much pressure to bear on the market.[1] Raising production capacity to 10 million tons means that the industry must be largely remodelled, which requires heavy investment in industrial equipment. This decision, taken in 1963, seems to have been strongly influenced by the conditions prevailing on the world sugar market at that time, when prices were spiralling at a rate unequalled since the 1920s. The rise in prices was attributable partly to the temporary decline in European beet production and partly to the diversion of sugar produced by other Latin American countries from the *free market* to the United States market at a time when the fall in Cuban production could not be offset. There was an underlying conviction that the reduction in Cuba's sugar-cane production would be permanent, since the revolutionary government had decided to diversify crop production in order to free the island from dependence on imports of food. The change in policy altered the picture, all the more so in that Cuba proposed to return to the world market with even larger quantities of sugar. Despite the 1965 fall in prices, the revolutionary government insisted on pressing ahead with its aims, even going so far as to claim their political significance in provoking a confrontation with capitalist producers (Fidel Castro's speech at the Antonio Guiteras sugar mill, 7 July 1965). However, the facts of the situation are that for the majority of sugar-producing countries exports are marginal, since the domestic consumer covers the difference between the export price and the country's average production costs. The system is justified from the social point of view by the dearth of external means of payment afflicting the sugar exporters, which are nearly all underdeveloped countries. For countries linked to a specific market, such as Puerto Rico or the Antillean countries that are part of the British Commonwealth, the consumer in the preferential market pays the indirect subsidy. In the case of Cuba, the brunt must be borne by consumers in the Socialist countries, a circumstance which will by no means help to strengthen Cuba's bargaining position in negotiations with the governments of those countries. The difficulties that arose in 1967 affecting Cuba's trade with China, from whom Cuba had hoped to obtain the bulk of her rice supply, have demonstrated once again the risks attached to over-specialisation in the agricultural sector. Consequently, despite the fact that in 1968 the Cuban government was still adhering to its targets for the sugar sector, it will not be surprising if the period fixed for their attainment is extended.

[1] Cf. Michel Gutelman, *L'Agriculture Socialisée à Cuba.*

Economic Development of Latin America

A decade after the revolution, the Cuban economy appears still to be seeking an individual path of development.[1] The socialist ideals of its leaders, whose egalitarian aims have been given tangible expression in the concerted effort to bring about rapid improvements in the living conditions of the masses, affect the entire economic process. The remarkable victories scored in raising the educational levels of the masses and improving their health conditions, together with the mobilisation of the people and their integration into the political process, are ample proof of the outstanding ability of the revolutionary leaders. None the less, the basic economic problem continues to stand: when will the country be able to count on a productive system capable of providing an increasing flow of goods and services that will allow the Cuban population to have access to the benefits of the technological revolution taking place on a world-wide scale? The plans currently being implemented characterise an intermediate stage: they aim to recover the capacity to import, thus reducing dependence on foreign aid, which for some time was a necessary condition for survival. Everything indicates that a new stage of development should begin within the next decade. A substantial rise in the technical standards of the agricultural and livestock sectors should reconcile a reduction of employment in these sectors with a more rational use of natural resources. Only then will the country be able to diversify agricultural production so as to increase supplies for the domestic market while maintaining the volume of exports. On the other hand, there will have to be rapid growth in the industrial sector since the role of the external sector in the diversification of supply will tend to have diminishing importance. Both these developments presuppose the existence of an efficient economic system. Up to now the prevailing orientation has been towards growing *budgetisation* of economic activities, that is, economic problems have been transformed into problems of operational research. To be reasonably effective, this system involves a *standardisation* of all tasks and a refinement of means of control conceivable only at the highest level of technological development.[2] In an economy subject to multiple limitations of a physical order and innumerable unforeseeable contingencies, such a system tends inevitably to involve high social costs and inhibits the formation of genuine managerial cadres. In the agricultural sector the situation is further complicated by the coexistence of a completely centralised public sector

---

[1] A summary of the recent evolution of the Cuban economy (up to the beginning of 1967) is found in Robin Blackburn's article, 'The Economics of the Cuban Revolution', in Claudio Veliz (ed.), *Latin America and the Caribbean: A Handbook*.

[2] I am, of course, disregarding the problem of the *substantive rationality* of the system, i.e. of the criteria used to define the final demand schedule.

with a private sector consisting of some 150,000 small farmers largely responsible for supplying the domestic market. In 1965 the private sector supplied 69 per cent of the vegetables, 68 per cent of the fruit, 58 per cent of the yams and tubers, 40 per cent of the milk and 32 per cent of the rice available for domestic consumption. Despite the fact that 43 per cent of the agricultural land is in the hands of the private sector, the latter cannot be successfully integrated in agricultural planning, which tends to be over-rigid and does not easily adapt itself to production units responsive solely to economic incentives. The decision announced in January 1968, to do away with the system whereby small private farmers were under contract to the State and had to hand over their surplus produce to public pooling and purchasing centres, regardless of fixed prices[1] and in exchange for standard inputs, seems to indicate that Cuba is moving towards complete collectivisation of the agricultural sector. The experience of other Socialist countries has shown that this will prove by no means an easy task. These observations are enough to confirm the statement made above that the Cuban Revolution is still trying to find a model for its economic organisation. This search has been prolonged by the philosophical conflict underlying all socialist revolutions, between those who believe that fundamental cultural changes—the ultimate task of revolution—can only be accomplished if formal rationality criteria are not too heavy a constraint during the first stages of the process and those who feel that no victory in the human sphere can be lasting if the material basis of society is not substantially broadened from the outset. After ten years of revolution, there seems little doubt that the time to broaden the material basis of society cannot long be delayed. And this objective can be achieved only if the country is provided with a truly effective economic system.

[1] Cf. Henri Denis, 'Le Socialisme Cubàin à la Recherche d'un Modèle Economique', *Le Monde*, 10 January 1968.

CHAPTER 25

PRESENT TRENDS AND PROSPECTS

In the present phase, after a century and a half of separation from their former European metropolises, the Latin American countries still present, jointly or severally, a profile not yet fully delineated. Each sub-region is at a different stage of a process of cultural homogenisation, of social and political modernisation and of an economic process that is in many respects *sui generis*. The institutions that formed the substratum of colonial society— the *hacienda*, the dependent indigenous community and the agricultural enterprise producing for export—remained virtually intact in the period that followed and it was on this foundation that the nation-states were built. Economic development, insignificant in the three preceding centuries, gained momentum in the mid-nineteenth century, taking the form of integration into the international system of division of labour constituted as a projection of the Industrial Revolution. Economic development in Latin America up to the beginning of the present century consisted in making extensive use of available land and labour resources to gain a place in the world market for primary products. In many cases this required substantial infrastructural investment, generally financed abroad. Thus, modern technology penetrated the sectors creating external economies for overall economic activities rather than the directly productive sectors.

Modernisation of infrastructures made it possible to reap economies of agglomeration favouring the urban populations, which began to increase in the last quarter of the nineteenth century as a reflexion of the expanding external sector and the final consolidation of the nation-states. With urbanisation, the transplanting of private and public consumption standards from countries with an industrial-based civilisation was intensified. Hence, modernisation was accomplished through the adoption of finished products and the transplantation of behaviour patterns related to the *use* of the product rather than through the assimilation of modern technology related to productive forms and processes. Adoption of higher standards of consumption, particularly in the public health sector, had a marked impact on the demographic situation. Death rates declined steadily, falling to levels similar to those obtaining in countries with far higher standards of living. On the other hand, birth rates remained very high since, in many essential respects, the living conditions of the broad mass of the population were unaffected by development. The growth of large urban nuclei, bringing changes in the process of capital formation—particularly with regard to building techniques—and the rising levels of living of part of the population, set in train an industrialisation process that was to open out in a number of directions and gain in depth as a result of the structural tensions created by the crisis in the export sector.

Given that the assimilation of technological progress is the basis of economic development, it will be useful to approach the Latin American process from this particular angle. I have pointed out that in the phase of expanding primary exports the penetration of modern technology was virtually confined to the infrastructure sector. In the mineral-exporting economies, the enclave nature of the export sector prevented technical progress in this sector from having any significant effect on the economy as a whole. In the case of the farming and cattle-raising economies producing for export, whether because their comparative advantages were based on extensive use of resources or because their agrarian organisation did not favour the introduction of improvements in productive techniques, experience showed that the assimilation of technical innovations in the sector responsible for exports would be slow or non-existent. The role of opening the door to the assimilation of modern technology on a wide front fell to the industrialisation process. Simplifying, it can be said that in Latin America modernisation was at first confined to the forms of consumption and that, strictly speaking, the word 'modernisation' can only be applied to forms of production after industrialisation had started. However, this modernisation was not accomplished without creating a number of problems and it was precisely at this point that economic development assumed the peculiarities characteristic of the region. Transplantation of a highly complex technology gave rise to a new type of dualism between highly capitalised productive units employing modern technical processes and productive sectors employing traditional techniques and having a low level of capital investment, a dualism superimposed on the former polarisation between market-economy sector and subsistence-economy sector.

Latin American industrialisation was just beginning when the international economy entered a phase of important changes. The international system of division of labour, based on the exchange of raw materials for manufactures, began to break down, giving way to the decentralisation of industrial activity on a worldwide scale following the lead of large enterprises creating or controlling new productive processes. In Latin America this process largely took the form of a progressive control of local manufacturing activities, in sectors in which technological progress was most rapid, by large enterprises with head offices in the United States. The process of transmitting progress in technology, formerly implicit in the exportation of equipment and machinery traded for raw materials, now tended to take the form of international decentralisation by the big industrial groups. This new form of technological deployment aggravated the disequilibrium at the factor level already evident in the preceding period. Since technical progress implies, first and foremost, a rise in the capital outlay per person employed—reflecting the particular conditions of the highly developed countries—assimilation of this progress may lead to serious structural distortions, particularly if it is not accompanied by a significant increase in the overall product or if it means that a growing share of income accrues to foreign-owned factors and generates a flow of payments to be made abroad. In countries with a structural manpower surplus, where wage rates reflect the living conditions of the bulk of the population and not the degree to which technological progress has been assimilated, the benefits of increased productivity will tend to be concentrated in the hands of owners and entrepreneurs. Hence the characteristic discontinuities in the demand schedule, representing a large group whose consumption remains undiversified and grows by the addition of new individuals only, and a minority whose demand is highly dynamic both qualitatively and quantitatively.

Thus, we find a pattern in which the assimilation of technology is decidedly slow, particularly in the directly productive activities, and the benefits of increased productivity are very poorly distributed. The result is that large sections of the population remain marginalised masses, virtually unaffected by progress. Even in countries where development has been most rapid, as in the case of Mexico, a large part of the population has failed to gain access to the benefits of economic development and the gap between this group and the medium- and high-income groups is constantly widening. The marginalised rural population is composed of minifundists and seasonal farm labourers, generally extremely undernourished and having a life expectancy far below the national mean. In the urban areas, the phenomenon of marginalisation is more visible because of the precarious housing conditions.

In examining the evolution of the Latin American economy in the postwar period we find a pronounced downward trend in the rate of growth. This decline is largely attributable to the performance of economies that have exhausted the import-substitution process. There is nothing to indicate, however, that this trend will lead to a stagnation resembling the

Presents Trends and Prospects

TABLE 25.1. *GDP Per Capita in 1960 and Projections for 1970 in Selected Countries (in 1960 dollars)*

	1960	estimated annual rate of increase	1970
Argentina	868	1·3	990
Venezuela	809	1·9	971
Chile	658	1·3	750
Mexico	518	2·8	683
Peru	338	2·8	447
Colombia	336	1·2	380
Brazil	289	1·8	343

SOURCE: For the 1960 estimates, see Table 6.2 (page 46).

stationary state of the classical economic texts. It can be assumed that the mere renewal of existing equipment will enable productivity to be raised. In countries where the import coefficient has remained high (such as Venezuela, Peru and Chile) or where it has levelled off (as in the case of Mexico), there is every indication that a rise in productivity can be achieved, in the immediate future, along more or less traditional lines. Nevertheless, a certain slackening in the tempo of growth is a fairly generalised phenomenon and since this tapering off has been most marked in countries with the highest degree of industrialisation, it is conceivable that the others will follow suit. If we assume that growth rates in the second half of the current decade will remain at roughly the levels recorded for the 1960–5 period, the value of the per capita domestic product in 1970 would be as shown in the table above. The figures have probably been overestimated in the case of Peru and underestimated in the case of Chile.

Taking into account the income levels estimated for 1970 and the pace of growth of the present decade, it becomes apparent that in Argentina, Venezuela and Mexico average productivity levels now lag roughly one generation (three decades) behind the average prevailing in the European Common Market countries. Brazil, Colombia and Peru are critical under-developed areas. If Brazil and Colombia were to grow at a cumulative annual rate of 2 per cent in the next three decades—which would mean speeding up the growth rate of the present decade—by the year 2000 they would achieve a per capita product corresponding to that of Mexico in 1970 and that of Chile in 1960.

The decline in the growth rate observable in many countries of the region has been accompanied by mounting social tensions, a situation which has helped to foster awareness of the problem and its projections on the political plane. It should be borne in mind that rates of population increase and urbanisation have not been affected by fluctuations in the growth rate of the gross domestic product. On the other hand, given the low living levels of the broad masses of the population in most of the countries concerned, an inadequate increase in the supply of staple foods tends in certain areas to assume the character of social calamity. Consider a typical case in the region in which the annual rate of population growth is 3 per cent, with the rural population increasing at the rate of 1·5 per cent, the urban population at a rate of 4·5 per cent and the population equally divided between the two sectors. We will assume that, in conditions of sluggish growth of the product, the increase in productivity would be the same in the agricultural and non-agricultural sectors, which is an optimistic hypothesis. On the basis of this hypothesis, the per capita product would have to increase at a rate of at least 1·5 per cent a year if output of agricultural and livestock products is to keep pace with the growth of the population. Since agricultural production would be growing at a rate of 3 per cent, in other words just keeping pace with the population increase, the income-elasticity of demand for foodstuffs among the rising-income groups would have to be negative if there were to be no reduction in the already low levels of food consumption of the bulk of the population or if food imports were to be kept from increasing more than the population. If the growth rate of the per capita product is less than 1·5 per cent, productivity in the agricultural sector would have to rise faster than in the economy as a whole if there is to be no decline in the food supply, assuming that imports of food cannot be increased or that exports of agricultural commodities for which there is a domestic market cannot be curtailed.

This example is intended only to show that, given certain demographic parameters, a given rate of growth must be attained simply to keep the population from becoming subject to a constant deterioration in its living conditions. This barrier, beyond which a slackening in the pace of economic growth seems to create acute social tensions, will be higher or lower according to specific factors in the individual countries. Confining ourselves to the most significant factors, we should mention the differences in the rates of population increase, which are much higher in Brazil and Colombia than in Argentina, Chile and Uruguay; the availability of an exportable surplus of food products, which places Argentina and Uruguay in a position to absorb the impact of far lower growth rates for the product than the rate postulated above; a high import coefficient, which enables countries such as Venezuela, Peru and Colombia to increase their domestic food supply by cutting down on other imports, thus cushioning the social impact of a slow rate of growth of the product. In the case of countries with more flexible economic structures and hence greater capacity to absorb social unrest, the 'tolerance threshold' could be around 1 per cent. Since countries with a low rate of tolerance account for a larger proportion of the population, the critical rate for the region as a whole is probably nearer 1·5 than 1 per cent. As we have seen, there has been a persistent loss of momentum in the region's tempo of growth, the rate having declined from 2·2 per cent in the first half of the 1950s to 1·8 per cent in the latter half and to 1·7 per cent in the first half of the present decade. Even if we allow for the fact that these figures apply to the region as a whole and that the problem of social tensions has real meaning only within the particular context of the individual national societies, there can be little doubt that forces creating a tendency towards stagnation are bringing the region perilously close to the limits of tolerance of its social structures.

Economic analysis is merely a first approach to the study of complex historical processes currently under way in Latin America. We must not forget that what is happening in this region is largely conditioned by exogenous variables, since it continues to be largely dependent on exports of raw materials and imported technology. Moreover, the most up-to-date industrial sectors are integrated in financially powerful international consortia, operating with equally powerful political backing. On the other hand, the disparities among countries at different stages of economic growth and cultural homogenisation considerably limit the scope of any attempt to forecast trends. None the less, there can be no doubt that developmental possibilities based on exports of raw materials and import-substituting industrialisation controlled from abroad are reaching or have already reached their limits. At the same time, the institutional framework inherited from the colonial period or built shortly after separation from the mother countries seems to have exhausted its possibilities of adaptation to development needs. It is understandable, then, that problems relating to structural reform should have become the region's foremost concern and that even its most obscurantist governments should have repeatedly expressed their determination to carry out structural economic reforms. Definition of these new policy directives, even when merely rhetorical, is a clear indication of the psycho-social climate prevailing in the region. This is why discussion has focused increasingly on the means to be used for a structural reconstruction, the basic lines of which are being progressively more clearly defined. Among the most relevant points emerging

Economic Development of Latin America

from the list of topics being debated in the region the following are worth singling out:

1. Re-entry of the regional economies into the expanding lines of the international economy. The organisation of commodity markets so as to assure relative stability for commodity prices and the possibility of establishing medium-term forecasts of demand are minimum objectives. The effort to attain these objectives is helping to create a united front among the countries of the region and to promote a more broadly-based understanding with the other countries of the Third World. The definition of a common trade policy vis-à-vis the outside world will considerably enhance the region's bargaining position in its negotiations with other major blocs, such as the United States, the European Common Market, the Soviet Union and Japan.

2. Reshaping of economic relations with the United States. The recent evolution of such relations indicates that the region is becoming a source of foreign exchange earnings which the United States uses to cover part of its balance of payments deficit with other regions of the world. Latin America's share of U.S. imports has been declining persistently, falling from around one-third in the early 1950s to one-quarter of the total by the end of that decade and to 15 per cent in 1967. In the 1962–6 period, Latin America had to achieve a positive balance of 1·5 billion dollars a year in its commercial relations with the rest of the world in order to cover a balance of trade deficit with the United States amounting to 100 million dollars and to meet the servicing of foreign capital, primarily North American, invested in the region. The situation has been deteriorating as a result of the measures taken by the United States government to cope with its own balance of payments difficulties. Norms, recommended in 1965 and made compulsory on 1 January 1968, limit investments made in the region by U.S. enterprises to 110 per cent of the 1965–6 level and to 65 per cent in the case of the petroleum sector. In addition, parent companies are to guarantee credits obtained on the local markets by their subsidiaries. Finally, commercial and investment banks must cut back their liquid financial assets to the 1965–6 level. ECLA has estimated that the application of these norms will limit total U.S. private investments in the region to 250 million dollars a year. Since profits on capital already invested average no less than 1,000 million dollars, we must conclude that enterprises operating in the region will be obliged to pursue a policy of self-financing corresponding to a retention of profits of 25 per cent, whereas in the United States profit-retention policy envisages the ploughing back of not less than 50 per cent. The strong financial position of the U.S.

subsidiaries assures them of ample local credit facilities, which means that these measures will not imply a slackening in their rate of growth but increased competition for limited local savings resources. To come to grips with these problems, a united national front must be formed and economic relations with the United States must be placed on a common footing for the region as a whole, a proposition which clearly has considerable political implications.

3. Reshaping of relations with the big international consortia. We have already seen that the structure of the Latin American economy tends to be increasingly controlled by international consortia, a situation which introduces new disintegrating elements into the national economies. Apart from problems relating to allocation of investments, orientation of technology and application of resources to research within the individual countries, there is the more general problem of the appropriation by foreign groups of a considerable proportion of the benefits of increased productivity. Given the oligopolistic positions they occupy and the price-leadership policies they pursue, foreign enterprises are in a position to plan their expansion on the basis of self-financing, complemented where necessary by recourse to local banking systems. In other words, in economies characterised by a sizeable structural manpower surplus, the enterprises that dominate the market are in a privileged position for retaining all the benefits of increased productivity, whether deriving from advances in technology or from the pecuniary external economies which the enterprises are able to reap. Such a situation implies that economic development would not benefit the country itself, if we take this to mean the bulk of its population, but the foreign groups in control of the enterprises. Its repercussions on the balance of payments position are obvious, a circumstance which in itself could unleash forces capable of acting as a brake on development. An exceptionally complex problem is involved and it cannot be solved at the cost of obstructing the channels that at present permit, however well or ill, the transmission of technological progress. Although discussion of this problem is still at the preliminary stage, there is every indication that the solution must be sought in the creation of new forms of enterprise, which will enable private or national organisations to co-operate with foreign groups. Joint-production ventures, already tried out in some areas, reflect the efforts being made to find a way out of the present impasse.

A move towards the solution of some of the problems indicated would be inconceivable without a parallel effort to reconstruct several other structural features in the countries carrying most weight in the region and to create new forms of co-operation among such countries. Of the items included in this second part of the agenda, particular significance attaches to the following:

(*a*) Reconstruction of economic structures with a view to intensifying the assimilation of modern technology in all productive sectors. In most of the countries concerned, the intensification of technological progress in the agricultural sector has now become an unavoidable necessity. To achieve this desideratum without incurring increasing social costs, profound and rapid changes must be introduced into the agrarian structure. It was in some ways by having overcome this obstacle a generation ahead of the other countries that Mexico gained a considerable lead in the region as a whole. The solution found to this problem will leave a decisive mark on the socio-economic evolution of countries such as Brazil, Colombia and Peru in the next few decades.

(*b*) Formulation of employment policies capable of putting an end to the present process of growing social marginalisation. The penetration of modern technology in an underdeveloped economy, within the *laissez-faire* framework, creates or aggravates the type of dualism on the social plane which has been described as 'marginalisation'. The problem is all too familiar. It cannot be solved except by a policy designed to ensure the distribution of development gains among the population as a whole, while at the same time safeguarding the rate of capital formation. The solution to this complex problem calls for a minimum of autonomous technology which the countries of the region at present do not possess.

(*c*) Reorganisation of the public sector. Since the State must assume growing responsibility for promoting development, it will have to undergo profound modifications. New forms of organisation that make it possible to reconcile adequate standards of efficiency with the coherence of purpose inherent in public action are already being developed in the region. However, overall planning is still in an embryonic state, a situation attributable mainly to the fact that the structures of strategic sectors did not undergo the initial preparation that would have enabled them to respond to the dynamisation aimed at through the introduction of planning.

(*d*) The achievement of a minimum of technological autonomy. Given the peculiarities of the region's natural resources, particularly in the case of the tropical and subtropical areas, and in view of the *sui generis* aspects of its economy, Latin America's development calls for a concerted effort in promoting technological research and the background sciences required to consolidate and develop research findings. This effort will have to be carried out almost exclusively by the public sector or in State-financed university institutions, inasmuch as control of a large part of the private sector by foreign groups tends to make enterprises dependent on research centres located outside the region.

(e) Co-operation at the regional level. Most of the problems referred to can be adequately approached only within a framework of effective regional co-operation. On the other hand, co-operation presupposes the existence of viable national structures from the point of view of development. In other words: structural reconstruction, the reorganisation of the State so as to equip it to take command of national development processes, and the attainment of forms of closer co-operation at the regional level are interdependent problems, for which solutions can be arrived at only by approximations based on parallel efforts. In present conditions of inadequate structures and external dependence, *integration* could lead the region to a new impasse in underdevelopment. At the same time, existing national decision-centres would be even further deflated. In view of the marked disparities in present levels of development and of the magnitude of the internal structural reconstruction effort required, there is every indication that a very long path is still to be travelled in the search for increasingly complex and effective forms of economic co-operation before the creation of an integrated economic structure can be considered an effective instrument for regional development.

(f) Reintegration of Cuba in the regional economy. After the second half of the coming decade, there is every indication that Cuba will have to turn to industrialisation as the most effective means of furthering her development. This industrialisation could be carried out at very low cost within the framework of co-operation with the other countries of the region, particularly those of the Caribbean area. Preferential trading with the Socialist countries is economically justifiable to the extent that Cuba can make full use of the comparative advantages of tropical agricultural production. When it comes to manufactured products, these advantages cease to operate and trade would be carried out at a level of prices that would make it non-viable over the long term. That Cuba should be trading extensively with the Eastern European countries and Canada and not with Latin America is a consequence of the evolution of her relations with the United States, of the hegemony which this country exercises over the region and of the way in which the Cuban revolutionary government responded to this situation. Once the emotional overtones of the current approach to the problem have been overcome, we can take it that relations of mutual interest will develop with due allowance for differences in economic, social and political organisation.

259

Economic Development of Latin America

The observations made above refer only to hypotheses selected from a wide range of historical possibilities. It is perfectly possible that history will choose quite another path. For instance, there is a possibility that the present phase of stagnation will be prolonged for a considerable time, followed by the onset of a process of acute social tensions, which could cost the region an increase in its relative backwardness in a fast-developing world. It is also possible that a period of indecision will be followed by a process of drastic social change, giving way in due course to a phase of accelerated development.

Moving out of the realm of conjecture, it is reasonable to assume that the forces which presently offer most resistance to structural reconstruction are beginning to weaken, both as a reflexion of the urbanisation process and as a consequence of the tensions created over the last decade by the decline in the rate of growth. On the other hand, there is now a better understanding of the nature of the problems to be faced and a firmer grasp of the techniques that can successfully be used to intervene in complex social processes. Since economic stagnation does not provide social stability—quite the contrary—defending the *status quo* will become an increasingly difficult task. As problems become more complex, options become fewer and there is greater likelihood that any step forward will start cumulative processes in the directions indicated or provoke retrogressions that may come to make the initial position deteriorate still further. In other words, the cost of social immobilism will become increasingly high for those who benefit from it.

BIBLIOGRAPHY

1. UNITED NATIONS DOCUMENTS

UNITED NATIONS, ECONOMIC COMMISSION FOR LATIN AMERICA (ECLA)
América Latina y la Política Comercial Internacional, UN (E/CN.12/773), 1967.
Analyses and Projections of Economic Development, UN (E/CN.12/363), 1955.
La CEPAL y el Análisis del Desarrollo Latino-americano, UN (E/CN.12/AC.61/10), 1968.
Contribución a la Política de Integración Económica de América Latina, UN (E/CN.12/728), 1965; also included in ECLA, *Hacia la Integración Acelerada de America Latina*.
El Desequilibrio Externo en el Desarrollo Económico Latinoamericano: el Caso de México, UN (E/CN.12/428), 1957.
Las Economias de Escala en Plantas Siderurgicas, UN, 1967.
The Economic Development of Latin America in the Post-War Period, UN, 1964.
Economic Bulletin for Latin America, UN, monthly.
Economic Survey of Latin America, UN, annual. *1949, 1963, 1965, 1966, 1967.*
Estudio sobre la Distribución del Ingreso en América Latina, UN, 1967.
Evolución de la Integración Económica en Centroamérica, UN, 1966.
Hacia la Integración Acelerada de América Latina, Mexico, 1967.
La Industria Petroquimica en América Latina, vol. I of ECLA, *El Proceso de Industrialización en América Latina*.
La Industria Quimica Latinoamericana en 1962-64, UN (E/CN.12/756), 1966.
La Industria Textil en América Latina, XII: *Informe Regional*, UN, 1968.
Integración, Sector Externo y Desarrollo Económico de America Latina, 1966.
An Introduction to the Technique of Programming, UN, 1953; also abbreviated as vol. I of ECLA, *Analyses and Projections*.
Latin America and the Second Session of UNCTAD, UN (E/CN.12/803), 1968.
Latin America and the U.N. Conference on Trade and Development, UN (E/CN.12/693), 1964.
Latin American Symposium on Industrialization, UN, March 1966.
Las Máquinas-herramientas en el Brasil, UN (E/CN.12/633), 1962.
Las Máquinas-herramientas en la Argentina, UN (ST.ECLA/Conf.23/L 18), 1966.
El Proceso de Industrialización en América Latina, UN (E/CN.12/716 rev. 1), 1966.
Theoretical and Practical Problems of Economic Growth, UN (E/CN.12/221), 1951.
ECLA and BANCO NACIONAL DE DESENVOLVIMENTO ECONOMICO. *Analise e Projeções da Economia Brasileira*, issued as vol. II of ECLA, *Analyses and Projections*.
A Evolução Recente da Economia Brasileira, Rio de Janeiro 1967.
ECLA, FAO and INTERAMERICAN DEVELOPMENT BANK. *El Uso de Fertilizantes en América Latina*, UN, 1966.
UNITED NATIONS. *Monthly Bulletin of Statistics: December 1967*, New York, July 1968.
Yearbook of International Trade Statistics, New York, 1964.

Bibliography

2. OTHER WORKS

ABREU, J. Capistrano de. *Capítulos de História Colonial*, 5th ed. Rio de Janeiro, 1934.

ARAGÃO, José Maria. 'La Teoría Económica y el Proceso de Integración de América Latina', in *Integración*, no. 2, Buenos Aires, 1968.

BAER, Werner. 'The Inflation Controversy in Latin America: A Survey', *Latin American Research Review*, II, no. 2, 1967.

BAER, Werner and MANESCHI, Andrea. *Import-substitution, Stagnation and Structural Change: an Interpretation of the Brazilian Case* (mimeograph), 1968.

BARRACLOUGH, Solon L. and DOMIKE, Arthur L. 'La Estructura Agrária en Siete Paises de América Latina', *El Trimestre Económico*, April–June 1966.

BLACKBURN, Robin. 'The Economics of the Cuban Revolution', in Claudio Veliz (ed.), *Latin America and the Caribbean: A Handbook*, London, 1968.

BOXER, C. R. *The Golden Age of Brazil, 1695–1750: Growing Pains of a Colonial Society*, Berkeley, Univ. of California Press, 1962.

CAMACHO, Hugo Dario Montiel. *La Explotación del petróleo en Venezuela y la capitalización Nacional*, Mexico, 1967.

CECEÑA, José Luis. *Los Monópolios en México*, Mexico, 1962.

Centre National de la Recherche Scientifique. *Colloques Internationaux: Paris 11–16 October, 1965: Les Problèmes Agraires des Amériques Latines*, Paris, 1967.

CHEVALIER, François. 'The *Ejido* and Political Stability in Mexico', in Claudio Veliz (ed.), *The Politics of Conformity in Latin America*, London, 1967.

CHONCHOL, Jacques. 'Land Tenure and Development in Latin America', in Claudio Veliz (ed.), *Obstacles to Change in Latin America*, London, 1965.

CORTÉS CONDE, R. 'Problemas del Crecimiento Industrial, 1870–1914', S. Torcuato di Tella and others, *Argentina, Sociedad de Masas*, Eudeba, Buenos Aires, 1965.

CÓSIO VILLEGAS, Daniel. *História Moderna de México*, VII, *El Porfiriato: Vida Económica*, Mexico, 1965.

CUNNINGHAM, W. *The Growth of Modern Industry and Commerce: Modern Times*, Part I, Cambridge Univ. Press, 1921.

DENIS, Henri. 'Le Socialisme Cubain à la Recherche d'un Modèle Economique', *Le Monde*, 10 Jan. 1968.

DÍAZ-ALEJANDRO, Carlos F. 'El Grupo Andino en el Proceso de Integración Latino-americano', in *Estudios Internacionales*, July–September 1960.

'An Interpretation of Argentine Economic Growth since 1930', *Journal of Development Studies*, Oct. 1966 and Jan. 1967.

DUMONT, René. *Cuba, Socialisme et Développement*, Editions du Seuil, Paris, 1964.

ELLICOT, Gerald. 'The Fishing Industry of Peru', in Claudio Veliz (ed.), *Latin America and the Caribbean: A Handbook*, London, 1968.

ENJALBERT, Henri. 'Réforme Agraire et Production Agricole au Mexique (1910–1965)' in Centre National de la Recherche Scientifique, *Les Problèmes Agraires des Amériques Latines*.

Bibliography

FERNANDEZ Y FERNANDEZ, Ramón. 'La Reforma Agraria Mexicana: una Gran Experiencia', in Centre National de la Recherche Scientifique, *Les Problèmes Agraires des Amériques Latines*.

FERRER, Aldo. *La Economía Argentina*, Mexico, 1963. English edition: *The Argentine Economy*: translated by Marjorie M. Urquidi, Berkeley, Univ. of California Press, 1967.

FURTADO, Celso. 'The External Disequilibrium in the Underdeveloped Economies', *The Indian Journal of Economics*, April 1958.

Formação Econômica do Brasil, Rio, 1959. English edition: *The Economic Growth of Brazil: a Survey from Colonial to Modern Times*, tr. by Richard W. de Aguiar and Eric Charles Drysdale, Berkeley, Univ. of California Press, 1963.

Subdesenvolvimento e Estagnação na América Latina, Rio de Janeiro, 1967.

Teoria e Politica do Desenvolvimento Econômico, Editora Nacional, São Paulo, 1967.

Um Projeto para o Brasil, Rio, 1968.

GERMANI, Gino. *Política y Sociedad en una Época de Transición*, ed. Paidos, Buenos Aires, 1962.

GONZALEZ CASANOVA, Pablo. *La Democracia en México*, Mexico, 1965.

Government of Cuba. 'El Desarollo Industrial de Cuba', in ECLA, *Latin American Symposium on Industrialization*.

GUERRA Y SÁNCHEZ, Ramiro. *Azúcar y Población en las Antillas*, Havana, 1944: translated as *Sugar and Society in the Caribbean: an Economic History of Cuban Agriculture*, New Haven, Yale University Press, 1964.

GUMBAU, Henri. 'Les Changements de Structure à la suite de la Reforme Bollivienne' in Centre National de la Recherche Scientifique, *Les Problèmes Agraires des Amériques Latines*, Paris, 1967.

GUTELMAN, Michel. *L'Agriculture Socialisée à Cuba*, Maspero, Paris, 1967.

HARLOW, V. T. *A History of Barbados*, Oxford, 1926.

HUMPHREYS, Robert A. *Latin American History: a Guide to the Literature in English*, Oxford, London, 1960.

Instituto Brasileiro de Geografia e Estatística. *Anuário Estatístico do Brasil, Quadros Retrospectivos, 1939–40*.

Instituto Interamericano de Estudios Jurídicos Internacionales. *Instrumentos Relativos a la Integración Económica en América Latina*, Washington, 1964: translated as Inter-American Institute of International Legal Studies, *Instruments Relating to the Economic Integration of Latin America*, Oceana Publications, Dobbs Ferry, 1968.

Instituto Interamericano de Estadística, *América en Cifras*, 1965.

Instituto Latinoamericana de Planificación Económica y Social. *Discusiones sobre Planificación*, Mexico, 1966.

Interamerican Committee for Agricultural Development. *Posse e Uso da Terra e Desenvolvimento Sócio-Econômico do Sétor Agricola à Brasil*, Washington, 1966.

Interamerican Development Bank. Montague Yudelman (ed.), *Agricultural Development in Latin America: Current Status and Prospects*, 1966.

263

Bibliography

JARA, Alvaro. *Problemas y Métodos de la História Económica Hispanoamericana*, 2nd ed., Universidad Central de Venezuela, Caracas, 1969.

Guerre et Societé au Chili, translated by Jacques Lafayette, Paris, 1961.

Tres Ensaios sobre Economía Minera Hispanoamericana, Santiago, 1966.

KINDLEBERGER, C. P. *Foreign Trade and the National Economy*, Yale University Press, 1962.

KUZNETS, Simon. *Modern Economic Growth*, Yale University Press, 1966.

LAMBERT, Jacques. *Amérique Latine: Structures Sociales et Institutions Politiques*, Paris, 1963, 2nd ed. 1968. English ed. *Latin America: Social Structure and Political Institutions*, translated by Helen Katel, Berkeley, Univ. of California Press, 1967.

LARRALDE, W. 'Primeiros Ensaios de Reforma Agraria en Venezuela' in Centre National de la Recherche Scientifique, *Les Problèmes Agraires des Amériques Latines*.

LE RIVEREND, Julio. 'Conclusiones sobre la Reforma Agrária en Cuba' in Centre National de la Recherche Scientifique, *Les Problèmes Agraires des Amériques Latines*.

MARTNER, Gonzalo. *Planificación y Presupuesto por programas*, Mexico, 1967.

MELLAFE, Rolando. 'Problemas Demográficos e História Colonial Hispanoamericana' in *Temas de História Ecónomica Hispanoamericana*, Paris, 1965.

NAVARETTE, Ifigenia N. de. *La Distribución del Ingreso en el Desarrollo Económico de México*, Instituto de Investigaciones Económicas, Mexico, 1960.

NOYOLA, Vazquez, Juan. 'El Desarrollo Económico y la Inflación en México y Otros Paises Latinoamericanos', *Investigación Económica*, XVI, no. 4, Mexico, 1965.

NURKSE, Ragnar. 'Trade Theory and Development Policy', in H. Ellis (ed.), *Economic Development for Latin America*, International Economic Association Conference 1957, Macmillan, London, 1961.

OLIVEIRA, Julio. 'La Teoria no Monetaria de la Inflación', *El Trimestre Económico*, Jan.–Mar. 1960.

PENA, Moisés T. de la. *Mito y Realidad de la Reforma Agrária en México*, Mexico, 1964.

PEREIRA, José C. *Estrutura e Expansão da Industria em São Paulo*, São Paulo, 1967.

PICÓ, Rafael. *Puerto Rico: Planificación y Acción*, San Juan de Puerto Rico, 1962.

PINTO SANTA CRUZ, Aníbal. *Chile, un Caso de Desarrollo Frustrado*, ed. Universitaria, Santiago de Chile, 1962.

'Estabilidad y Desarrollo', *El Trimestre Económico*, Jan.–Mar. 1960.

POBLETE TRONCOSO, Moisés. *La Reforma Agraria en América Latina*, Bello, Santiago dê Chile, 1961.

PREBISCH, Raúl. 'El Falso Dilema entre Desarrollo Económico y Estabilidad Monetaria', *Boletín Económico de América Latina*, March 1961.

Nueva Politica Comercial para el Desarrollo, Fondo de Cultura Económica, Mexico, 1964.

REYNOLDS, Clark Winston. *Essays on the Chilean Economy*, 1965.

SEERS, Dudley. 'Inflación y Crecimiento: Resumen de la Experiencia Latinoamericana' in *Boletín Económico de América Latina*, Feb. 1962.

SEERS, Dudley, and others. *Cuba: the Economic and Social Revolution*, London, 1964.

Bibliography

SILVA HERZOG, Jesús. *História de la Expropriación de las Empresas Petroleras*, Mexico, 1964.

SÓLIS, M. Leopoldo. 'Hacia un Análisis General a Largo Plazo del Desarrollo Económico de México' in Colégio de México, *Demografía y Economía*, I, no. I, Mexico, 1967.

SOZA VALDERRAMA, Hector. *Planificación del Desarrollo Industrial*, Mexico, 1966.

STAVENHAGEN, Rodolfo. 'Aspectos Sociales de la Estrutura Agrária en México' in Centre National de la Recherche Scientifique, *Les Problèmes Agraires des Amériques Latines.*

STEIN, Stanley J. *The Brazilian Cotton Manufacture: Textile Enterprise in an Underdeveloped Area, 1850–1950*, Harvard University Press, 1957.

SUNKEL, Osvaldo. 'La Inflación Chilena: un Enfoque Heterodoxo', *El Trimestre Económico*, Oct.–Dec. 1958.

TAMAGNA, Frank. *Central Banking in Latin America*, Mexico, 1965.

TAPIÉ, Victor-L. *Histoire de l'Amérique Latine au XIXe Siècle*, Paris, 1945.

URQUIDI, Victor, L. *Teoría, Realidad y Posibilidad de la ALALC en la Integración Económica Latinoamericana*, Mexico, 1966.
Viabilidad Económica de América Latina, Mexico, 1962.
The Challenge of Development in Latin America, translated by Marjorie M. Urquidi, Pall Mall Press, London, 1964.

URQUIDI MORALES, A. 'Las Comunidades Indígenas y su Perspectiva Histórica' in Centre National de la Recherche Scientifique, *Les Problèmes Agraires des Amériques Latines*, Paris, 1967.

VÉLIZ, Claudio (ed.). *Latin America and the Caribbean: A Handbook*, London, 1968.
Obstacles to Change in Latin America, London, 1965.
The Politics of Conformity in Latin America, London, 1967.

VICENS VIVES, Jaime. *Bibliógrafía Histórica de Espana y Hispanoamérica*, Barcelona, 1953.

VIGNOLS, Léon. 'Les Antilles Françaises sous l'Ancien Régime', *Revue d'Histoire Economique et Sociale*, 1928.

VILLA MARTINEZ, Rosa Olivia. *Inflación y Dessarollo: el Enfoque Estructuralista* (Thesis), Universidad Nacional Autónoma de México, 1966.

VILLANUEVA, Javier. *The Inflationary Process in Argentina, 1943–1960* (mimeographed), Buenos Aires, 1964.

WIONCZEK, Miguel S. 'Central Banking', in C. Veliz (ed.), *Latin America and the Caribbean: A Handbook*, London, 1968.

WIONCZEK, M. S. and others. *Latin American Economic Integration*, Praeger, New York, 1966.

YATES, P. L. *Forty Years of Foreign Trade*, Allen and Unwin, London, 1959.

ZAVALA, Silvio. *Las Instituciones Jurídicas en la Conquista de América*, Madrid, 1935.

INDEX

N.B. For commodities, the reader should refer to the separate countries. The analytic list of contents and the list of tables should also be consulted.

Index

Index

General Agreement on Tariffs and Trade (GATT), 198
Gold Exchange Standard, 68, 70–2
Great Depression, 39, 73, 82, 85, 91 n, 160, 205
Guatemala, 191; *minifundio*, 54; *microfincas*, 55; free trade, 192; Economic Association, 193; taxes, 211–13

Haiti: population, 4 n; incomes, 45; health, 47; education, 48; War of Liberation, 232
hacienda, 215–20, 223–5
Hawaii: sugar, 237, 245
Herzog, Jesús Silva, 159
Hojalata y Laminas, 133
Honduras: free trade, 192; Economic Association, 193
Huachipato, 133

Indians (South American), 12–15; in Mexico, 21
Industrial Revolution, 2, 19, 27, 29
Institute for the Promotion of Foreign Trade (IAPI), 158
Instituto Nacional de la Reforma Agraria (INRA), Cuba, 240
Interamerican Development Bank (IDB), 139, 167–8, 186
International Monetary Fund (IMF), 74, 104

Kennecott Copper Corporation, 165
Korean War, 102, 157, 162–3

labour, international division of, 29, 32, 39, 42, 151
latifundio, 26, 52–8, 224; –Indian community, 15, 52–3; –*minifundio*, 15–16, 52–8

Maranhão, 6
Mateos, López, 220, 222
Mesa Central, 62, 102
Methuen Treaty, 20
Mexico, 1, 4, 17, 35, 65, 101, 105, 142, 167, 222–3, 258; population, 5, 7, 35, 63–4; mineral products, 12, 22, 34–5, 78, 80, 90; Revolution, 20–1, 217–18; petroleum, 35, 91, 102, 139, 159–61, 166, 174; agriculture, 35, 54, 78, 105, 114–18, 149, 209, 217–22; foreign capital, 39, 174; trade, 41, 87, 110, 160; industrialisation, 44, 78–81, 83, 88, 92, 107, 109–12, 170; health, 47; education, 48; incomes, 60–1, 63–4, 252; banks, 71 n, 91, 221; crafts, 79; Porfiriato era, 79; Federal Electricity Commission, 91; tourism, 102, 185–6, 210; various products, 120–40, 183–4, 244; constitution, 166; and Central America, 191 n; taxes, 211–13; productivity, 253
minifundio, 216, 224, 227, 232
Monclova, 133
Monterrey, 133
Montevideo, Treaty of, 198–201
Movimiento Nacionalista Revolucionário, Bolivia, 224–5

Napoleonic Wars, 19, 24
New Granada, 17, 22
Nicaragua, 193

269

Index